Structure for Architects

A PRIMER

Ramsey Dabby

Ashwani Bedi

WILEY

John Wiley & Sons, Inc.

Copyright © 2012 by John Wiley & Sons, Inc. All rights reserved

Published by John Wiley & Sons, Inc., Hoboken, New Jersey

Published simultaneously in Canada

For general information about our other products and services, please contact our Customer Care Department within the United States at (800) 762-2974, outside the United States at (317) 572-3993 or fax (317) 572-4002.

Wiley publishes in a variety of print and electronic formats and by print-on-demand. Some material included with standard print versions of this book may not be included in e-books or in print-on-demand. If this book refers to media such as a CD or DVD that is not included in the version you purchased, you may download this material at http://booksupport.wiley.com. For more information about Wiley products, visit www.wiley.com.

Library of Congress Cataloging-in-Publication Data:

Dabby, Ramsey.
    Structure for architects : a primer / Ramsey Dabby and Ashwani Bedi.
        p. cm.
    Includes index.
        ISBN 978-0-470-63376-2 (hardback); ISBN 978-0-470-90294-8(ebk);
        ISBN 978-0-470-90246-2 (ebk); ISBN 978-0-470-90249-3(ebk);
        ISBN 978-0-470-95096-8(ebk); ISBN 978-0-470-95113-2(ebk)
    1. Architecture. 2. Structural engineering. 3. Thought and thinking. I. Bedi, Ashwani. II. Title.
        TH845.D33 2011
        624.1'7–dc22
                                                                          2010054173
Printed in the United States of America

10 9 8 7 6 5 4 3 2 1

Contents

Preface

The concept for this preliminary textbook arose a few years ago when we jointly taught a Structures course to architectural students in the Architectural Technology Department at The New York City College of Technology. Noting the lack of an appropriate introductory text covering the intended topics, we decided to draw upon our professional and classroom experiences and began work on a structures textbook primarily aimed at the architectural student. Thus began a journey that has spanned over several years and continues to evolve.

Architects tend to think visually, in concepts, while engineers tend to think mathematically, in details. The disparity between the way architects and engineers perceive and process information is not addressed by most structural engineering textbooks, which focus heavily on technical aspects and often intimidate the architectural student. Actually, structures is the most intuitive of engineering disciplines, its principles easily perceived and visible in countless everyday situations. Our intent in this work is to de-mystify structural principles and present them in an intuitive, easy-to-read, and graphically friendly format.

We wish to thank Tim Maldonado, former Dean of the School of Technology at The NYC College of Technology, for his encouragement and guidance especially during the early stages of development. We also wish to thank Stella Deporis, R. Elias Dabby, and Latif Dabby for their advice and inspiration, as well as Andrzej Flakowicz, and Rodrigo da Silva (our former student and now graduate architect) for their much-valued early assistance on the illustrations.

While we collaborated with and also thank our many other academic and professional colleagues, we would not have imagined this work to be complete without the thoughts and reviews from two very talented engineers—our dear friends, Tom Michon and Sunil Saigal. Tom is simply one of the most brilliant practicing structural engineers with whom we've ever had the pleasure of knowing and working. Sunil, Dean of The Newark College of Engineering at NJIT and Distinguished Professor of Structures, has always placed his students before anything else. With an avid passion for structures and academics, Tom and Sunil's primary desire was to help develop quality technical material for students, while keeping it easy-to-understand.

We would like to express our appreciation to Wiley Acquisitions Editor Paul Drougas and Senior Production Manager Kerstin Nasdeo for their confidence, patience, and publishing guidance.

Finally, we wish to thank our families who wondered about, and put up with, our discussions lasting hours on end. Barbara and Kiran, we could not have accomplished this without your support and understanding—we lovingly dedicate this to you.

We welcome and appreciate any comments, suggestions, or corrections by the reader.

Ramsey Dabby, RA
Ashwani K. Bedi, PE
StructureForArchitects@gmail.com

Architects, Engineers, and Design

To the general public the distinction between architects and engineers, and their relationship to design, is blurred. What exactly is the difference between an architect and an engineer? Between architecture and engineering? Don't architects, after all, study engineering? What do engineers have to do with design? Isn't design what architects do? And if architects and engineers are so highly trained in design and construction, why is a third group—contractors—needed to construct buildings? The confusion is understandable.

For centuries, there was little, if any, distinction among architects, engineers, and builders. With the advent of the Industrial Revolution, the world became increasingly complex. The guild and trades system, in which skills and techniques were handed down from generation to generation, began to break down. By the mid-1800s, architecture in the United States evolved into a profession distinct from engineering and construction.

There are many ways to define architecture, but perhaps the most expressive definition was the one provided by Marcus Vitruvius Pollio, a first-century AD Roman writer, architect, and engineer. Vitruvius wrote *De architectura*, a Latin

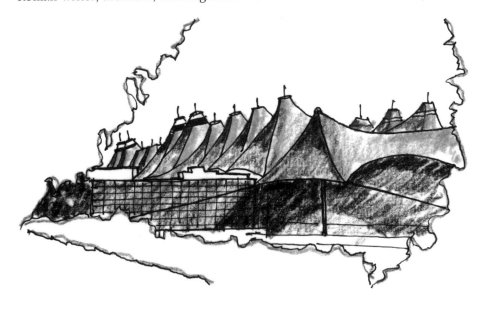

Figure 1.1 Denver International Airport, Denver, CO

treatise on architecture, in which he asserted that a structure (architecture) must exhibit the three qualities of *firmitas, utilitas,* and *venustas,* loosely translated as strength, having soundness of construction; usefulness, having practical value or purpose; and beauty, giving pleasure and delight to those who experience it.

Determining strength and usefulness is relatively easy. Determining beauty is more difficult, since each of us is free to decide what gives us visual pleasure and delight. With all due respect to Vitruvius, perhaps another way to define architecture is to simply call it the *art* and *science* of constructing.

Figure 1.2 Puente de la Mujer, Buenos Aires, Argentina

In modern practice, the knowledge and information needed to design and construct a large building requires many areas of expertise, too much for any one profession to know. The entire process of determining a building's appearance, the materials and systems to be used, and their configurations and sizes is broadly called *design.* Design falls mainly on the shoulders of architects and engineers. Architects have primary responsibility for determining the building's size and

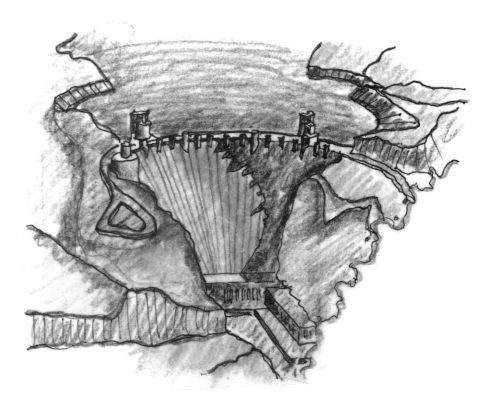

Figure 1.3 Hoover Dam, Boulder City, NV

shape, along with the myriad architectural materials, finishes, and details. Engineers have primary responsibility for determining the mechanical, electrical, and structural systems, along with the many engineering calculations and details.

Contemporary architects, as the leaders and orchestrators of most building projects, are trained as generalists and humanists conversant with aesthetics, planning, sociology, and economics, as well as engineering. By contrast, the training of contemporary engineers is highly technical and focused on a specific engineering discipline. Early engineering had only two disciplines, *military* and *civil*. As technology advanced, new branches of engineering such as mechanical, electrical, and chemical engineering emerged from civil engineering as individual disciplines. Structural engineering, however, the branch of engineering concerned with designing buildings and other types of structures to stand up and resist loads, has always been considered a part of civil engineering and remains so today.

Structural engineering is the engineering discipline most closely intertwined with architectural form. The best architecture exhibits a strong understanding of how forces move through a structure. Toward that end, the primary intent of this book is to increase the structural vocabulary of future architects. It is our hope that by doing so, the architect's dialogue with the structural engineer will be enriched, thereby affording architecture the opportunity to reach its fullest potential.

Figure 1.4 CN Tower, Toronto, Canada

Stability and Strength

CHAPTER **2**

In a broad sense, all structural engineering can be reduced to satisfying two basic conditions: stability and strength.

Through *stability*, the various forces that act on a structure are kept in balance, preventing the structure from toppling, sliding, bending, or twisting.

Through *strength*, the size and physical makeup of the structural materials are made sufficient to withstand the various forces acting on them.

Let's use an example of a weightlifter, Andre, holding a barbell over his head in order to illustrate the concepts of stability and strength. Suppose that the barbell has a 100 lb weight on each end and that Andre is well trained and intuitively keeps his hands evenly spaced. Since the barbell is balanced by the spacing of his hands, and since Andre has the strength to support the 200 total lbs, Andre stands upright, in firm control of the barbell and weights (Figure 2.1).

Figure 2.1 Lifter Supporting Barbell and Weights

Now suppose that Andre's hands are not evenly spaced. The barbell would tend to tilt and eventually topple. Although he would be strong enough to support the 200 total lbs, he would be unable to control the load due to a *failure of stability* (Figure 2.2).

Figure 2.2 A Failure of Stability

Now suppose that Andre's hands are evenly spaced but that the weight on each end is increased from 100 lbs to 200 lbs. His arms and legs would tend to bow and eventually would buckle beneath the increased weight. Although he would be sufficiently well balanced to control the 400 total lbs, he would be unable to support the load due to a *failure of strength* (Figure 2.3).

Figure 2.3 A Failure of Strength

Without stability, the strongest of buildings will fail, and without strength, the most stable of buildings will fail. Not only must the building as a whole satisfy these two conditions, but every one of its components must do so as well.

Loads

Structures are subject to numerous and sometimes complex forces, called *loads*, that exert pressure vertically, horizontally, or at some angle in between. Loads can be predictable, such as fixed mechanical equipment on a roof, or unpredictable, such as wind on a façade; they can be concentrated, such as a column supported by a beam, or distributed over a wide area, such as snow falling on a roof. Loads can be static and subject to little or no change over time, or dynamic and subject to rapid change. With respect to the engineering analysis of structures, however, all loads are ultimately analyzed as acting statically in either a vertical or a horizontal direction. For this reason, perhaps the best way to categorize loads is by grouping them into vertical gravity loads and horizontal lateral loads.

3.1 Gravity Loads

Gravity loads act downward, pulling all objects toward the center of the Earth. They may be classified as dead loads or live loads.

Dead loads are those that are built into a structure, such as the weight of permanent floors, roofs, walls, and fixed mechanical equipment. Dead loads are finite and can be accurately determined.

Live loads are variable, unpredictable, and mobile, such as people, furniture, snow, rain, and ice. These loads can vary at any given moment, so building codes specify minimum live loads to be used for the design of floors and roofs. Live loads are expressed in pounds per square foot (psf), such as 40 psf for office floors or 150 psf for warehouse storage floors (Figure 3.1).

3.2 Lateral Loads

Lateral loads are caused by wind and seismic movement (earthquake) and, in general, are considered to act horizontally. Although wind and seismic loads are unpredictable, codes account for their complexity by prescribing equivalent static lateral loads based upon geographic zones.

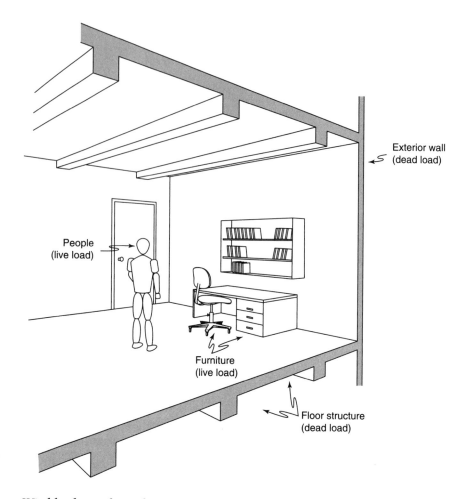

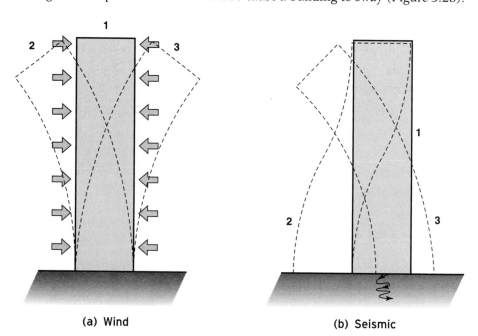

Figure 3.1 Live and Dead Gravity Loads

Wind loads are dependent upon many factors such as velocity and the shape and height of the building, as well as the geometry and proximity of adjacent buildings. Wind loads exert pressure on the sides of a building, causing it to sway (Figure 3.2a).

Seismic loads are created by random, variable, and erratic motions of the ground during an earthquake. Seismic loads also cause a building to sway (Figure 3.2b).

Figure 3.2 Behavior of Buildings under lateral Loads

(a) Wind

(b) Seismic

Although the behavior of a building under wind and seismic loads is different, the net effect is similar in that both types of lateral loads create conditions of (a) bending and (b) base shear on the building (Figures 3.3 and 3.4).

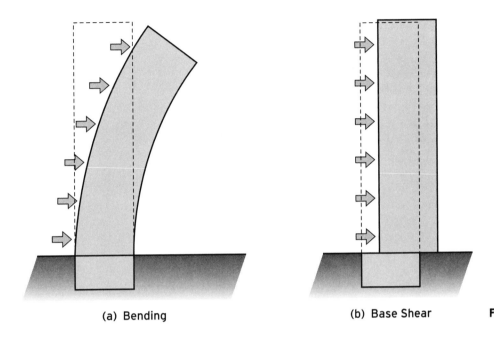

(a) Bending   (b) Base Shear   **Figure 3.3** Effect of Wind Load

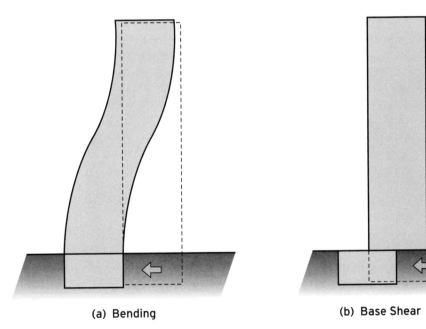

(a) Bending   (b) Base Shear   **Figure 3.4** Effect of Seismic Load

Wind loads create positive pressure by pushing inward against the building's exterior surfaces on the windward side, and negative pressure (suction) by pulling outward on the building's exterior surfaces on the leeward side (Figure 3.5). For very tall or irregularly shaped structures, wind tunnel tests are often used to supplement information provided in codes and to predict actual aerodynamic forces more precisely.

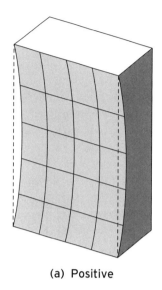 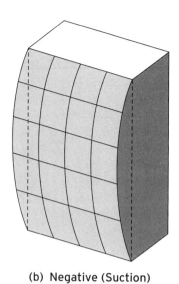

Figure 3.5 Wind Pressures   (a) Positive   (b) Negative (Suction)

Wind and seismic loads also tend to twist a structure, creating torsion, a complex behavior in a building (Figure 3.6).

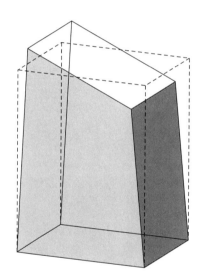

Figure 3.6 Torsion on a Structure

Wind and seismic loads can also create uplift forces at the base of a structure, tending to overturn it. Communications towers, which are relatively lightweight, are particularly susceptible to uplift and overturning (Figure 3.7).

Structural systems that resist lateral loads will be examined more closely in Chapter 15.

3.3 Dynamic Loads

Loads that change rapidly, that are applied suddenly, or that are the result of an amplified rhythmic movement are called *dynamic loads*. Examples of dynamic loads include heavy vibrating machinery, an elevator starting and stopping in its shaft, a vehicle starting or stopping in a garage, and soldiers

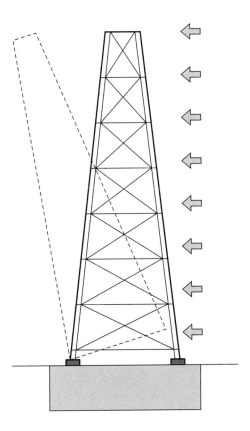

Figure 3.7 Uplift and Overturning of a Tower

marching in rhythm on a bridge (Figure 3.8). The net effect of a dynamic load is that it increases its actual static load. Since the analysis of dynamic loads is complex, codes typically account for them by substituting additional equivalent static loads.

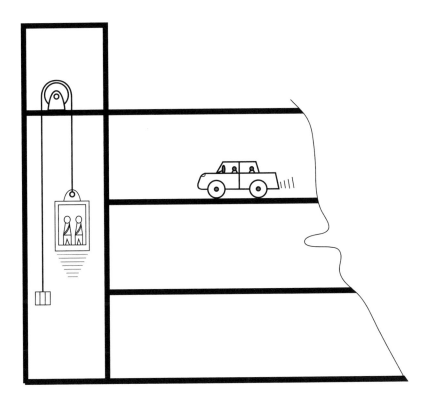

Figure 3.8 Dynamic Loads

3.4 Impact Loads

Loads that result from a sudden collision or an explosion are called *impact loads*. For example, columns in a garage are normally designed to withstand a moderate impact force from an automobile. Blast-resistant design must consider the impact force of the explosion as well as the impact force from projectiles being hurtled about. Codes typically account for impact loads by prescribing additional factors of safety on the static loads.

3.5 Load Paths

All loads applied to a structure, whether gravity or lateral, eventually make their way down through the structure's components to the ground. Let's take the simple example of a man sitting on a four-legged stool. The man's weight is transferred from the seat of the stool to the legs, and from the legs to the ground. If the man weighs 200 lbs, the seat will transmit 50 lbs to each leg, and each leg will transmit 50 lbs to the floor. The flow of loads through a structure, in this case the stool, is called the *load path* (Figure 3.9).

The most efficient load path is a direct line to the ground (Figure 3.10).

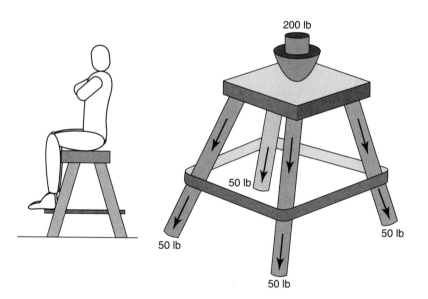

Figure 3.9 Load Path of a Man on a Stool

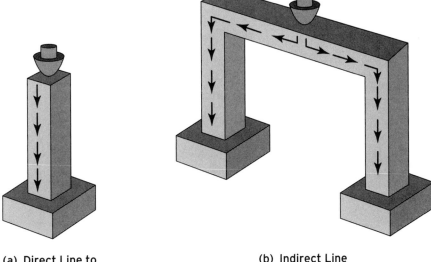

**(a) Direct Line to
Ground**

**(b) Indirect Line
to Ground**

Figure 3.10 Load Paths

In framed buildings, loads applied to the roof, floors, and vertical supports make their way down through the structure to the foundations and ultimately to the ground. The ground, in turn, exerts resisting forces against the foundations, continuing through the structure and opposing the downward flow of loads—in a sense, a reverse load path (Figure 3.11).

In a cable suspension bridge (Figure 3.12), the vehicle loads from the roadway are supported by vertical suspension cables (in tension) extending up to the main cable (in tension), down through the towers (in compression) to the foundations, and ultimately to the ground. The main cable is held in tension by attachments in the anchorage abutments. The concepts of tension and compression will be explored more fully in Chapter 4.

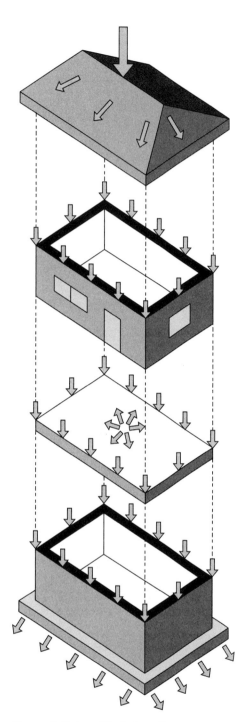

Figure 3.11 Load Path in a Simple Building

ROOF

- Live load weight from roof (snow, wind, etc.)

- Dead load weight of roof (structural materials, etc.)

VERTICAL SUPPORTS (bearing walls, columns, etc.)

- Live and dead loads from above

- Dead load weight of vertical supports

FLOORS

- Live and dead loads from above

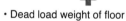

- Dead load weight of floor

- Live load weight on floor (people, furniture, etc.)

FOUNDATIONS

- Live and dead loads from above

- Dead load weight of foundations

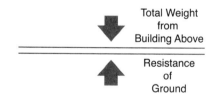

Total Weight from Building Above

Resistance of Ground

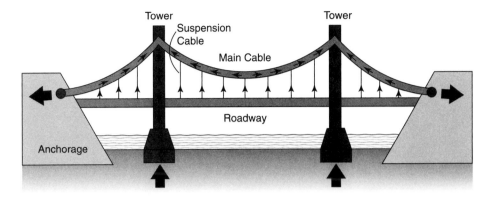

Figure 3.12 Load Path in a Suspension Bridge

For any structure to be stable and not move, all of the forces acting on it and all of its components must be in equilibrium (i.e., in balance).

We'll examine equilibrium and how this balance of forces is analyzed in Chapter 6.

States of Stress

While loads are external forces applied to a body, *stress* is the internal resistance of the body to those forces. There are three basic types of stress: *tension, compression,* and *shear*. All stress consists of these three basic types or some combination thereof.

4.1 Tension

Tension is the tendency of a body to be pulled apart. The rope in Figure 4.1a has direct tensile stress acting on it (the two men pulling on each end) in a direction perpendicular to its cross section (Figure 4.1b).

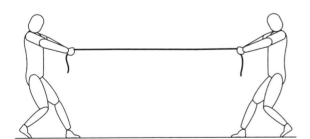

Figure 4.1a A Rope in Tension

Figure 4.1b Direct Tensile Stress

4.2 Compression

Compression is the tendency of a body to be crushed. The post in Figure 4.2a has direct compressive stress acting on it (the downward force and the upward resistance of the ground) in a direction perpendicular to its cross section (Figure 4.2b).

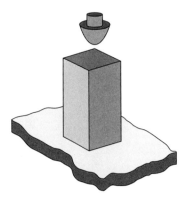

Figure 4.2a A Post in Compression

Figure 4.2b Direct Compressive Stress

4.3 Shear

Shear is the tendency of a body to be sliced. The bolt in Figure 4.3a has direct shear stress acting on it (the two bars pulling in opposition to each other) in a direction parallel to its cross section (Figure 4.3b).

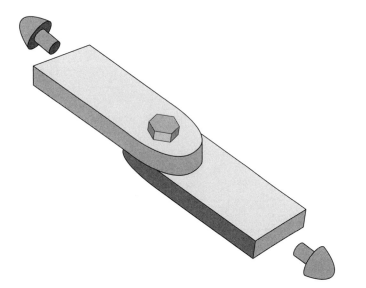

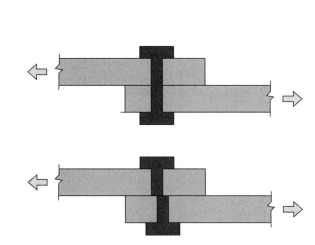

Figure 4.3a A Bolt under Shear

Figure 4.3b Direct Shear Stress

4.4 Torsion

Torsion is a type of shear in which a body tends to be twisted, resulting in shear stresses (Figures 4.4 and 4.5).

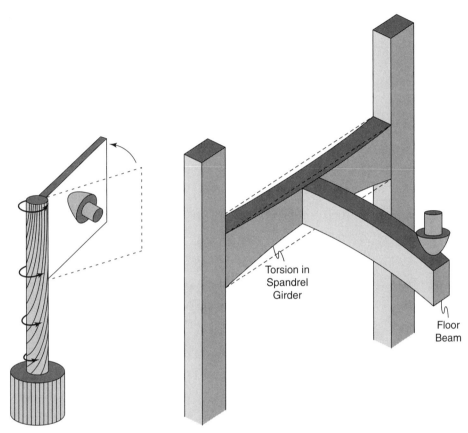

Figure 4.4 A Pole Sign under Torsion

Figure 4.5 A Spandrel Girder under Torsion

Torsion in Spandrel Girder

Floor Beam

4.5 Bending

Bending is the tendency of a body, such as a beam, to bow, thereby creating stress in the body. When bowed, the body compresses along one edge and stretches along the other. The bending of a simply supported beam under load produces tension along the bottom of the beam and compression along the top (Figure 4.6). Moving away from the tension and compression edges toward the centerline of the beam, the tensile and compressive stresses gradually diminish until they reach zero. The imaginary plane passing through the centerline of a beam along its length, at which no tension or compression occurs, is called the *neutral plane* or *neutral axis*. Although bending is of paramount importance in beams, it may occur in any structural member, including columns. Bending is also referred to as *flexure*.

In addition to producing tensile and compressive stresses from bending, a beam under load will produce shear stress, both perpendicular (i.e., vertical) and parallel (i.e., horizontal) to the length of the beam (Figures 4.7 and 4.8).

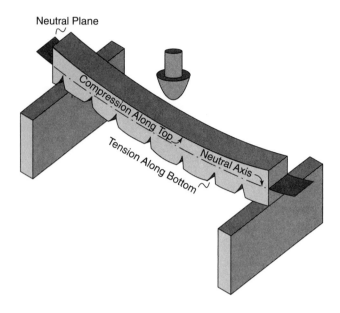

Figure 4.6 Tension and Compression in a Beam

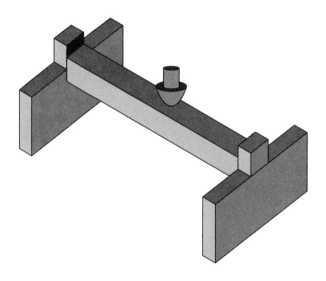

Figure 4.7 Vertical Shear Perpendicular to the Length of a Beam

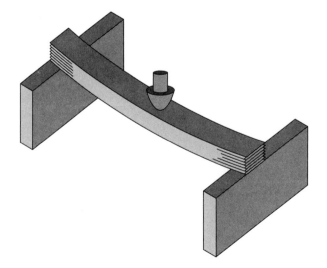

Figure 4.8 Horizontal Shear Parallel to the Length of a Beam

With a load placed at the center of a span, the maximum bending stresses in a beam occur at the center of the span (Figure 4.9), with the maximum compressive stress at the top edge and the maximum tensile stress at the bottom edge (Figure 4.10).

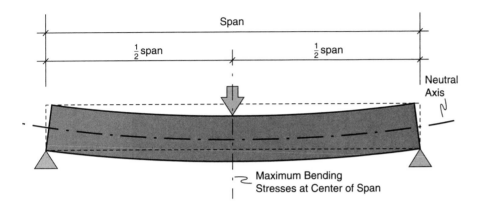

Figure 4.9 Maximum Bending Stresses at the Center of a Span

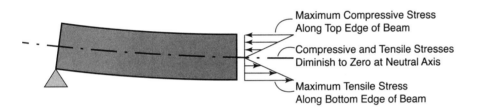

Figure 4.10 Maximum Compressive and Tensile Stresses at the Edges of a Beam

Since tensile, compressive, and shear stresses vary for any point along the length of a beam, their computation in beams is more complex than in members under direct stress. Beam analysis, as well as the analysis of members under direct stress, will be examined more closely in subsequent chapters.

Forces, Movement, Levers, and Moment

Dynamics and especially statics are the two branches of *mechanics* (which, in turn, is a branch of physics) that are most applicable to structural design. *Dynamics* concerns objects in motion, while *statics* concerns objects at rest. In the next few chapters, we'll examine some of the basic principles of mechanics as they relate to structures.

5.1 Applied and Reactive Forces

We all have an intuitive understanding of what a force is, but we need to be more specific. Sir Isaac Newton in the seventeenth century defined a force by relating it to motion. Depending on the situation, a force can cause motion on a body (e.g., make a stationary wagon roll), change motion (make the wagon speed up, slow down, or change direction), or stop motion (bring the wagon to a stop). A push, a pull, gravity, and friction are a few common examples of forces.

For building structures, the typical concern is to assure that the structure and its various components remain stationary and do not move. Therefore, any force applied on a stationary body (tending to cause it to move) must be opposed (resisted) by an equal and opposite force for that body to have no movement. The force tending to cause the movement is called the *applied force*, and the force resisting the movement is called the *reactive force* (or reaction).

Let's examine the two basic types of movement, translational and rotational, to see how this works.

5.2 Translational Movement

In Figure 5.1, a crate on wheels is being pushed by a man. Under the force exerted by the man (the applied force), the crate moves from left to right. This type of movement, in this case hori-zontally, is called *translational movement*.

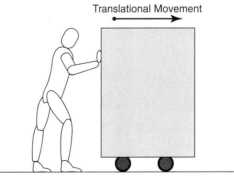

Figure 5.1 Translational Movement

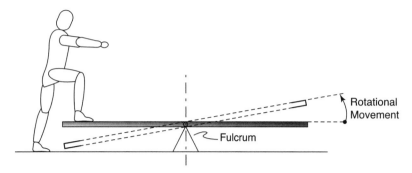

Figure 5.2 Rotational Movement

5.3 Rotational Movement

In Figure 5.2, a man is stepping on the left side of a horizontal seesaw. Under the force exerted by the man's foot (the applied force), the seesaw rotates about the support (fulcrum). This type of movement, in this case counter-clockwise, is called *rotational movement*.

5.4 Levers

The rotational movement of the seesaw underlies the familiar principle of the lever. Levers allow heavy objects to be moved with much less force than their weight alone. By doing so, the lever is said to produce a mechanical advantage. In Figure 5.3a, a long crowbar, acting as a lever, enables a man to move a heavy rock with less force than if he tried to move it directly out of place. The longer the crowbar, the greater the mechanical advantage, or leverage, and the easier it is to move the rock. The distance between the point of rotation (the fulcrum) and the force being applied (the man pushing down) is called the *lever arm* (Figure 5.3b).

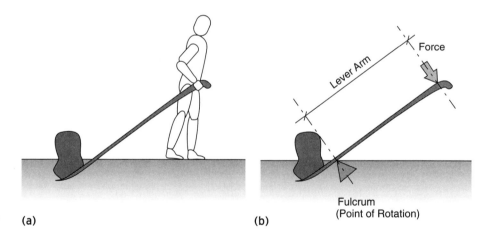

Figure 5.3 Principle of the Lever   (a)   (b)

Note that the lever arm is the *perpendicular* distance between the line of action of the force and the point of rotation. In order to lift the rock, a given force applied at 90 degrees to the crowbar (Figure 5.4a) is the most efficient way to do so since it has the greatest perpendicular distance (i.e., the greatest lever arm) between the line of action of the force and the point of rotation (see Figures 5.4b and 5.4c for comparison).

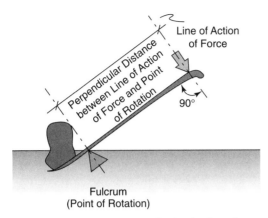

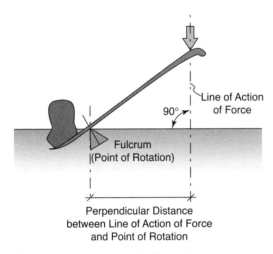

(a) Force Applied Perpendicular to Crowbar

(b) Force Applied Vertically to Crowbar

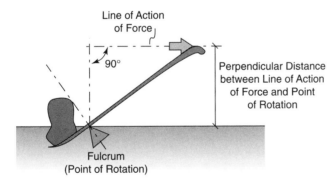

(c) Force Applied Horizontally to Crowbar

Figure 5.4 Forces on a Crowbar

5.5 Moment

The lever underlies the important structural concept of moment. *Moment* is the tendency of a force on a body to produce rotational movement about any chosen point. In mathematical terms, moment is the product of a force times the distance of the force about a chosen point of rotation. (*Torque*, a term similar to moment, is used more often in mechanical engineering applications.)

Moment = Force × Distance

■ EXAMPLE 5a: Moment on a Crowbar

The man attempting to lift the rock applies a 20 lb force perpendicular to one end of a 6 ft long crowbar. The crowbar is embedded 1 ft under the rock, creating a fulcrum 1 ft from the other end of the crowbar. What is the moment about the fulcrum created by the 20 lb force?

Moment = Force x Distance

Moment = 20 lb (force) x 5 ft (distance, i.e., lever arm)

Moment = 100 lb-ft (in the clockwise direction)

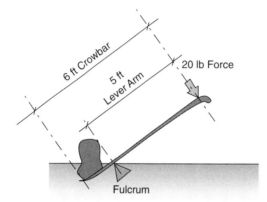

Figure 5.5 Moment from a Crowbar

■ EXAMPLE 5b: Torque (Moment) on a Bolt

A carpenter applies a 10 lb force perpendicular to the end of a 2 ft long wrench to tighten a large bolt. What is the torque (moment) on the bolt created by the 10 lb force on the wrench?

Torque (Moment) = Force × Distance

Torque = 10 lb (force) × 2 ft (distance, i.e., lever arm)

Torque = 20 lb-ft (in the clockwise direction)

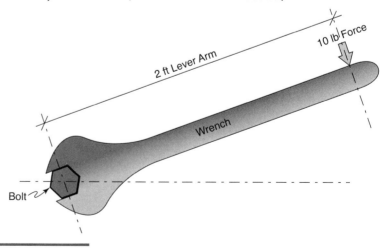

Figure 5.6 Torque on a Bolt

We'll see how translational movement, rotational movement, and moment apply to structural analysis in Chapter 6.

Stability and Equilibrium

CHAPTER **6**

Authors' Note: *Stability* and *equilibrium* are closely related terms, frequently used interchangeably. The difference is semantically debatable and not particularly relevant to the larger concepts of structural engineering. At times the use of the terms may seem inconsistent or blurred, but for our purposes we'll generally use *stability* when referring to structures as a whole and *equilibrium* when referring to individual members within a structure. Although equilibrium can be dynamic or static, we'll use the term to refer to static equilibrium, the typical condition of concern for structures.

6.1 Introduction

Stability is the condition in which gravity and lateral loads that tend to crush, slide, bend, or topple a structure are resisted so that the structure, as a whole, does not move. *Equilibrium* is the condition in which all forces acting on a body are in balance so that the body does not move.

Structural engineering is primarily concerned with applying the principles of stability and equilibrium to calculate all forces acting on a structure and its individual members, then selecting the size, shape, and material to resist those forces with a reasonable margin of safety.

Let's continue with our Chapter 5 examples of the crate and the seesaw in order to demonstrate the conditions for equilibrium.

6.2 Translational Equilibrium

In Figure 6.1a, the crate in Chapter 5 continues to be pushed by the man until it comes up against a wall and can go no further. The applied force on the crate (the man's push) is resisted by a reactive force on the crate (the wall) acting in an equal and opposite direction. In addition, the downward force of gravity (the crate's weight) is resisted by the reactive upward force of the ground (through the crate's wheels) acting in an equal and opposite direction (Figure 6.1b). No matter how hard the man pushes or how heavy the crate is, the wall prevents horizontal movement and the ground prevents vertical movement. The crate is said to be in equilibrium.

27

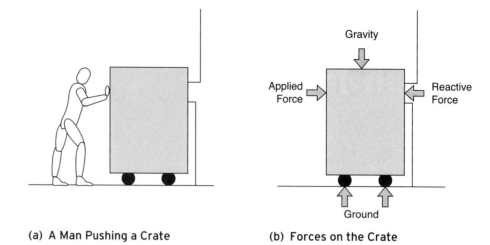

Figure 6.1 Translational Equilibrium

(a) A Man Pushing a Crate

(b) Forces on the Crate

6.3 Rotational Equilibrium

In Figure 6.2a, the man steps onto one end of a horizontal seesaw, which begins to rotate until the other end comes up against the underside of a ledge and can rotate no further. The applied force on the seesaw (the man's weight) is resisted by a reactive force on the seesaw (the ledge) acting in an equal and opposite direction. In addition, the downward forces of the man's weight and the ledge are resisted by the upward force of the ground (acting through the fulcrum). No matter how much the man weighs, the ledge prevents rotational movement and the ground prevents vertical translational movement. The seesaw is said to be in equilibrium.

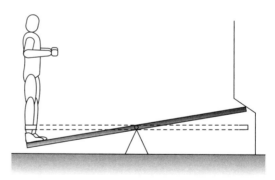

(a) A Man Standing on a Seesaw

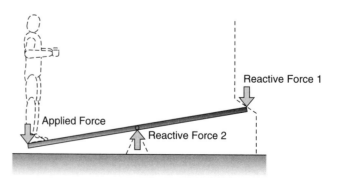

Figure 6.2 Rotational Equilibrium

(b) Forces on the Seesaw

6.4 Sign Conventions

For consistency in algebraic computations, the direction of forces and moments are given signs by convention. For our purposes, we'll only analyze forces and moments in two directions, x and y (the xy plane). In more complex analyses, the third direction, z, must also be considered (Figure 6.3a).

Vertical (y) forces acting upward are positive, and vertical forces acting downward are negative (Figure 6.3b).

Horizontal (x) forces acting to the right are positive, and horizontal forces acting to the left are negative (Figure 6.3c).

Moments that tend to produce clockwise rotation are positive, and moments that tend to produce counterclockwise rotation are negative (Figure 6.3d). (Note that *clockwise* and *counterclockwise directions* are relative terms dependent upon the viewer's position in relation to the object being viewed. With this understanding, we'll refer to clockwise and counterclockwise based upon the viewpoint of our illustrations.)

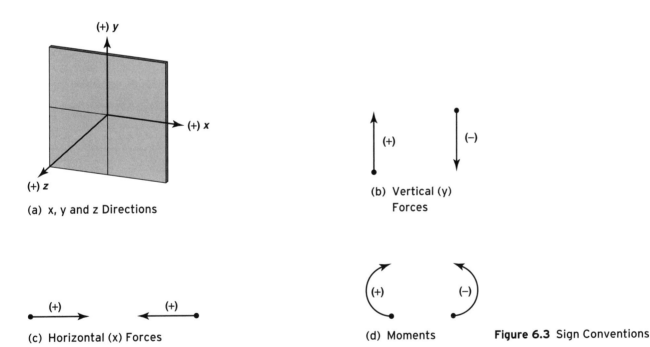

(a) x, y and z Directions

(b) Vertical (y) Forces

(c) Horizontal (x) Forces

(d) Moments

Figure 6.3 Sign Conventions

6.5 The Equilibrium Equations

Our examples of the crate and the seesaw illustrate the two basic and simultaneous conditions that must be met in order for equilibrium to exist on a body: that there be *no translational movement* and that there be *no rotational movement*. Stated mathematically:

- For there to be no translational movement, the algebraic sum of all forces acting in the (x) direction must equal zero, and the algebraic sum of all forces acting in the (y) direction must equal zero:

$$\Sigma F_x = 0$$

$$\Sigma F_y = 0$$

- For there to be no rotational movement, the algebraic sum of all moments about any chosen point must equal zero:

$$\Sigma M = 0$$

Note that the equation for rotational equilibrium, $\Sigma M = 0$, applies to moments taken about *any chosen point*. Although the seesaw rotates about the fulcrum, and you could certainly choose to calculate moments about that point, the equation is equally valid should you choose to calculate moments about any other point. (Try it in any of the examples that follow.)

6.6 Free-Body Diagrams and Familiar Examples of Equilibrium

Let's analyze several common examples to see how to apply the equilibrium equations. We'll examine (1) a log, (2) a barbell, (3) our familiar seesaw, (4) a diving board, and (5) a fishing pole, all under load. As we examine these examples, think of each of these five objects as a beam with applied and reactive forces acting on it. To keep our analyses simple, we'll ignore the actual weights of the objects, and to help visualize the forces acting on the objects, we'll create free-body diagrams for each situation.

Free-body diagrams simplify the structural analysis of an individual member (in our case, the objects) by isolating it, essentially showing it "cut free" from other members or conditions attached to it. The other members or conditions are then replaced by forces representing their effect on the member.

Generally, the most efficient way to apply the equilibrium equations to a free-body diagram is through a $\Sigma M = 0$ calculation about each support. By doing so, a result is obtained for the reaction at each support. The results should then be verified through a $\Sigma F_y = 0$ calculation. (Note that our five examples have forces acting only in the vertical (y) direction. Since there are no forces acting in the horizontal (x) direction, there is no need to use the equation ΣF_x.) The equilibrium equations will be applied in this manner in our examples. While the verification will be performed only on the first example, you are encouraged to do so on your own in the subsequent examples.

Once you are comfortable with the idea of free-body diagrams, you may often find yourself mentally reducing common, everyday situations to free-body conditions.

■ EXAMPLE 6a: The Log

A thick log, 20 ft long, is spanning a ditch. A 200 lb man starting at the right bank traverses the log. How much weight is supported at each bank when he reaches the middle (Figure 6.4)?

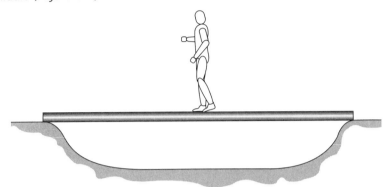

Figure 6.4 A Man on a Log

With the man standing at the middle of the log, it's easily visualized that each bank carries half of his weight, or 100 lbs. Nevertheless, let's create a free-body diagram to see how the equilibrium equations work. We'll call the reaction at the left bank R_1 and the reaction at the right bank R_2 (Figure 6.5).

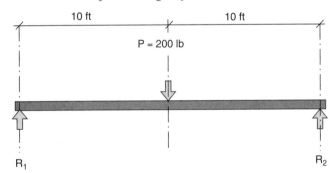

Figure 6.5 Free-body Diagram

Applying the equilibrium equations to the free-body diagram:

$\sum M_{R1} = 0$ (choosing R_1 as the point about which moments are calculated)

$\sum M_{R1} = -(R_2 \times 20 \text{ ft}) + (200 \text{ lb} \times 10 \text{ ft}) = 0$

$\sum M_{R1} = -(20R_2) + (2000) = 0$

$R_2 = 100$ lb

$\sum M_{R2} = 0$ (choosing R_2 as the point about which moments are calculated)

$\sum M_{R2} = +(R_1 \times 20 \text{ ft}) - (200 \text{ lb} \times 10 \text{ ft}) = 0$

$\sum M_{R2} = +(20R_1) - (2000) = 0$

$R_1 = 100$ lb

Verifying the results:

$\sum F_y = 0$

$\sum F_y = +(R_1) + (R_2) - (200 \text{ lb}) = 0$

$\sum F_y = +(100) + (100) - (200) = 0$

0 = 0; therefore, the support reactions are correct

Now let's suppose that the man is standing 5 ft from the left bank. How much weight is now supported at each bank (Figure 6.6)?

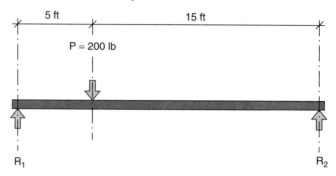

Figure 6.6 Free-body Diagram

Applying the equilibrium equations to the free-body diagram:

$\sum M_{R1} = 0$ (choosing R_1 as the point about which moments are calculated)

$\sum M_{R1} = -(R_2 \times 20 \text{ ft}) + (200 \text{ lb} \times 5 \text{ ft}) = 0$

$\sum M_{R1} = -(20R_2) + (1000) = 0$

$R_2 = 50$ lb

$\sum M_{R2} = 0$ (choosing R_2 as the point about which moments are calculated)

$\sum M_{R2} = +(R_1 \times 20 \text{ ft}) - (200 \text{ lb} \times 15 \text{ ft}) = 0$

$\sum M_{R2} = +(20R_1) - (3000) = 0$

$R_1 = 150$ lb

Verifying the results (by the reader)

DISCUSSION

When the man begins his traverse, the right bank (R_2) carries all of his weight, decreasingly so until he reaches the middle, when both banks carry his weight equally. As he passes the middle, the left bank (R_1) begins to carry most of his weight, increasingly so until he completes his traverse, when the left bank then carries all of his weight.

If we now imagine that the log is not very thick (i.e., has a small cross-sectional area), the log will noticeably bend. The thinner the log (i.e., the smaller the cross-sectional area), the more it will bend. As the man begins his traverse, the log begins to bend–not very much at first but increasingly so as he approaches the middle. When he reaches the middle, the log is at its point of maximum bending, or maximum bending moment (Figure 6.7). As the man continues past the middle, the bending gradually decreases until he reaches the left bank.

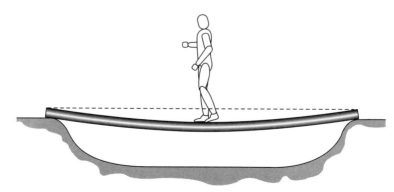

Figure 6.7 A Log Bending under the Weight of a Man

The bowed shape of the log under the man's weight is called its *deformation*. The maximum vertical distance that the deformation deviates from its original true shape is called its *deflection* (Figure 6.8). These two terms are sometimes used interchangeably.

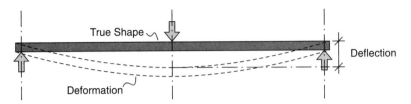

Figure 6.8 Deformation and Deflection of the Log

■ EXAMPLE 6b: The Barbell

A barbell, 6 ft long with a 100 lb weight on each end, is held overhead by a weight-lifter whose hands are evenly spaced 1 ft from each end. How much weight is supported by each hand (Figure 6.9)?

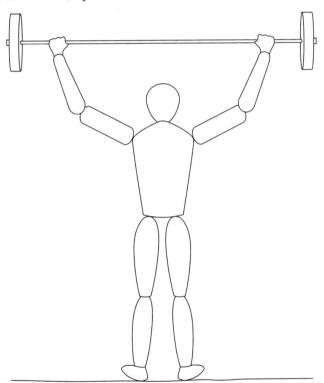

Figure 6.9 A Weightlifter Supporting a Symmetrically Loaded Barbell

Although we could apply the equilibrium equations, it's easy visualized from the free-body diagram that each hand, R_1 and R_2, carries half of the 200 lb total weight, or 100 lbs (Figure 6.10).

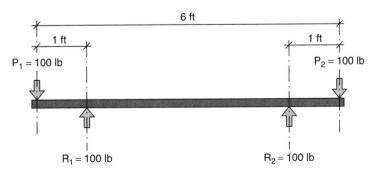

Figure 6.10 Free-body Diagram

The deformation and deflection of the barbell are shown in Figure 6.11.

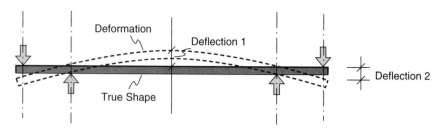

Figure 6.11 Deformation and Deflection of the Barbell

Now suppose that a 175 lb weight is on the left end and a 25 lb weight is on the right. How much weight is now supported by each hand (Figures 6.12 and 6.13)?

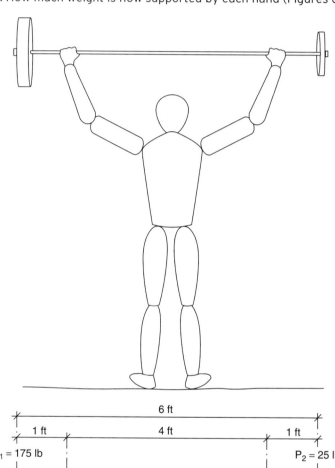

Figure 6.12 A Weightlifter Supporting an Asymmetrically Loaded Barbell

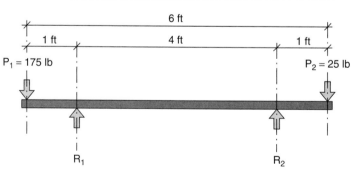

Figure 6.13 Free-body Diagram

Applying the equilibrium equations to the free-body diagram:

$\sum M_{R1} = 0$ (choosing R_1 as the point about which moments are calculated)

$\sum M_{R1} = -(175 \text{ lb} \times 1 \text{ ft}) - (R_2 \times 4 \text{ ft}) + (25 \text{ lb} \times 5 \text{ ft}) = 0$

$\sum M_{R1} = -(175) - (4R_2) + (125) = 0$

$-(4_{R2}) - (50) = 0$

$R_2 = -12.5 \text{ lb}$

$\sum M_{R2} = 0$ (choosing R_2 as the point about which moments are calculated)

$\sum M_{R2} = -(175 \text{ lb} \times 5 \text{ ft}) + (R_1 \times 4 \text{ ft}) + (25 \text{ lb} \times 1 \text{ ft}) = 0$

$\sum M_{R2} = -(875) + (4R_1) + (25) = 0$

$- (4_{R1}) - (850) = 0$

$R_1 = 212.5 \text{ lb}$

Verifying the results (by the reader)

DISCUSSION

With the condition of uneven weights, it's easily visualized, as well as apparent from the calculations, that the weightlifter's left hand (R_1) carries a much heavier load than the weightlifter's right hand (R_2). We also notice that R_2 is a negative number. This is because, in our free-body diagram, we assumed that the weightlifter's right hand would be pushing upward to support the barbell. The negative number tells us that our assumption was wrong and that the weightlifter's right hand actually exerts a downward force on the barbell, preventing it from rotating counter-clockwise around the weightlifter's left hand. Also note that the force exerted by the weightlifter's left hand (R_1) is 212.5 lb, a force greater than the combined 200 lbs of weight on the barbell!

■ EXAMPLE 6c: The Seesaw

A seesaw, 12 ft long with the fulcrum in the middle, has a 100 lb boy sitting on the left end balanced by a 100 lb girl sitting on the right end. How much weight is supported by the fulcrum (Figure 6.14)?

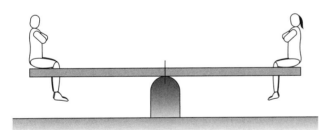

Figure 6.14 A Boy and a Girl on a Seesaw

Although we could apply the equilibrium equations, it's easily visualized from the free-body diagram that the fulcrum (R) would support the total weight of the boy and girl, or 200 lbs (Figure 6.15).

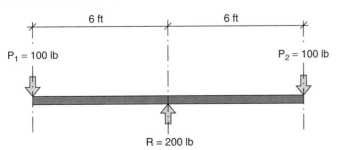

Figure 6.15 Free-body Diagram

The deformation and deflection of the seesaw are shown in Figure 6.16.

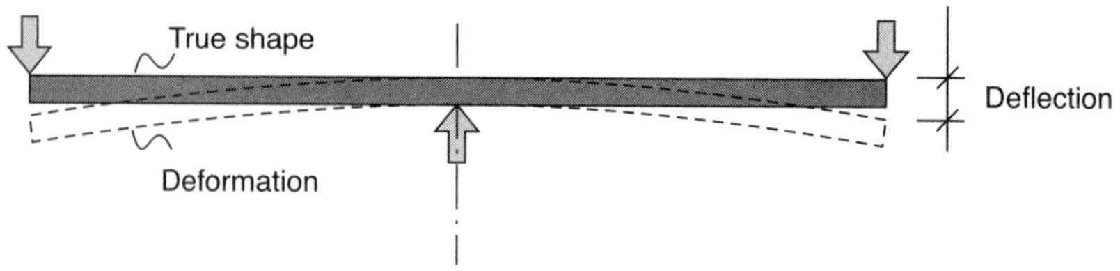

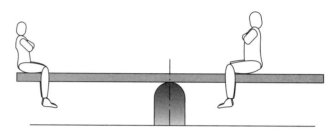

Figure 6.16 Deformation and
Deflection of the Seesaw

Now suppose that the 100 lb boy is sitting on the left end and a 200 lb man is
sitting on the right end. What distance (d) must the man sit from the fulcrum to
keep the seesaw in balance, and what total weight (R) does the fulcrum support
(Figures 6.17 and 6.18)?

Figure 6.17 A Boy and a Man on
a Seesaw

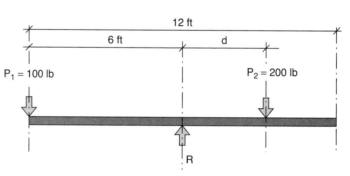

Figure 6.18 Free-body Diagram

Applying the equilibrium equations to the free-body diagram:

$\Sigma M_R = 0$ (choosing R as the point about which moments are calculated)

$\Sigma M_R = -(100 \text{ lb} \times 6 \text{ ft}) + (200 \text{ lb} \times d) = 0$

$\Sigma M_R = -(600) + (200d) = 0$

d = 3 ft

$\Sigma F_y = 0$

$\Sigma F_y = +(R) - (100 \text{ lb}) - (200 \text{ lb}) = 0$

$+(R) - (300) = 0$

R = 300 lb

Verifying the results (by the reader)

DISCUSSION

The heavier weight of the man requires a shorter lever arm (the distance of the
man from the fulcrum) to balance the lighter weight of the boy with the longer
lever arm.

■ EXAMPLE 6d: The Diving Board

A diving board, 12 ft long, has a 100 lb diver standing on the diving end and a roller support 4 ft from the other end, which has a pinned support. How much weight is carried by the roller and pinned supports (Figures 6.19, 6.20, and 6.21)? (The support conditions described as *roller* and *pinned* in this example will be explained more fully in Chapter 8.)

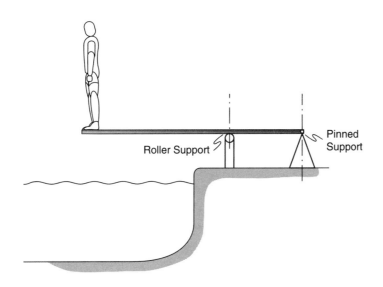

Figure 6.19 A Diver Standing on a Diving Board

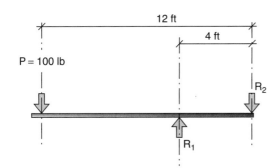

Figure 6.20 Free-body Diagram

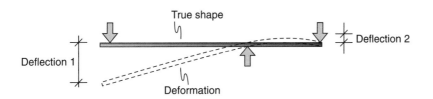

Figure 6.21 Deformation and Deflection of the Diving Board

Applying the equilibrium equations to the free-body diagram:

$\sum M_{R1} = 0$ (choosing R_1 as the point about which moments are calculated)

$\sum M_{R1} = -(100 \text{ lb} \times 8 \text{ ft}) + (R_2 \times 4 \text{ ft}) = 0$

$-(800) + (4R_2) = 0$

$\mathbf{R_2 = 200\ lb}$

$\Sigma M_{R2} = 0$ (choosing R_2 as the point about which moments are calculated)

$\Sigma M_{R2} = -(100 \text{ lb} \times 12 \text{ ft}) + (R_1 \times 4 \text{ ft}) = 0$

$-(1200) + (4R_1) = 0$

$R_1 = 300$ lb

Verifying the results (by the reader)

DISCUSSION

It's easily visualized from the free-body diagram that the pinned support (R_2) exerts a downward force on the diving board to prevent it from rotating counter-clockwise around the roller support (R_1). By comparing the free-body diagrams, we see that this situation is somewhat similar to that of a seesaw, except that in this case, no matter how much the diver weighs, the reactive forces at R_1 and R_2 will increase to compensate and keep the diving board in equilibrium. The heavier the diver, the greater the downward reactive force at R_2 and the greater the upward reactive force at R_1.

■ EXAMPLE 6e: **The Fishing Pole**

An old-fashioned 6 ft long fishing pole, held horizontally by a strong fisherman on a pier, has snagged a 50 lb tire (P). What are the reactions needed by the fisherman's hands to hold the pole level (Figures 6.22, 6.23, and 6.24)?

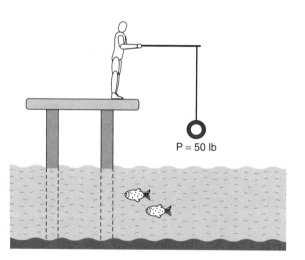

P = 50 lb

Figure 6.22 Fisherman Catching a Tire

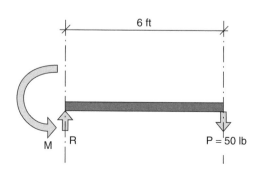

6 ft

M   R   P = 50 lb

Figure 6.23 Free-body Diagram

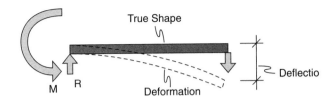

True Shape

Deflectio

Deformation

M R

Figure 6.24 Deformation and Deflection of the Fishing Pole

Applying the equilibrium equations to the free-body diagram:

$$\Sigma F_y = 0$$

$$\Sigma F_y = +(R) - (P) = 0$$

$$+(R) - (50 \text{ lb}) = 0$$

R = 50 lb

Using $\Sigma F_y = 0$, we quickly see from the free-body diagram that the fisherman must exert an upward force R of 50 lbs to oppose P, the 50 lb weight of the tire.

But with no other forces at play, R and P would cause the pole to rotate in the clockwise direction. Therefore, some other reaction is being developed to keep the pole from rotating. This reaction is a *resisting moment* exerted by the fisherman's hands. We can determine the magnitude of this resisting moment by using $\Sigma M = 0$.

$$\Sigma M_R = 0 \text{ (choosing R as the point about which moments are calculated)}$$

$$\Sigma M_R = +(P \times 6 \text{ ft}) - (M) = 0$$

$$(50 \text{ lb} \times 6 \text{ ft}) - (M) = 0$$

$$+(300) - (M) = 0$$

M = 300 lb-ft (in the counterclockwise direction)

Verifying the results (by the reader)

DISCUSSION
R and P are two equal forces acting in opposite directions, having parallel lines of action. R and P, called a *force couple*, tend to produce pure rotation. With no other forces at play, a force couple can only be resisted by a pure moment. Not all types of support are capable of providing resisting moment but, in this case, you can well imagine the fisherman's strong hands being capable of doing so. His hands exert a counterclockwise 300 lb-ft moment on the pole to counteract the clockwise rotational tendency of force couple R and P. Note that M, the resisting moment, is considered to be a reaction along with R.

6.7 Introduction to Bending in Beams

With an understanding of how to create free-body diagrams and apply the equilibrium equations, let's again use the example of the log to visualize several basic factors affecting bending in the log:

1. The more the man weighs, the more the log bends. Where the man stands also affects how much the log bends. If the man were to lie down, thereby spreading out his weight, the log would bend less.
2. The greater the distance between the shorelines, the more the log bends.

3. The thinner the log, the more the log bends.
4. If the log has begun to decay, making it less strong than when freshly fallen, the more the log bends.

If we state the above factors in more technical terms, considering the log as a beam, we can describe several important factors that affect the amount of bending in a beam, and consequently its design:

1. The magnitude of the load on the beam, where it's placed, and how it's distributed
2. The span of the beam (or, more generally, the conditions of support)
3. The cross-sectional shape and dimensions of the beam
4. The strength of the material of which the beam is made

We'll examine these factors, as well as other considerations for beam design, more closely in subsequent chapters.

Working with Forces | CHAPTER **7**

7.1 Forces, Vectors, and Lines of Action

From Chapter 5 we have a basic understanding of a force. A force is also a vector quantity, meaning that it has magnitude (e.g., pounds, kips) and direction (e.g., up, down, left, right). Because it is a vector, a force can be represented graphically by being drawn to size at a particular scale and in a particular direction (bearing). The infinite imaginary line passing through a vector force is called its *line of action* (Figure 7.1).

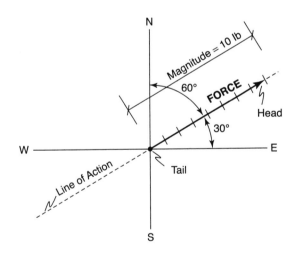

Figure 7.1 Force as a Vector Quantity. A 10 lb force with a line of action having a bearing from (0, 0) of N 60 degrees E.

Principle of Transmissibility

The principle of transmissibility states that a given force can be applied on a body (the point of application) anywhere along the force's line of action without causing any external effect on that body. Note *external* effect! In fact, changing the point of application can have a marked change on the *internal* effect on that body. Let's use the following example of a load on a truss to see the difference between the external and internal effect of a point of application.

■ EXAMPLE 7a: **Principle of Transmissibility**

A 4 kip downward vertical force P is applied at point M (the point of application) on the top chord of a truss (Figure 7.2). What are reactions R_1 and R_2?

Using the equilibrium equations, R_1 and R_2 are readily determined to be 3 kips and 1 kip, respectively.

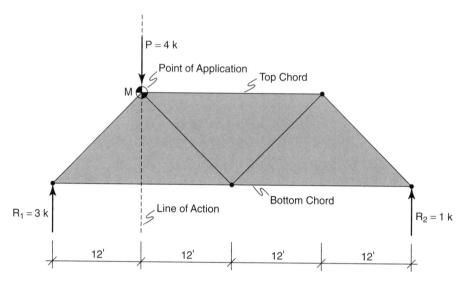

Figure 7.2 Point of Application of Force on Top Chord

P is now applied along the same line of action at point N on the bottom chord of the truss (Figure 7.3). What are reactions R_1 and R_2?

Using the equilibrium equations, R_1 and R_2 are readily determined to be the same 3 kips and 1 kip, respectively.

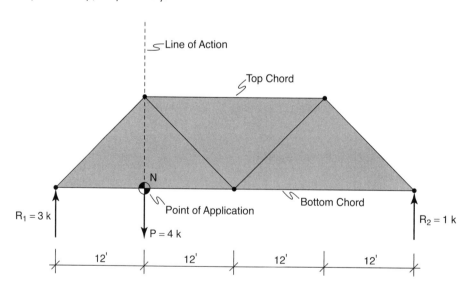

Figure 7.3 Point of Application of Force on Bottom Chord

Discussion

Whether force P is applied at the top chord or the bottom chord, as long as the points of application are on the same line of action, the external effects on the truss (i.e., the support reactions) are the same. However, the internal effect on the truss (i.e., the forces within the individual members of the truss) is obviously quite different.

Collinear Forces

When two or more forces have the same line of action, they are said to be *collinear* (Figure 7.4).

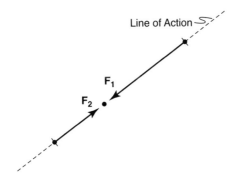

Figure 7.4 Collinear Forces F_1 and F_2

Parallel Forces

Parallel forces have lines of action that never intersect (Figure 7.5). Until now, we've only examined examples of parallel force systems. The log, the barbell, the seesaw, and the diving board are all such examples. Of course, not all force systems are parallel.

Figure 7.5 Parallel Forces F_1 through F_4

Concurrent Forces

Concurrent forces have lines of action that intersect (Figure 7.6). When two or more forces are not parallel, their lines of action will eventually intersect at one common point, the *point of concurrency*.

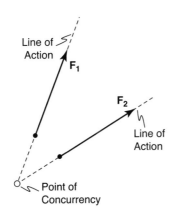

Figure 7.6 Concurrent Forces F_1 and F_2

Any two or more forces having the same point of concurrency are said to be *concurrent forces* (Figure 7.7).

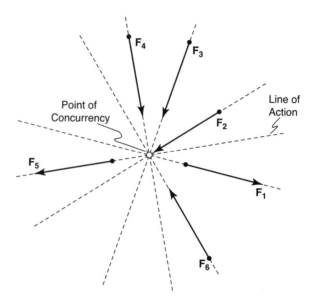

Figure 7.7 Concurrent Forces F_1 through F_6

In order to analyze concurrent forces, we'll first need to understand how to combine and resolve forces.

7.2 Combining and Resolving Concurrent Forces

Resultant, Component, and Equilibrant Forces

Many functions can be performed on forces, including adding and subtracting them. Two or more forces can be combined into a single force, called the *resultant*. A resultant is equivalent in all respects to the sum of its component forces. Conversely, a force can also be broken down into two or more *component* forces. Separating a force into component forces is called *force resolution*. Combining or resolving forces may be performed algebraically or graphically by drawing to scale.

A force equal and opposite to one or more forces, maintaining equilibrium, is called an *equilibrant*.

The Parallelogram Method of Combining and Resolving Forces

The parallelogram method is a graphic technique for combining or resolving forces.

The Parallelogram Method of Combining Forces

The parallelogram method may be used to combine two forces into a single resultant.

Figure 7.8 shows F_1 and F_2 combined into their resultant F_r.

$$\mathbf{F_1} + \mathbf{F_2} = \mathbf{F_r}$$

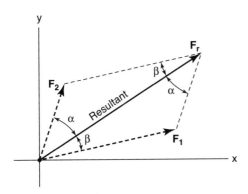

Figure 7.8 Parallelogram Method of Combining Forces into a Resultant

The Parallelogram Method of Resolving Forces

The parallelogram method may also be used to resolve a force into any two components along any two lines of action, typically the x and y axes in order to facilitate structural analyses.

Figure 7.9 shows F_r resolved into components F_x and F_y along the x and y axes.

$$\mathbf{F_r} = \mathbf{F_x} + \mathbf{F_y}$$

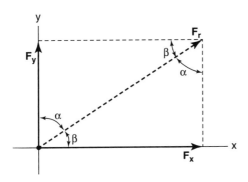

Figure 7.9 Parallelogram Method of Resolving a Force into *x* and *y* Components

Figure 7.10 shows F_r resolved into components F_3 and F_4 along two arbitrary axes.

$$\mathbf{F_r} = \mathbf{F_3} + \mathbf{F_4}$$

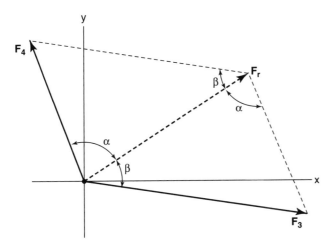

Figure 7.10 Parallelogram Method of Resolving a Force into Any Two Components

Figure 7.11 shows the equilibrant, F_e, of F_3 and F_4 (also the equilibrant of F_r).

$$\mathbf{F_e} = \mathbf{F_3} + \mathbf{F_4} = \mathbf{F_r}$$

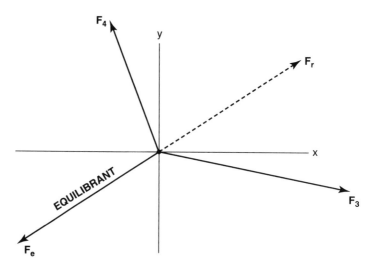

Figure 7.11 Equilibrant of Forces F_3 and F_4

The Polygon Method of Combining Forces

The polygon method is a graphic technique for combining concurrent forces.

Figure 7.12 shows four concurrent forces F_1, F_2, F_3, and F_4.

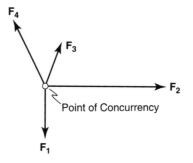

Figure 7.12 Concurrent Forces F_1 through F_4

Figure 7.13 shows the polygon method of combining these forces into a resultant, F_r. Starting at a point of origin, each force is drawn in succession, attaching the tail of one to the head of the other. The resultant is then determined by connecting the point of origin to the head of the last force.

$$\mathbf{F_r} = \mathbf{F_1} + \mathbf{F_2} + \mathbf{F_3} + \mathbf{F_4}$$

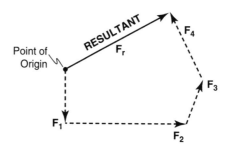

Figure 7.13 Polygon Method of Combining Forces into a Resultant

Figure 17.14 shows the equilibrant, F_e, of F_1 through F_4 (also the equilibrant of F_r).

$$\mathbf{F_e = F_1 + F_2 + F_3 + F_4 = F_r}$$

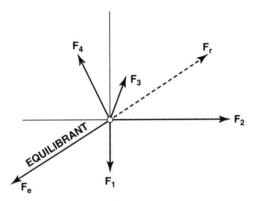

Figure 7.14 Equilibrant of Forces F_1 through F_4

■ EXAMPLE 7b: **Combining and Resolving Concurrent Forces**

Two collinear forces F_1 and F_2 are acting concurrently at point A at an angle of 30 degrees to the horizontal. F_1 is 10 lbs acting upward to the right and F_2 is 6 lbs acting downward to the left (Figure 7.15).

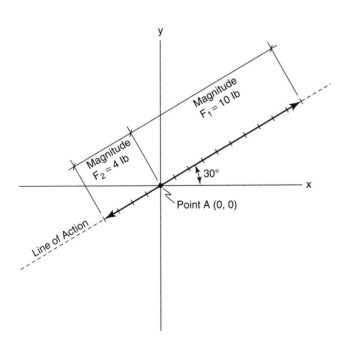

Figure 7.15 Collinear Forces F_1 and F_2

1. Graphically combine F_1 and F_2 into a resultant F_{r1} (Figure 7.16).

$$F_{r1} = F_1 + F_2 = + (10\ lb) + (-4\ lb) = 6\ lb$$

Combining F_1 and F_2 produces a resultant force F_{r1} of 6 lbs acting upward to the right at a 30 degree angle to the horizontal.

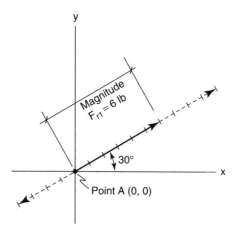

Figure 7.16 Graphically Combining F_1 and F_2 into Resultant Force F_{r1}

2. Algebraically resolve resultant F_{r1} into its horizontal and vertical component, F_x and F_y (Figure 7.17).

Solving for F_x:

$$\cos 30° = F_x / F_{r1}$$

$$F_x = (F_{r1}) \times (\cos 30°)$$

$$F_x = (6\ lb) \times (0.866)$$

$$\mathbf{F_x = 5.2\ lb}$$

Solving for F_y:

$$\sin 30° = F_y / F_{r1}$$

$$F_y = (F_{r1}) \times (\sin 30°)$$

$$F_y = (6\ lb) \times (0.5)$$

$$\mathbf{F_y = 3.0\ lb}$$

Resolving F_{r1} into its horizontal and vertical components produces a horizontal force F_x of 5.2 lbs acting to the right and a vertical force F_y of 3 lbs acting upward.

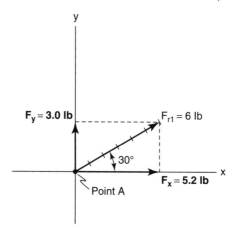

Figure 7.17 Algebraically Resolving F_{r1} into x and y Components

3. Combine F_{r1} with a new force F_3 of 8 lbs acting vertically downward, into a resultant force F_{r2} (Figure 7.18).

Combining F_{r1} and F_3 by the parallelogram method produces a resultant force F_{r2} of (approximately) 7 lbs acting downward to the right.

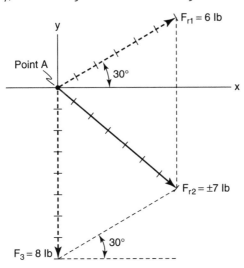

Figure 7.18 Combining F_{r1} and F_3 into Resultant Force F_{r2}

7.3 Familiar Examples of Concurrent Forces

Let's apply the principles of force resolution to the following familiar examples involving concurrent forces.

■ EXAMPLE 7c: Fido and His Leash

Rodrigo is holding his dog, Fido, on a leash, waiting for the light to change so that they can cross the street. The leash is held at a 30 degree angle to the ground. Although Rodrigo and Fido are standing still, Fido is pulling on the leash with an applied force equal to 8 lbs. How much reactive force must Rodrigo exert on the leash to resist being dragged across the street (Figure 7.19)?

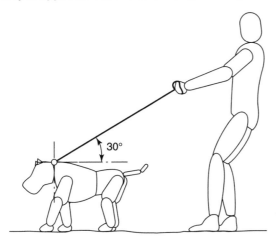

Figure 7.19 Fido's Collar and Leash

If your intuition tells you that Rodrigo would need to pull back on the leash with a force of 8 lbs, you'd be wrong. To help analyze the reason, we'll create a free-body diagram of Fido's collar showing the forces acting on it, and resolve all the forces algebraically into their vertical and horizontal components.

Starting our free-body diagram, we see that there are two obvious forces acting on the collar: Fido's pull, F_1, of 8 lbs and the leash, F_2 (Figure 7.20).

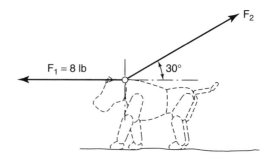

Figure 7.20 Obvious Forces Acting on the Collar

From Figure 7.21 we also see that F_2 has a horizontal component, F_{2x}, and a vertical component, F_{2y}. We know that F_{2x} must act equal and opposite to F_1 and, since F_1 equals 8 lbs acting horizontally to the left, F_{2x} must equal 8 lbs acting horizontally to the right.

We also know that F_2 has a vertical component F_{2y} acting vertically upward. If F_{2x} equals 8 lbs, and if the leash is at a 30 degree angle, we can then calculate F_{2y} algebraically.

Calculating F_{2y}:

$$\tan 30° = F_{2y}/F_{2x}$$
$$F_{2y} = (F_{2x}) \times (\tan 30°)$$
$$F_{2y} = (8 \text{ lb}) \times (0.577)$$
$$\mathbf{F_{2y} = 4.6 \text{ lb}}$$

Since all the forces acting on Fido's collar must be in equilibrium, we can readily see that there must be a third force F_3 acting on the collar, equal and opposite to F_{2y}. Since F_{2y} equals 4.6 lbs acting vertically upward, F_3 must equal 4.6 lbs acting vertically downward.

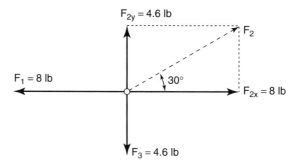

Figure 7.21 Free-body Diagram of All Forces Acting on the Collar

In order to determine the actual force F_2 exerted by the boy on the leash, we combine F_{2x} and F_{2y} into their resultant F_2.

Combining F_{2x} and F_{2y} into resultant F_2 (Figure 7.22):

$$\cos 30° = F_{2x}/F_2$$
$$F_2 = (F_{2x})/(\cos 30°)$$
$$F_2 = (8 \text{ lb})/(0.866)$$
$$\mathbf{F_2 = 9.2 \text{ lb}}$$

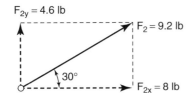

$F_{2y} = 4.6$ lb

$F_2 = 9.2$ lb

30°

$F_{2x} = 8$ lb

Figure 7.22 Combining F_{2x} and F_{2y} into Resultant Force F_2

DISCUSSION

As Fido pulls with 8 lbs of force, Rodrigo must pull back on the leash with a force of 9.2 lbs. F_{2x}, the horizontal component of F_2, is what resists Fido's 8 lb pull and keeps him from crossing the street. F_{2y}, the vertical component of F_2, simply makes Fido's life more difficult by pulling upward on his collar, which tends to choke him.

From this example, we can draw the conclusion that the most efficient way for Rodrigo to keep Fido from crossing the street (i.e., using the least amount of force) is by keeping the leash horizontal in direct opposition to Fido's pull.

■ EXAMPLE 7d: **A Hanging Sculpture**

An artist has suspended an 80 lb sculpture (P) from the ceiling of her studio with two equal-length cables. One end of each cable is attached to the ceiling, while the other end of each cable is attached to a small steel ring from which the sculpture is suspended. The cables are spaced 6 ft apart at the ceiling, and the center of the ring is suspended 4 ft from the ceiling (Figure 7.23). Determine:

1. The force resisted by each cable
2. The arrangement of the cables that puts the least stress on them

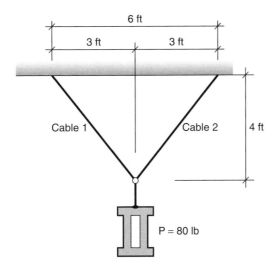

6 ft

3 ft   3 ft

Cable 1   Cable 2   4 ft

P = 80 lb

Figure 7.23 A Symmetrically Suspended Sculpture

If your intuition tells you each cable is supporting 40 lbs (i.e., half the 80 lb load), you'd be wrong. Let's analyze why.

Step 1: Draw the free-body diagram isolating the steel ring and the forces acting on it (Figure 7.24).

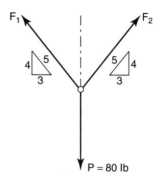

Figure 7.24 Free-body Diagram
of Ring

From the free-body diagram, we observe three forces acting on the ring:

- P, acting vertically downward, with a magnitude of 80 lbs.
- F_1, of unknown magnitude, acting along the line of action of cable 1.
- F_2, of unknown magnitude, acting along the line of action of cable 2.

We also observe that:

- The geometry of the suspended cables is that of a 3:4:5 right triangle.
- Since the sculpture is suspended symmetrically, each cable will carry the same load and therefore $F_1 = F_2$.

Step 2: Resolve all forces into their x and y components and apply the equilibrium equation $\Sigma F = 0$ to solve for unknown forces in the y direction (Figure 7.25).

$$\Sigma F_y = 0$$

$$+ (F_{1y}) + (F_{2y}) - (P) = 0$$

$$+ (F_{1y}) + (F_{2y}) - (80 \text{ lb}) = 0$$

(since the sculpture is suspended symmetrically, $F_{2y} = F_{1y}$)

$$+ (F_{1y}) + (F_{1y}) - (80) = 0$$

$$+ (2F_{1y}) = 80$$

$$\mathbf{F_{1y} = 40 \ lb = F_{2y}}$$

If $F_{1y} = F_{2y} = 40$ lb, then F_1 and F_2 can be determined by the proportions of a 3:4:5 right triangle:

$$F_1 = F_2 = (5/4) \times (40 \text{ lb})$$

$$\mathbf{F_1 = F_2 = 50 \ lb}$$

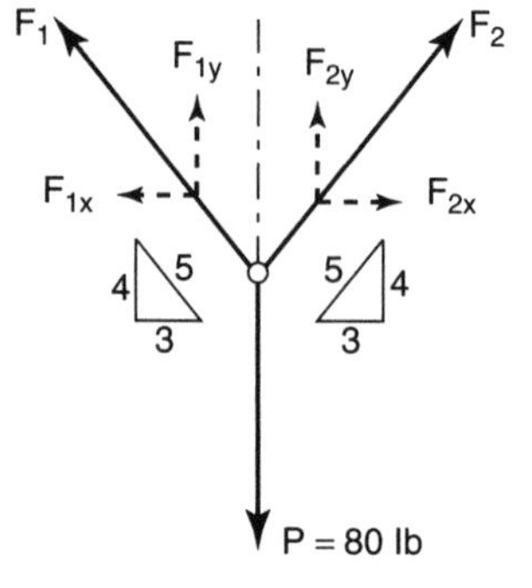

Figure 7.25 Resolving Forces F_1
and F_2 into x and y Components

DISCUSSION

We see from Figure 7.25 that only F_{1y} and F_{2y} (the vertical components of F_1 and F_2) are supporting the load. F_{1x} and F_{2x} (the horizontal components) do not contribute to supporting the load. We can therefore draw the following conclusions about the way the cables support the load:

- The closer the cables are to the vertical, the greater the vertical components of F_1 and F_2, and the more efficiently the cables support the load (Figure 7.26).

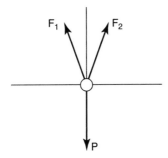

Figure 7.26 Efficient Cable Support

- The closer the cables are to the horizontal, the smaller the vertical components of F_1 and F_2, and the less efficiently the cables support the load (Figure 7.27).

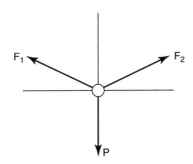

Figure 7.27 Inefficient Cable Support

Artistic considerations aside, to support the load in the most efficient manner and put the least stress on the cable, the artist should hang the cables vertically (Figure 7.28).

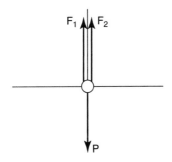

Figure 7.28 Most Efficient Cable Support

■ EXAMPLE 7e: A Practice Problem

The artist has now decided to hang her sculpture asymmetrically using a longer cable on the left as shown in Figure 7.29. What is the force now resisted by each cable?

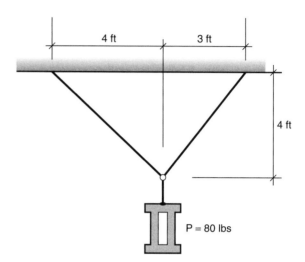

Figure 7.29 An Asymmetrically Suspended Sculpture

Supports, Reactions, and Restraint of Movement

A structural member such as a beam or column carries its load to other structural elements, or to the ground, through supports (also referred to as *connections, joints, or restraints*). Supports can be at the ends or at any intermediate point along the member. The type of support affects how reactions will act on the member and the kind of movement that the support will restrain. The actual conditions of a support can be quite complex; so, to facilitate structural analysis, the support is generally idealized and considered to act in a simplified and pure manner. We'll categorize supports into four idealized types: (1) roller and frictionless-surface, (2) pinned, (3) fixed, and (4) hanger. Keep in mind the word *idealized* and remember that the reality of a support can often be quite different than its idealized representation.

There are several ways to represent graphically the various support types. In the descriptions that follow, we've chosen a graphic representation that best displays the support functioning in its idealized manner.

8.1 Roller and Frictionless-Surface Supports

Roller and *frictionless-surface (F.S.) supports* can be found on one end of bridges to allow for thermal expansion and contraction of the span. Frictionless-surface supports in the form of rubber bearings are also used in foundations in zones of seismic activity to allow limited lateral movement. Although no surface is truly frictionless, a frictionless-surface support is idealized as such. In their idealized form, roller and frictionless-surface and supports behave exactly alike and exert the same reaction on a member.

Graphic Representation

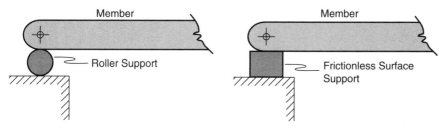

Figure 8.1a Roller Support　　　**Figure 8.1b** Frictionless-surface Support

Reaction on a Member

A roller and frictionless-surface support can only exert a force on a member acting normal (i.e., perpendicular) to it and away from the surface on which the member rests (Figure 8.2).

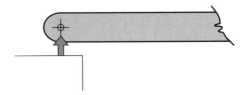

Figure 8.2 Possible Reactions

Restraint of Movement

A roller and frictionless-surface support cannot prevent translational movement in all directions and cannot prevent any rotational movement (i.e., cannot exert resisting moment). Examples of the types of movement allowed are shown in Figures 8.3a and 8.3b.

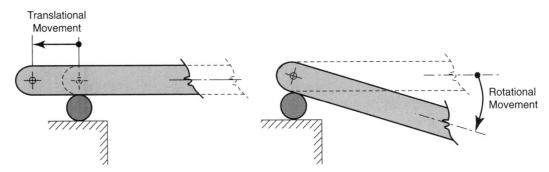

Figure 8.3a Translational Movement   **Figure 8.3b** Rotational Movement

8.2 Pinned Supports

Pinned supports (also referred to as *hinged supports*) are used in bridges and certain types of trusses. Some pinned supports are literally pins, as is readily visible in the bottom chord of the inverted bowstring truss in Figures 8.4 and 8.5.

Figure 8.4 An Inverted Bowing Truss

Figure 8.5 A Pinned Connection

Other pinned supports are idealized as being so, even though in reality they may resist a small amount of moment. The steel connection shown in Figure 8.6, attaching the web (only) of a beam to a girder, is called a *shear connection* and is an example of an idealized pinned support of a beam.

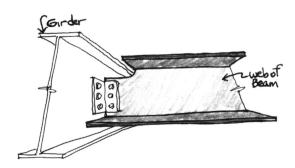

Figure 8.6 Shear Connection of a Steel Beam

Graphic Representation

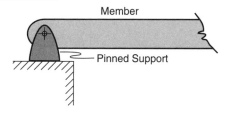

Figure 8.7 Pinned Support

Reactions on a Member

A pinned support can exert a force on a member acting in any direction (Figure 8.8).

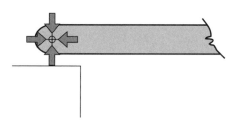

Figure 8.8 Possible Reactions

Restraint of Movement

A pinned support prevents translational movement in all directions but cannot prevent any rotational movement (i.e., cannot exert resisting moment). An example of the type of movement allowed is shown in Figure 8.9.

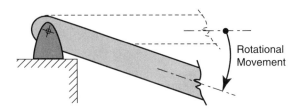

Figure 8.9 Rotational Movement

8.3 Fixed Supports

Fixed supports (also referred to as *rigid supports*) are commonly found in beam-to-column connections of moment-resisting steel frames as well as in beam, column, and slab connections in concrete frames. The connection of a cantilevered beam, projecting out from a building, is another example of a fixed support.

The steel connection shown in Figure 8.10, attaching the flange (and in this case, the web) of a girder to a column, is called a *moment connection* and is an example of an idealized fixed support.

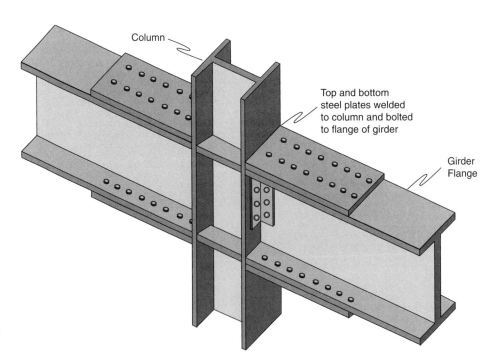

Figure 8.10 Moment Connection of a Steel Girder

Graphic Representation

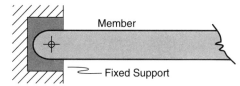

Figure 8.11 Fixed Support

Reaction on a Member

A fixed support can exert a force on a member acting in any direction and in addition can exert a resisting moment acting in either rotational direction (Figure 8.12).

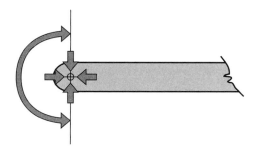

Figure 8.12 Possible Reactions

Restraint of Movement

A fixed support prevents all translational movement and all rotational movement (Figure 8.13).

Figure 8.13 No Movement

A member that has only a single fixed support is theoretically stable by itself, since all translational and rotational movements are prevented at the fixed support. However, the member may still deform under load. The member's deformation should not be confused with rotational movement at the fixed support, which does not occur (Figure 8.14).

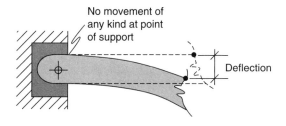

Figure 8.14 Deformation of a Member at a Fixed Support

8.4 Hanger Supports

Hanger supports can be found in suspension bridges, canopies, signs, and so on (Figures 8.15 and 8.16). Hanger supports can act only in tension. Steel cables, rods, and flat bars are typically used as hanger supports

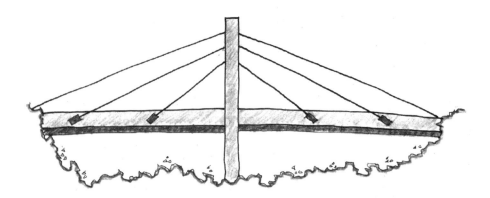

Figure 8.15 Hanger Supports on the Beam of a Bridge

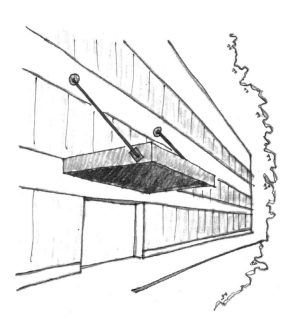

Figure 8.16 Hanger Supports on a Canopy

Graphic Representation

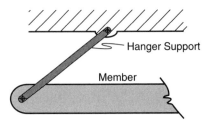

Figure 8.17 Hanger Support

Reaction on a Member

A hanger support can only exert a force on a member acting away from the member in the direction of the hanger (Figure 8.18).

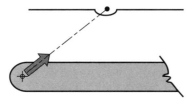

Figure 8.18 Possible Reactions

Restraint of Movement

A hanger support cannot prevent translational movement in all directions and cannot prevent any rotational movement (i.e., cannot exert resisting moment). Examples of the types of movement allowed are shown in Figures 8.19a and 8.19b.

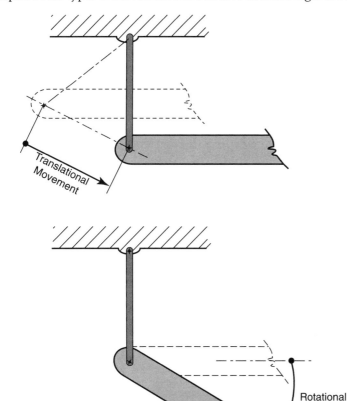

Figure 8.19a Translational Movement

Figure 8.19b Rotational Movement

8.5 Familiar Examples of Support Conditions

Let's analyze examples of support conditions for three familiar objects: (1) a skateboard, (2) a ladder, and (3) a beam supporting a suspended sign. Once again, think of each of these three objects as a beam, create a free-body diagram, and apply the equilibrium equations. As you review the examples, try to visualize the forces and reactions acting on the objects in order to understand how a support type affects reactions and restrains movement.

■ EXAMPLE 8a.1: A Skateboard

Wyatt's skateboard has a set of front and rear wheels 2 ft apart. Weighing 100 lbs and standing in the middle of his board, Wyatt starts his way down a ramp inclined at 4 horizontal to 3 vertical. Halfway down, the rear wheels fall off. What is the frictional force required by the ramp's surface to resist Wyatt's downward movement and bring him to a stop?

DISCUSSION

A skateboard is actually a beam on two sets of roller supports (i.e., wheels) designed not only to support the weight of a skateboarder, but also specifically designed to allow translational movement. When on the ramp, the skateboard fulfills its mission and rolls downward (Figure 8.20). Let's analyze why.

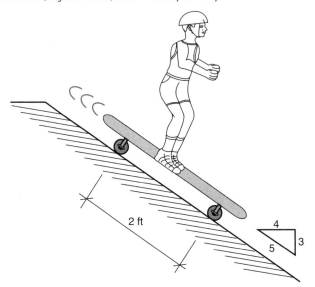

Figure 8.20 A Skateboard on a Ramp

Creating the free-body diagram (with both sets of wheels attached)

While Wyatt is rolling down the ramp, from the free-body diagram we see three forces acting on the skateboard (Figure 8.21a):

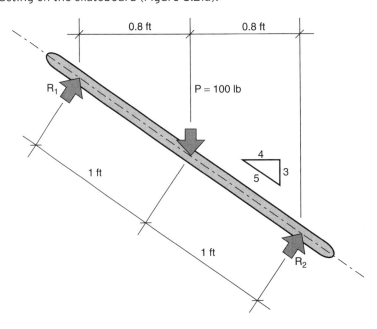

Figure 8.21a Free-body Diagram

- Wyatt's 100 lb weight, P, acting vertically downward at the center of the skateboard
- The two sets of wheels (i.e., roller supports), R_1 and R_2, acting normal to and away from the ramp (i.e., normal to and away from the surface on which the skateboard rests)

To simplify our visualization of forces, let's rotate the free-body diagram so that the axis of the skateboard is horizontal (Figure 8.21b). Resolving P into its vertical and horizontal components, we can readily determine that:

$$P_y = - 80 \text{ lb (vertically downward)}$$
$$P_x = + 60 \text{ lb (horizontally to the right)}$$
$$R_1 = + 40 \text{ lb (vertically upward)}$$
$$R_2 = + 40 \text{ lb (vertically upward)}$$

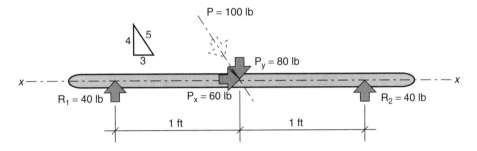

Figure 8.21b Rotated Free-body Diagram

What we observe is that there is no horizontal force capable of being applied to the skateboard to resist the 60 lb force of P_x. The equilibrium equations cannot be satisfied, and the skateboard rolls down the ramp.

Creating the free-body diagram (with the rear set of wheels detached)

With the rear wheels detached, the rear support comes in contact with the ground, creating a frictional force on the skateboard (Figure 8.22).

Fig. 8.22 A Skateboard on a Ramp (with rear wheels detached)

From the free-body diagram we see four forces acting on the skateboard (Figure 8.23a):

- Wyatt's 100 lb weight, P, acting vertically downward at the center of the skateboard
- The front set of wheels (i.e., roller supports), R_2, acting normal to and away from the ramp
- The rear support exerting a force R_1 acting normal to and away from the ramp, and also exerting a frictional component F acting uphill and parallel to the skateboard's axis

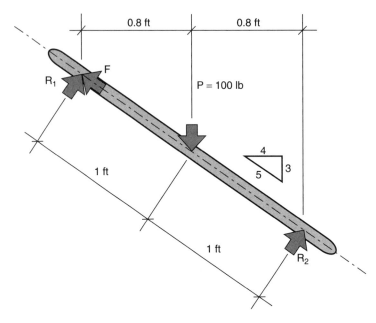

Figure 8.23a Free-body Diagram

To simplify our visualization of forces, let's again rotate the free-body diagram so that the axis of the skateboard is horizontal (Figure 8.21c). We can now readily determine all forces acting on the skateboard:

$$P_y = -80 \text{ lb (vertically downward)}$$
$$P_x = +60 \text{ lb (horizontally to the right)}$$
$$F = -60 \text{ lb (horizontally to the left)}$$
$$R_1 = +40 \text{ lb (vertically upward)}$$
$$R_2 = +40 \text{ lb (vertically upward)}$$

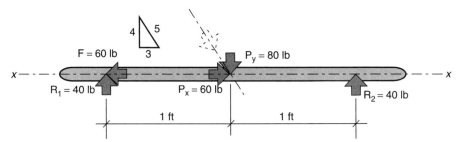

Figure 8.23b Rotated Free-body Diagram

DISCUSSION

The frictional force component F (60 lbs) of the rear support acts equal and opposite to P_x (60 lbs), keeping the skateboard in equilibrium and at rest. Had the ramp been covered by a sheet of ice, thereby creating a frictionless surface at the rear support (incapable of providing a frictional force F), Wyatt would have continued down the ramp just as if the rear wheels had remained in place.

■ EXAMPLE 8b.1: A Ladder

A 20 lb, 15 ft long ladder is resting on a concrete sidewalk covered by a sheet of ice and is leaning against a glass wall. The base of the ladder is 9 ft away from the wall, thereby putting the top of the ladder 12 ft above the sidewalk. Assuming that both the ice-covered sidewalk and the glass wall are frictionless-surface supports, what will happen to the ladder?

Creating the free-body diagram

We see that there are three forces acting on the ladder (Figure 8.24):

- The 20 lb weight of the ladder, P, acting vertically downward at the center of the ladder
- The glass wall, a frictionless-surface support exerting a reactive force on the ladder, R_{1x}, acting horizontally to the left normal to and away from the wall (i.e., perpendicular to and away from the surface on which that end of the ladder rests)
- The ice-covered sidewalk, a frictionless-surface support exerting a reactive force on the ladder, R_{2y}, acting vertically upward, normal to and away from the sidewalk (i.e., perpendicular to and away from the surface on which that end of the ladder rests)

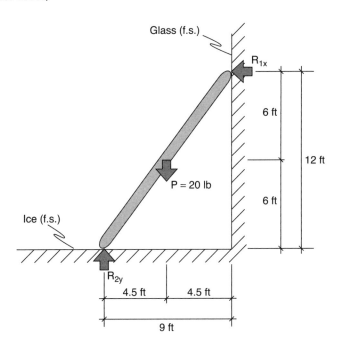

Figure 8.24 Free-body Diagram

DISCUSSION

Neither frictionless-surface support is capable of exerting a horizontal force to the right (to oppose R_{1x}) and keep the base of the ladder from sliding to the left. The frictionless-surface supports simply cannot exert the necessary reactions to satisfy the equilibrium equations. The ladder is unstable and falls (Figure 8.25).

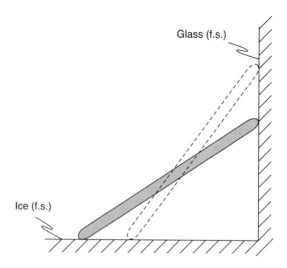

Figure 8.25 Movement of the Unstable Ladder

■ EXAMPLE 8b.2

Suppose that the ice has melted and the ladder now rests on the concrete sidewalk. We'll still assume that the glass wall is a frictionless-surface support but that the concrete sidewalk is capable of providing frictional resistance. If the frictional resistance of the sidewalk is great enough, we can visualize that the ladder could very well be stable. Let's modify the free-body diagram to account for this frictional resistance and apply the equilibrium equations.

Modifying the free-body diagram

See Figure 8.26.

1. The 20 lb weight of the ladder, P, is still acting vertically downward at the center of the ladder.

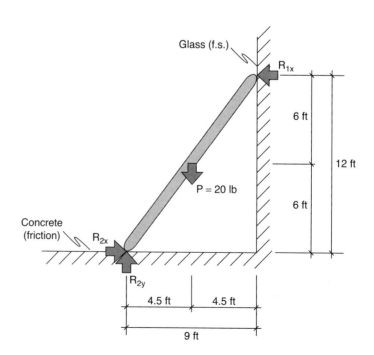

Figure 8.26 Free-body Diagram

2. The glass wall, a frictionless-surface support, is still exerting a reactive force on the ladder, R_{1x}, acting horizontally to the left.
3. But now, in addition to R_{2y} acting vertically upward, the concrete sidewalk also provides frictional resistance, R_{2x}, acting horizontally to the right.

Applying the equilibrium equations

$\Sigma M_{R2} = 0$ (choosing R_2 as the point about which moments are calculated)

$\Sigma M_{R2} = + (P \times 4.5 \text{ ft}) - (R_{1x} \times 12 \text{ ft}) = 0$

$\Sigma M_{R2} = + (20 \text{ lb} \times 4.5 \text{ ft}) - (R_{1x} \times 12 \text{ ft}) = 0$

$\Sigma M_{R2} = + (90) - (12R_{1x}) = 0$

$R_{1x} = 7.5 \text{ lb}$

$\Sigma F_x = 0$

$\Sigma F_x = + (R_{2x}) - (R_{1x}) = 0$

$\Sigma F_x = + (R_{2x}) - (7.5 \text{ lb}) = 0$

$R_{2x} = 7.5 \text{ lb}$

$\Sigma F_y = 0$

$\Sigma F_x = + (R_{2y}) - (P) = 0$

$\Sigma F_x = + (R_{2y}) - (20 \text{ lb}) = 0$

$R_{2y} = 20 \text{ lb}$

DISCUSSION

The 20 lb downward vertical weight of the ladder is resisted entirely by R_{2y}, the vertical component of the sidewalk's reaction acting upward. The weight of the ladder creates a reaction, R_{1x}, of 7.5 lbs from the glass wall that is opposed entirely by R_{2x}, the frictional horizontal component of the sidewalk's reaction. It is this force, R_{2x}, that keeps the ladder's base from sliding to the left. As long as the frictional resistance, R_{2x}, is large enough (a risky proposition), the equilibrium equations can be satisfied and the ladder made stable.

■ EXAMPLE 8b.3

Suppose that a 180 lb man is now carefully standing upright at the midpoint of the ladder. Since it is too risky to rely on the frictional resistance of the concrete sidewalk to keep the ladder stable, the base of the ladder is attached to the concrete sidewalk with a pinned support (Figure 8.27). What are the forces and reactions acting on the ladder?

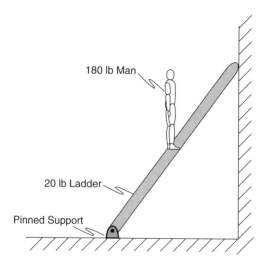

Figure 8.27 Ladder with Pinned Support at Base

Creating the free-body diagram

See Figure 8.28:

- The 20 lb weight of the ladder and the 180 lb man combine for a total load, P, of 200 lbs acting vertically downward at the center of the ladder.
- The glass wall, a frictionless-surface support, is still exerting a reactive force on the ladder, R_{1x}, acting horizontally to the left.
- The pinned support exerts a reactive force on the ladder having a vertical component, R_{2y}, acting upward and a horizontal component, R_{2x}, acting to the right.

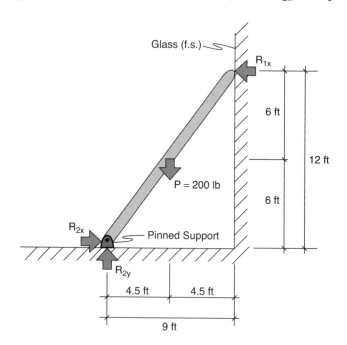

Figure 8.28 Free-body Diagram

Applying the equilibrium equations

$\sum M_{R2} = 0$ (choosing R_2 as the point about which moments are calculated)

$\sum M_{R2} = + (P \times 4.5 \text{ ft}) - (R_{1x} \times 12 \text{ ft}) = 0$

$\sum M_{R2} = + (200 \text{ lb} \times 4.5 \text{ ft}) - (R_{1x} \times 12 \text{ ft}) = 0$

$\sum M_{R2} = + (900) - (12 R_{1x}) = 0$

$R_{1x} = 75$ lb

$$\Sigma F_x = 0$$

$$\Sigma F_x = + (R_{2x}) - (R_{1x}) = 0$$

$$\Sigma F_x = + (R_{2x}) - (75 \text{ lb}) = 0$$

$$\mathbf{R_{2x} = 75 \text{ lb}}$$

$$\Sigma F_y = 0$$

$$\Sigma F_y = + (R_{2y}) - (P) = 0$$

$$\Sigma F_y = + (R_{2y}) - (200 \text{ lb}) = 0$$

$$\mathbf{R_{2y} = 200 \text{ lb}}$$

DISCUSSION

Aside from the increased weight and greater reactions on the ladder, the forces in this example are exactly analogous to those in Example 8b.2 (the exposed concrete sidewalk). The difference is that the pinned connection at the base of the ladder can, of course, provide much higher horizontal resistance than friction, thereby allowing the ladder to carry much heavier loads. The supports are able to exert the necessary reactions to satisfy the equilibrium equations and keep the ladder stable.

■ EXAMPLE 8b.4

With a pinned support at the base of the ladder, describe the effect on the reactions at the wall and base with the man standing near the bottom of the ladder and with the man standing near the top of the ladder.

DISCUSSION

Although we could apply the equilibrium equations to prove it, we understand intuitively that as the man starts to climb near the bottom of the ladder, relatively little force is exerted by the wall (R_{1x}) and equally little force is exerted by the horizontal component of the pinned support (R_{2x}) (Figure 8.29a).

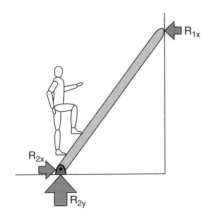

Figure 8.29a Free-body Diagram: Man near Bottom of Ladder

As the man approaches the top of the ladder, the force exerted by the wall (R_{1x}) increases, as does the horizontal component of the reactive force at the pinned support (R_{2x}). No matter where he stands, however, the vertical component of the reaction at the pinned support (R_{2y}) is the only force capable of providing the vertical resistance to carry the weight of the man and the ladder (Figure 8.29b). Therefore, this vertical force component (R_{2y}) remains the same in both cases.

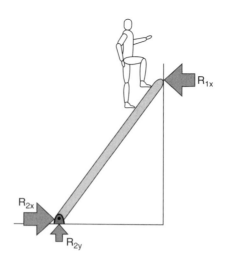

Figure 8.29b Free-body Diagram: Man near Top of Ladder

■ EXAMPLE 8c.1: **A Suspended Sign**

A 4 ft long horizontal beam has a pinned support at the left end attached to a wall. A cable support at the right end is attached to the wall 3 ft above the beam. A 1000 lb sign is suspended from the midpoint of the beam (Figure 8.30). Ignoring the weight of the beam, what are the reactions on it?

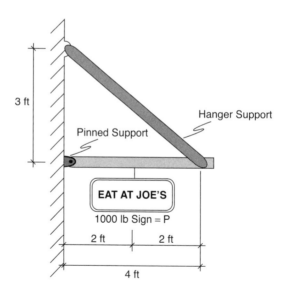

Figure 8.30 A Suspended Sign

Creating the free-body diagram

See Figure 8.31:

- The sign at the midpoint of the beam exerts a 1000 lb load, P, acting vertically downward.
- The cable support at the right end exerts a reactive force, R_2, acting away from the beam in the directional line of the cable. R_2 has a vertical component, R_{2y}, and a horizontal component, R_{2x}.
- The pinned support at the left end exerts a reactive force on the beam, having a vertical component, R_{1y}, and a horizontal component R_{1x}

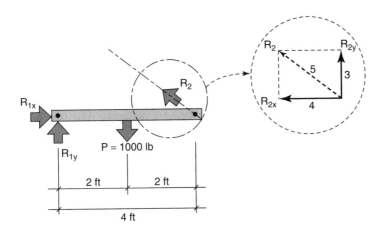

Figure 8.31 Free-body Diagram

Applying the equilibrium equations

$\Sigma M_{R2} = 0$ (choosing R_2 as the point about which moments are calculated)

$\Sigma M_{R2} = + (R_{1y} \times 4 \text{ ft}) - (P \times 2 \text{ ft}) = 0$

$\Sigma M_{R2} = + (R_{1y} \times 4 \text{ ft}) - (1000 \text{ lb} \times 2 \text{ ft}) = 0$

$\Sigma M_{R2} = + (4R_{1y}) - (2000) = 0$

$R_{1y} = 500 \text{ lb}$

$\Sigma F_y = 0$

$\Sigma F_y = + (R_{1y}) - (P) + (R_{2y}) = 0$

$(500 \text{ lb}) - (1000 \text{ lb}) + (R_{2y}) = 0$

$- (500) + (R_{2y}) = 0$

$R_{2y} = 500 \text{ lb}$

If R_{1y} is 500 lb, then R_{2x} can be determined from the proportions of a 3:4:5 right triangle:

$R_{2x} = (4/3) \times (500 \text{ lb})$

$R_{2x} = 667 \text{ lb}$

$\Sigma F_x = 0$

$\Sigma F_x = + (R_{1x}) - (R_{2x}) = 0$

$\Sigma F_x = + (R_{1x}) - (667 \text{ lb}) = 0$

$R_{1x} = 667 \text{ lb}$

DISCUSSION

The 1000 lb sign placed at the middle of the beam is carried equally by the vertical components of the reactions at the cable (R_{2y}) and pinned (R_{1y}) supports. In addition, opposing horizontal components of the reactions at both supports (R_{1x} and R_{2x}) are developed. The supports are able to exert the necessary reactions to satisfy the equilibrium equations and keep the beam stable.

■ EXAMPLE 8c.2

Instead of pinned and cable supports, suppose that the beam now has a single fixed support at the left end (Figure 8.32). What are the reactions on the beam?

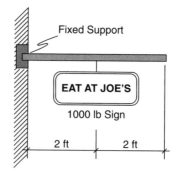

Figure 8.32 A Suspended Sign

Creating the free-body diagram

See Figure 8.33.

1. The sign at the midpoint of the beam exerts a 1000 lb load, P, acting vertically downward.
2. The fixed support at the left end exerts a vertical reactive force, R_{1y}, acting upward to oppose the weight of the sign. Since there are no horizontal forces on the beam, there is no horizontal component for the reaction at the fixed support.
3. The fixed support, however, must also develop a counterclockwise resisting moment, M, to keep the beam stable.

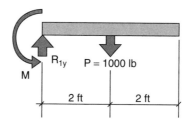

Figure 8.33 Free-body Diagram

Applying the equilibrium equations

$\sum M_{R1} = 0$ (choosing R_1 as the point about which moments are calculated)
$\sum M_{R1} = -(M) + (P \times 2\text{ ft}) = 0$
$\sum M_{R1} = -(M) + (1000\text{ lb} \times 2\text{ ft}) = 0$
$\sum M_{R1} = -(M) + (2000) = 0$

$M_{R1} = 2000$ lb-ft

$\sum F_y = 0$
$\sum F_y = +(R_{1y}) - (P) = 0$
$\sum F_y = +(R_{1y}) - (1000\text{ lb}) = 0$

$R_{1y} = 1000$ lb

DISCUSSION

This example is exactly analogous to the fishing rod example in Chapter 6. Since the sign exerts no horizontal force on the beam, there is no horizontal component of the reaction at the fixed support. The beam is kept stable by the combination of R_{1y} and the counterclockwise moment M. If there were a different load on the beam, one having a horizontal as well as a vertical component, then the fixed support would have exerted a reaction having a horizontal as well as a vertical component. The supports are able to exert the necessary reactions to satisfy the equilibrium equations and keep the beam stable.

■ EXAMPLE 8c.3

Let's take the suspended sign and move it to the right side of the beam at the cable support (Figure 8.34). What are the reactions on the beam?

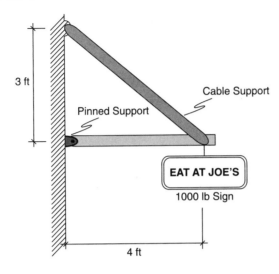

Figure 8.34 A Suspended Sign

Modifying the free-body diagram

See Figure 8.35.

1. The sign, now at the right end of the beam, exerts a 1000 lb load, P, acting vertically downward.
2. The cable support still exerts a reactive force, R_2, acting away from the beam in the directional line of the cable. R_2 has a vertical component, R_{2y}, and a horizontal component, R_{2x}.
3. The pinned support still exerts a reactive force on the beam, which we will assume has a vertical component, R_{1y}, and a horizontal component, R_{1x}.

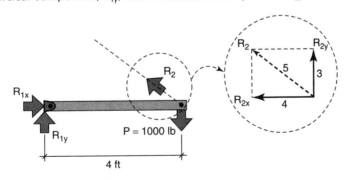

Figure 8.35 Free-body Diagram

Applying the equilibrium equations

$\sum M_{R2} = 0$ (choosing R_2 as the point about which moments are calculated)

$\sum M_{R2} = + (R_{1y} \times 4 \text{ ft}) = 0$

$\sum M_{R2} = + (4R_{1y}) = 0$

   $R_{1y} = 0$

$\sum F_y = 0$

$\sum F_y = + (R_{1y}) + (R_{2y}) - (P) = 0$

$\sum F_y = + (0) + (R_{2y}) - (1000 \text{ lb}) = 0$

   $R_{2y} = 1000 \text{ lb}$

If R_{2y} is 1000 lb, then R_{2x} can be determined from the proportions of a 3:4:5 right triangle:

$$R_{2x} = (4/3) \times (1000 \text{ lb})$$

$$\mathbf{R_{2x} = 1333 \text{ lb}}$$

$$\Sigma F_x = 0$$
$$\Sigma F_x = + (R_{1x}) - (R_{2x}) = 0$$
$$\Sigma F_x = + (R_{1x}) - (1333 \text{ lb}) = 0$$

$$\mathbf{R_{1x} = 1333 \text{ lb}}$$

DISCUSSION

With the sign suspended at the right side of the beam, we see that its entire weight is carried by the vertical component of the reaction at the cable support (R_{2y}) and that there is no vertical component of the reaction at the pinned support ($R_{1y} = 0$). On the other hand, the horizontal components of the reactions at both supports (R_{1x} and R_{2x}) are twice as much as when the sign was at the midpoint in Example 8c.1 (1333 lb vs. 667 lb). The supports are able to exert the necessary reactions to satisfy the equilibrium equations and keep the beam stable.

8.6 Stable or Unstable?

Analyze the support and loading conditions of the members in Figures 8.36 through 8.44 to determine whether they are stable or unstable. Start with your intuition and try to visualize the forces at play. Then create free-body diagrams, showing the reactions developed by each support type, to see if the supports are able to exert the necessary reactions to keep the member stable. (Try doing this first on your own without looking at the solutions.)

Remember that these are theoretical examples to help familiarize you with *idealized* support types and the reactions they exert. Even though a member may be theoretically stable, it may not necessarily be supported wisely. Also remember that the stability of a member can be very much dependent on the specific loading condition. Therefore, while some of these examples may be stable under the given loading condition, they may not be so under a different loading condition.

Finally, keep in mind that these examples are about *stability*. Although a long cantilever beam having a fixed support may be theoretically stable under load (Figure 8.44), it would still have to be designed with the proper material and cross section to provide the *strength* to resist the stresses and deflection. Therefore, the reader should be aware that the longer the cantilever is, the more challenging is its design!

In Figure 8.36 neither the frictionless-surface support on the left nor the roller support on the right can provide the horizontal restraint to oppose the horizontal component of P (i.e., P_x). Since the supports cannot restrain the translational movement shown, the member is *unstable*.

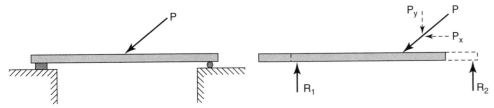

Figure 8.36
(a) Support and Loading Condition   **(b)** Free-body Diagram

In Figure 8.37 the pinned support on the right can provide the horizontal restraint (i.e., R_{2x}) to oppose the horizontal component of P (i.e., P_x). Since the supports can restrain movement, the member is *stable*.

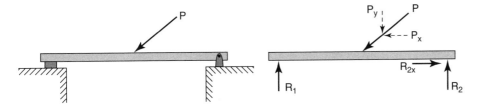

Figure 8.37
(a) Support and Loading Condition   **(b)** Free-body Diagram

In Figure 8.38 neither the frictionless-surface support on the left nor the pinned support on the right can provide the rotational restraint to oppose the moment caused by P. Since the supports cannot restrain the rotational movement shown, the member is *unstable*.

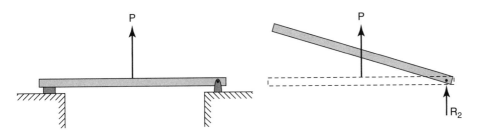

Figure 8.38
(a) Support and Loading Condition   **(b)** Free-body Diagram

In Figure 8.39 neither the hanger support on the left nor the frictionless-surface support on the right can provide the translational and rotational restraint to oppose P. Since the supports cannot restrain the translational and rotational movement shown, the member is *unstable*.

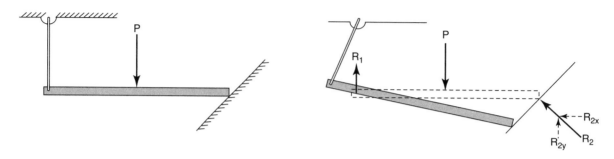

Figure 8.39
(a) Support and Loading Condition

(b) Free-body Diagram

In Figure 8.40 the frictionless-surface supports on the left and right can provide both the vertical and horizontal restraint to oppose P. Since the supports can restrain movement, the member is *stable*.

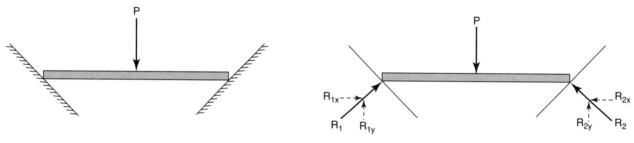

Figure 8.40
(a) Support and Loading Condition

(b) Free-body Diagram

In Figure 8.41, neither frictionless-surface support on the left or right can provide the restraint to oppose P and the member will start translational and rotational movement. The closer P is to the horizontal, the greater the tendency for the movement. Since the supports cannot restrain the translational and rotational movement shown, the member is *unstable*.

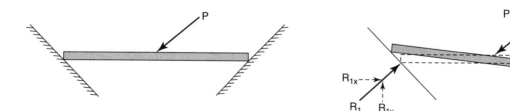

Figure 8.41
(a) Support and Loading Condition

(b) Free-body Diagram

In Figure 8.42 the pinned support on the top and the hanger support on the bottom can provide the translational restraint to oppose P_1 and P_2, but the supports cannot provide the rotational restraint to oppose the moment caused by P_1. Since the supports cannot restrain the rotational movement shown, the member is *unstable*.

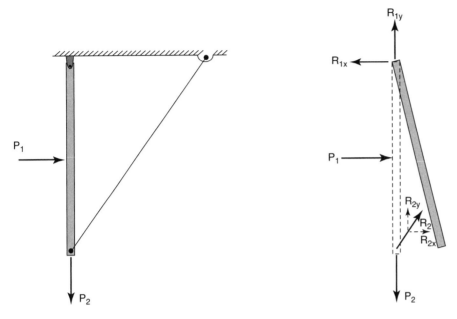

Figure 8.42
(a) Support and Loading Condition   **(b)** Free-body Diagram

In Figure 8.43 the pinned support on the top and the hanger support on the bottom can provide the translational and rotational restraint to oppose P_1 and P_2. Since the supports can restrain movement, the member is *stable*.

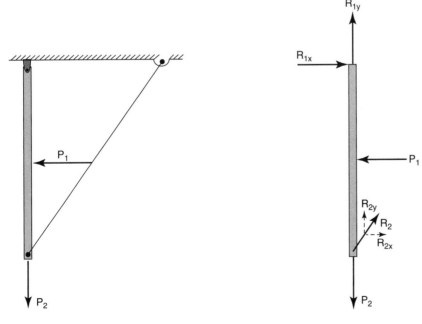

Figure 8.43
(a) Support and Loading Condition   **(b)** Free-body Diagram

In Figure 8.44 the fixed support on the left, by itself, can provide the translational and rotational restraint to oppose P. Since the support can restrain movement, the member is *stable*.

Figure 8.44

(a) Support and Loading Condition   **(b)** Free-body Diagram

Load Distribution

As we know from Chapter 3, the load path conducts various loads through a structure from their place of origin (roofs, walls, floors) through beams, girders, columns, foundations, and ultimately to the ground. Loads can be applied in several different ways.

9.1 Point Loads

Point loads occur at a single location. A beam framing into a girder, a column seated atop a girder, and the man standing on the log in Chapter 6 are examples of point loads. Appropriately enough, point loads are also called *concentrated loads* (Figures 9.1a and 9.1b).

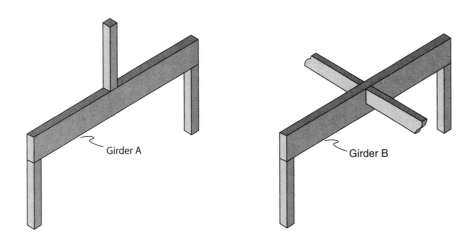

Girder A

Girder B

Free-body Diagram

Figure 9.1a Point Loads on Girder A and B

79

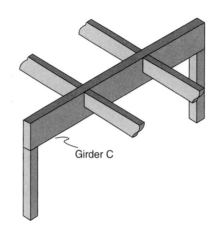

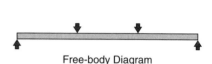

Figure 9.1b Point Loads on Girder C

Free-body Diagram

9.2 Distributed Loads

Distributed loads are spread out over an area of floor or over a length of a member. Distributed loads are expressed in *weight per unit of area*, such as pounds per square foot (psf); or *weight per unit of length*, such as pounds per linear foot (plf) or kips per linear foot (klf) (1 kip = 1000 lbs).

To illustrate the distinction between a point load and a distributed load, let's use an example of a man, 6 ft tall and weighing 180 lbs, standing at the center of a 20 ft log spanning a ditch. When standing, his weight is a point load (Figure 9.2).

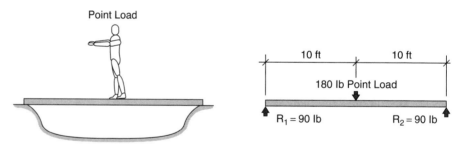

Figure 9.2 A Point Load

(a) A Man Standing on a Log

(b) Free-body Diagram

If the man lies down, however, his weight spreads out (i.e., is distributed) over a 6 ft length of log. His weight then changes from a point load of 180 lbs to a distributed load of 30 plf (i.e., 180 lb/6 ft) (Figure 9.3).

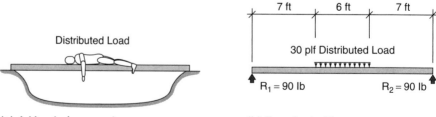

Figure 9.3 A Distributed Load

(a) A Man Lying on a Log

(b) Free-body Diagram

In either case, whether the man is standing or lying down at the center of the span, it's easily visualized that each reaction will support half of the man's total weight, or 90 lbs.

It's also easily visualized that, with the man's weight concentrated as a point load (i.e., while standing), the beam will have a greater deflection than if his weight is distributed (i.e., while lying down) (Figures 9.4 and 9.5).

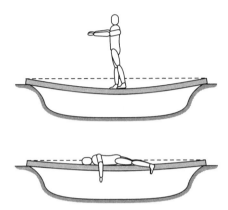

Figure 9.4 Larger Deflection under a Point Load

Figure 9.5 Smaller Deflection under a Distributed Load

While a point load and a distributed load have the same effect for a beam's reactions, we see that they have a quite different effect on a beam's behavior.

9.3 Equivalent Point Loads

See Appendix A5.1 for a review of centroids.

■ EXAMPLE 9a: Calculating Reactions Using an Equivalent Point Load

As we know from Chapter 6, wherever the man stands (i.e., as a point load) along the length of the 20 ft log, we can use the equilibrium equations to determine the reactions. Suppose, however, that the man is standing 6 ft from the left end and then decides to lie down (i.e., become a distributed load). How would we then calculate the reactions?

For the purpose of calculating reactions on a beam, and only for that purpose, the effect of a distributed load is equivalent to a point load acting through its centroid.

Determining the Equivalent Point Load and Reactions

Assuming that the man's 180 lb weight is equally (i.e., uniformly) distributed throughout his 6 ft height, his centroid and equivalent point load would be located as shown in Figures 9.6a and b, and we can readily determine by using the equilibrium equations that $R_1 = 126$ lbs and $R_2 = 54$ lbs.

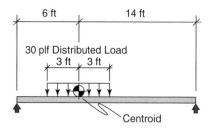

Figure 9.6a The Centroid of the Distributed Load

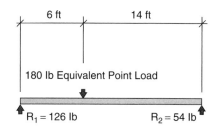

Figure 9.6b Free-body Diagram with the Equivalent Point Load

9.4 Uniformly Distributed Loads

If a distributed load is the same over each square foot of an area, or the same along each linear foot of a beam, it is called a *uniformly distributed load* (UDL). Live loads, such as people and furniture on a floor or snow on a roof, are examples of uniformly distributed loads over an area of floor. A wall of uniform height supported by a beam is an example of a uniformly distributed load over the length of a beam. In Example 9b, we'll analyze how a uniformly distributed load develops onto a beam from an area of floor. In Example 9c, we'll analyze how a uniformly distributed load develops onto a beam from a superimposed wall.

■ EXAMPLE 9b: A Uniformly Distributed Load on a Beam (from an area of floor)

A 20 ft beam is supporting a 20 ft long by 10 ft wide section of floor. The combined live and dead load of the floor is 100 psf (Figure 9.7). Determine: (1) the uniformly distributed load on the beam from the live and dead loads and (2) the reactions at each end of the beam .

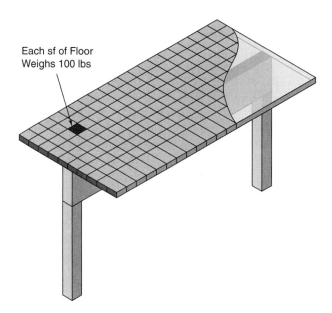

Each sf of Floor Weighs 100 lbs

Figure 9.7 A Uniformly Distributed Floor Load

1. Determining the uniformly distributed load on the Beam

Since each sq ft of floor surface weighs 100 lbs (i.e., 100 psf), each 1 ft long (by 10 ft wide) strip of floor weighs 1000 lbs, or 1 kip (i.e., 1 ft x 10 ft x 100 psf). Therefore, the uniformly distributed load on the beam from the live and dead floor loads is 1000 plf, or 1 klf (Figures 9.8a and 9.8b).

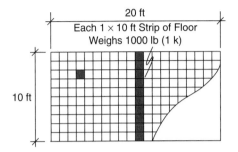

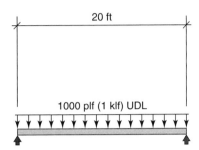

Figure 9.8a Plan of Uniformly Distributed Floor Load

Figure 9.8b Free-body Diagram of the Beam under the UDL

2. Determining the Reactions

Since the uniformly distributed load is 1 klf and since the loading condition is symmetrical, we know that the centroid and the equivalent point load of 20 kips (i.e., 1 klf × 20 ft) are located at the center of the span. Using the equilibrium equations, or simply by inspection for this simple example, it can readily be determined that R_1 and R_2 each equal 10 kips (Figures 9.9a and 9.9b).

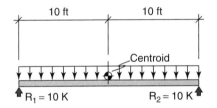

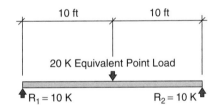

Figure 9.9a The Centroid of the UDL

Figure 9.9b Free-body Diagram of the Beam under the Equivalent Point Load

■ EXAMPLE 9c: A Uniformly Distributed Load on a Beam (from a superimposed wall)

A 20 ft beam is supporting a 20 ft long by 5 ft high rectangular wall. The weight of the wall is 200 psf of vertical wall surface (Figure 9.10). Determine: (1) the uniformly distributed weight on the beam from the weight of the wall and (2) the reactions at each end of the beam.

1. Determining the Uniformly Distributed load on the Beam

Since each sq ft of wall surface weighs 200 lbs (i.e., 200 psf), each 1 ft long (by 5 ft high) vertical strip of wall surface weighs 1000 lbs, or 1 kip (i.e., 1 ft × 5 ft × 200 psf). Therefore, the uniformly distributed load on the beam from the weight of the wall is 1000 plf, or 1 klf (Figures 9.11a and 9.11b).

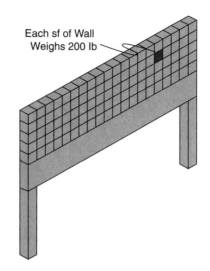

Figure 9.10 A Uniformly
Distributed Wall load

Each sf of Wall
Weighs 200 lb

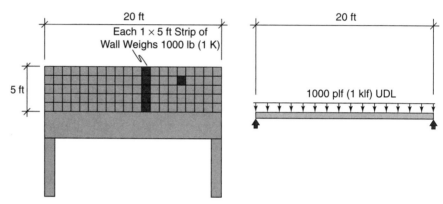

Figure 9.11a Elevation of Uniformly
Distributed Wall Load

Figure 9.11b Free-body Diagram of
the Beam under the UDL

2. Determining the Reactions

The area of the wall is 100 sq ft (i.e., 20 ft × 5 ft). Since each sq ft of wall surface weighs 200 lbs (i.e., 200 psf), the total weight of the wall is 20,000 lbs, or 20 kips (i.e., 100 sq ft × 200 psf). Since the loading condition is symmetrical, we know that the centroid and equivalent point load of 20 kips are located at the center of the span (Figures 9.12a and 9.12b).

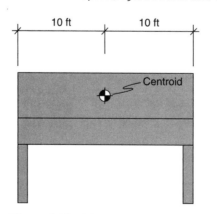

Figure 9.12a The Centroid of the UDL

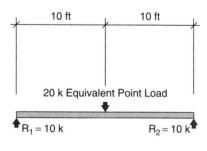

Figure 9.12b Free-body Diagram
of the Beam under the Equivalent
Point Load

Using the equilibrium equations, or simply by inspection for this simple example, it can readily be determined that R_1 and R_2 each equal 10 kips.

9.5 Non-Uniformly Distributed Loads

Distributed loads can also be *non-uniformly distributed*. Unevenly accumulated wind-blown snow is an example of a non-uniformly distributed load over an area of roof. If the wall supported by the beam in Example 9c was triangular, varying in height, it would be an example of a non- uniformly distributed load over the length of the beam.

■ EXAMPLE 9d: A Non-uniformly Distributed Load on a Beam (from a superimposed wall)

A 20 ft beam is supporting a triangular wall varying in height from zero at the left end to 5 ft at the right end. The weight of the wall is 200 psf of vertical wall surface (Figure 9.13). Determine: (1) the non-uniformly distributed load on the beam from the weight of the wall and (2) the reactions at each end of the beam.

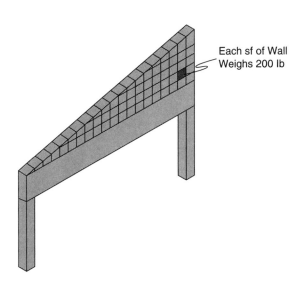

Each sf of Wall Weighs 200 lb

Figure 9.13 A Non-uniformly Distributed Wall Load

1. **Determining the Non-uniformly distributed load on the Beam**

   Each sq ft of wall surface weighs 200 lbs (i.e., 200 psf). Given the triangular shape of the wall, each 1 ft long vertical strip of wall surface varies in weight. Therefore, the non-uniformly distributed load on the beam from the weight of the wall varies linearly from zero at the left end to 1000 plf (i.e., 1 ft × 5 ft × 200 psf), or 1 klf, at the right end (Figures 9.14a and 9.14b). Although the load in this example is non-uniformly distributed, it is considered to be *uniformly varying* since the slope of the load is constant.

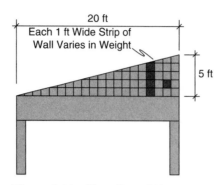

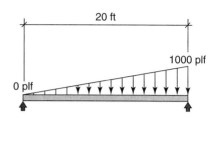

Figure 9.14a Elevation of Non-uniformly Distributed Wall Load

Figure 9.14b Free-body Diagram of the Beam under the Non-UDL

2. Determining the Reactions

The area of the wall is 50 sq ft (i.e., ½ × 20 ft × 5 ft). Since each sq ft of wall surface weighs 200 lbs (i.e., 200 psf), the total weight of the wall is 10,000 lbs, or 10 kips (i.e., 50 sq ft × 200 psf). The centroid and equivalent point load of 10 kips are located as shown (Figures 9.15a and 9.15b).

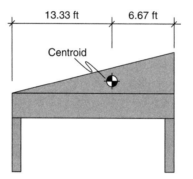

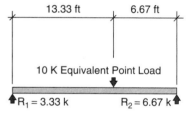

Figure 9.15a The Centroid of the Non-UDL

Figure 9.15b Free-body Diagram of the Beam under the Equivalent Point Load

Using the equilibrium equations, it can readily be determined that $R_1 = 3.33$ kips and $R_2 = 6.67$ kips.

Introduction to Beams

Beams are one of the most basic and common structural elements used in buildings. A beam may be generally defined as a horizontal member that supports loads, most often perpendicular to its length, by resisting bending. *Joists, girders, headers*, and *lintels* are simply names for specific uses of beams.

10.1 Beam Types

Beams are generally classified by the way they're supported (see Chapter 8). Although beams can be supported in many combinations of complex ways, we'll simplify their classification into four basic types: (1) *simple*, (2) fixed-end, (3) continuous, and (4) overhang (Figures 10.1 through 10.4). More important than a beam's name, however, is an understanding of its behavior.

1. *A Simple Beam:*
   A beam with simple supports (i.e., roller, frictionless-surface, or pinned) at each end. A simple beam is often referred to as a *simply supported beam* (Figure 10.1).

Figure 10.1 A Simple Beam

2. *A Fixed-end Beam:*
   A beam with a fixed support at one end, and no other support. A fixed-end beam is also referred to as a *cantilever beam* (Figure 10.2).

Figure 10.2 A Fixed-end Beam

3. *A Continuous Beam:*
   A beam with three or more supports (Figure 10.3).

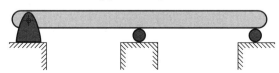

Figure 10.3 A Continuous Beam

4. An *Overhang Beam:*

A beam with one or both ends projecting (overhanging) beyond its support. Similar to a fixed-end beam, the overhanging section is also referred to as a cantilever (Figure 10.4).

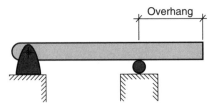

Figure 10.4 An Overhang Beam

10.2 Predicting Deformation, Deflection, and Beam Behavior

Predicting the way a beam deforms is often helpful when analyzing and understanding the internal shear and moment stresses within the beam. Through intuition and experience, the prediction will often be accurate, but even if it is not, mathematical analysis will still yield the correct results.

As we know from Chapter 6, when a member such as a beam is subjected to load, it deforms and creates deflection. The way a beam deforms is a function of:

- The loads—their type, magnitude, and location
- The supports—their type and location

In the following examples, we'll examine the four basic beam types under various load and support conditions.

■ Example 10a: A Simple Beam

A simple beam is subjected to two different loading conditions: (1) a point load at the midspan and (2) a uniformly distributed load having the same total magnitude as the point load (Figures 10.5a and 10.5b).

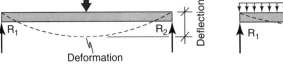 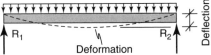

Figure 10.5 Deformation/ Deflection in a Simple Beam

(a) Under a Point Load

(b) Under a UDL

DISCUSSION

Since the total magnitude of the load is the same for these two conditions, reactions R_1 and R_2 are also the same (and equal) in each case. The beam deforms similarly under the two conditions, the difference being a greater deflection under a point load than under a uniformly distributed load.

■ Example 10b: A Fixed-End Beam

A fixed-end beam is subjected to a point load at its unsupported end (Figure 10.6).

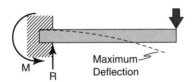

Figure 10.6 Deformation/ Deflection in a Fixed-End Beam

DISCUSSION

The beam deforms as shown with a maximum deflection at the unsupported (right) end. In addition to the vertical reaction R at the fixed end, a counterclockwise moment M is developed at the supported (left) end.

■ Example 10c: A Continuous Beam

A continuous beam is subjected to equal point loads at the two midspans (Figure 10.7).

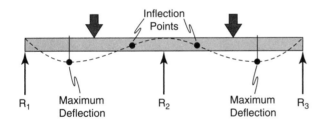

Figure 10.7 Deformation/ Deflection in a Continuous Beam

Note that there are two points at which deformational bending is reversed. These are called *inflection points* and are points of zero moment (i.e., points having no bending stress).

Compare the deformation and deflection of the continuous beam in Figure 10.7 with those of two separate, simple beams in Figure 10.8 having the same spans and loads.

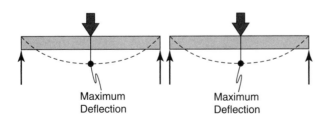

Figure 10.8 Deformation/ Deflection in Two Separate Simple Beams

DISCUSSION

In comparison to the two separate simple beams in Figure 10.8, the continuity of the continuous beam over R_2 in Figure 10.7 tends to (a) decrease the maximum deflection (i.e., decrease maximum bending in the spans between the supports) and (b) shift the points of maximum deflection closer to R_1 and R_3.

■ Example 10d: An Overhang Beam

An overhang beam having a pinned support at the left end is subjected to two different loading conditions: (1) a heavy point load at the midspan and a relatively light uniformly distributed load at the overhang (Figure 10.9a) and (2) a light point load at the midspan and a relatively heavy uniformly distributed load at the overhang (Figure 10.9b). Try to envision how the beam would deform under these two conditions.

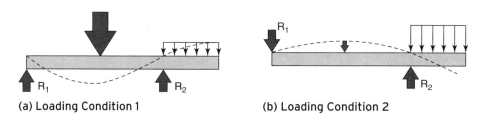

Figure 10.9 Deformation/ Deflection Comparison in an Overhang Beam

(a) Loading Condition 1   (b) Loading Condition 2

DISCUSSION

Note that the deformation, deflection, and reactions R_1 and R_2 can be dramatically different under these two loading conditions.

10.3 Statically Determinate and Statically Indeterminate Beams

Beams are also classified as statically determinate or statically indeterminate.

Statically determinate beams have reactions that can be determined by the equilibrium equations ($\Sigma F_{x,y} = 0$, $\Sigma M = 0$) alone. Simple, fixed-end, and overhang beams are statically determinate.

Statically indeterminate beams have reactions that cannot be determined by the equilibrium equations alone. A number of more complex formulae have been derived for the analysis of statically indeterminate beams that are beyond the scope of this book. Continuous beams are statically indeterminate.

The four basic beam types can be combined to create complex beam and support systems. Conversely, complex beam systems can sometimes be reduced to the four basic types in order to facilitate their analysis. The following are examples of various beam systems. We'll analyze their reactions and determinacy by creating free-body diagrams and reducing them, where possible, to the basic beam types. Beams can of course be loaded in innumerable ways so, to simplify our analysis, we'll assume a uniformly distributed load over the entire length of the beams. Note, however, that the determinacy of a beam will not be affected by different loading conditions, as long as the magnitude and locations of the loads are known and the support conditions are given. Since we're simply interested in understanding concepts in these examples, we'll stay away from any mathematical computations.

■ Example 10e: An Asymmetrically Supported Beam System

Analyze the asymmetrical beam system in Figure 10.10a to find its determinacy.

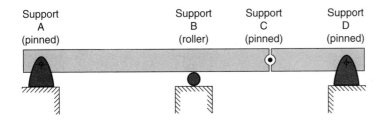

Figure 10.10a An Asymmetrically Supported Beam System

Begin by reducing this beam system to an overhang beam on the left (Beam AC) and a simple beam on the right (Beam CD), and then create a free-body diagram for each beam (Figure 10.10b).

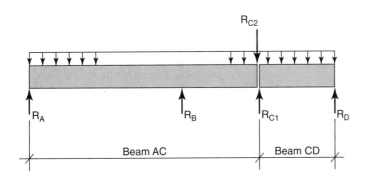

Figure 10.10b Free-body Diagram

Beam CD and the pin support at connection C hold the key to understanding the behavior of this beam system. By observation at connection C, we see that the right end of Beam AC supports the left end of Beam CD (reaction R_{C1}). As a result, the left end of Beam CD places a load (R_{C2}) onto the right end of Beam AC equal and opposite to R_{C1}. We must therefore first analyze Beam CD to determine the magnitude of R_{C1}.

Analysis of Beam CD

Beam CD has two unknown reactions (R_{C1} and R_D) that can readily be determined by applying the equilibrium equations.

Analysis of Beam AC

With R_{C1} now known, R_{C2} must be equal and opposite to it, and is therefore also known.

Beam AC therefore has two unknown reactions (R_A and R_B) that can be readily determined by applying the equilibrium equations.

DISCUSSION

Since all reactions can be determined by the equilibrium equations alone, this beam system is statically determinate.

■ Example 10f: A Symmetrically Supported Beam System

Analyze the symmetrical beam system in Figure 10.11a to find its determinacy.

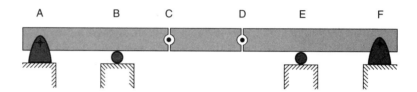

Figure 10.11a A Symmetrically Supported Beam System

Begin by reducing this beam system to an overhang beam on the left (Beam AC), a simple beam in the middle (Beam CD), and an overhang beam on the right (Beam DF), and then creating a free-body diagram for each beam (Figure 10.11b).

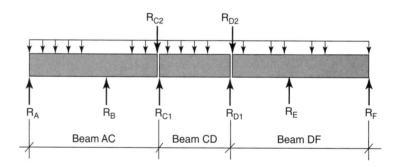

Figure 10.11b Free-body Diagram

Beam CD and the pin supports at connections C and D hold the key to understanding the behavior of this beam system. By observation at connections C and D, we see that the right end of Beam AC supports the left end of Beam CD (by reaction R_{C1}) and that the left end of Beam DF supports the right end of Beam CD (by reaction R_{D1}). As a result, the left end of Beam CD places a load (R_{C2}) onto the right end of Beam AC, and the right end of Beam CD places a load (R_{D2}) onto the left end of Beam DF. We must therefore first analyze Beam CD to determine the magnitudes of R_{C1} and R_{D1}.

Analysis of Beam CD

Beam CD has two unknown and equal reactions and equal (R_{C1} and R_{D1}) that can readily be determined by applying the equilibrium equations.

Analysis of Beams AC

With R_{C1} now known, R_{C2} must be equal and opposite to it, and is therefore also known.

Beam AC therefore has two unknown reactions (R_A and R_B) that can readily be determined by applying the equilibrium equations.

Analysis of Beams DF

The analysis of Beam DF, to determine reactions R_E and R_F, is similar to that of Beam AC.

DISCUSSION

Since all reactions can be determined by the equilibrium equations alone, this beam system is statically determinate.

■ Example 10g: An Asymmetrically Supported Beam

Analyze the asymmetrical beam in Figure 10.12a to find its determinacy.

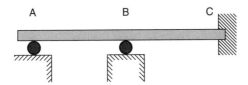

Figure 10.12a An Asymmetrically Supported Beam

Creating the free-body diagram, we see four reactions due to the vertical loading, R_A, R_B, R_C and M_C (Figure 10.12b).

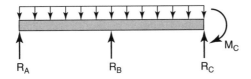

Figure 10.12b Free-body Diagram

DISCUSSION

Since the equilibrium equations alone are insufficient to solve for the reactions, this beam is statically indeterminate.

■ Example 10h: A Symmetrically Supported Beam

Analyze the symmetrical beam in Figure 10.13a to find its determinacy.

Figure 10.13a A Symmetrically Supported Beam

Creating the free-body diagram, we see four reactions due to the vertical loading, R_A, M_A, R_B, and M_B (Figure 10.13b).

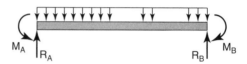

Figure 10.13b Free-body Diagram

DISCUSSION

Since the equilibrium equations alone are insufficient to solve for the reactions, this beam is statically indeterminate.

10.4 Other Considerations for Beams

Approximate Span-to-Depth Ratios

While several factors must be considered in order to establish the final depth of a beam, it's often useful to estimate their approximate depth during preliminary design. A good rule of thumb is to assume ½ in of depth for every 1 ft of span. In terms of the span-to-depth ratio, this can generally be expressed as:

$$D = L/24$$

where:

      D = depth (in inches)
      L = length (i.e., the span, in inches)(Figure 10.14)

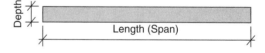

Figure 10.14 Span-to-Depth Ratio

For example, an 18 ft long beam would have an approximate depth of 9 in.
D = (18 × 12)/24 = 9 in

Lateral Buckling

Just as a column in compression has a tendency to buckle (Figure 10.15), a beam (especially a deep beam) subjected to bending has a tendency to buckle along the edge in compression.

For example, the simply supported beam in Figure 10.16 has its top edge in compression and its bottom edge in tension. The beam has a tendency to buckle laterally along the top compression edge, as shown.

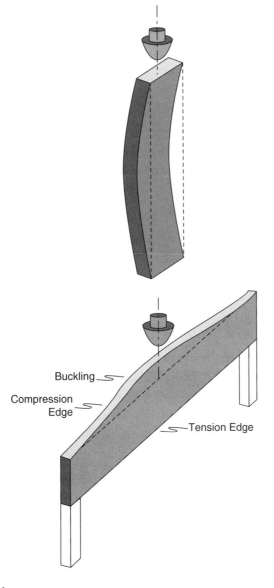

Figure 10.15 Buckling of a Column

Figure 10.16 Lateral Buckling of a Beam

Lateral Bracing

In order to prevent lateral buckling, additional members referred to as *lateral bracing* may be needed (Figure 10.17).

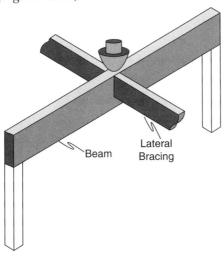

Figure 10.17 Lateral Bracing of a Beam

Another method used to prevent lateral buckling is *cross bracing*. This method is commonly used to laterally brace wood and open web steel joists (Figure 10.18).

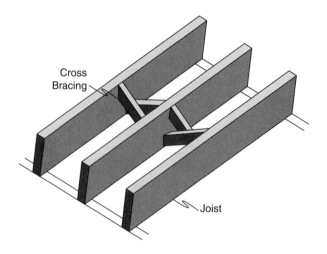

Figure 10.18 Lateral Cross Bracing of Joists

In steel construction, the compression flange of a typical wide flange beam tends to buckle as shown in Figure 10.19. The top compression flange of a steel beam, however, may be considered to be braced by the concrete slab if the beam and slab work together, as in composite construction (Figure 10.20).

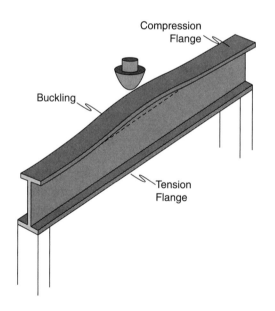

Figure 10.19 Lateral Buckling of a Steel Beam

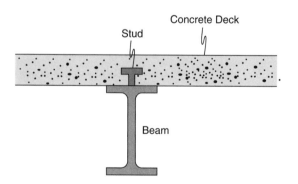

Figure 10.20 Lateral Bracing of a Steel Beam through Composite Construction

Web Stiffening

In steel construction, when large shear forces are transferred through a beam's web, the shear capacity of the web may need to be increased to prevent the web from buckling. Web buckling is referred to as *web crippling* and web reinforcing is referred to as *web stiffening* (Figure 10.21). Web buckling and web stiffening can also be factors in column design.

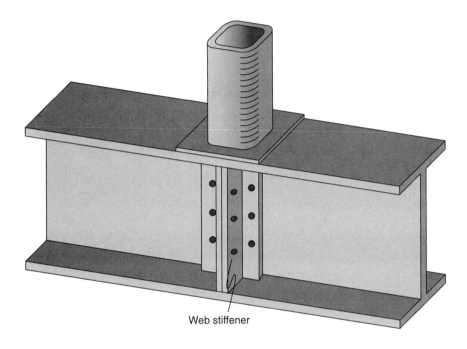

Web stiffener

Figure 10.21 Web Stiffening of a Steel Beam

Framing Systems and Load Tributary Areas

An individual member, such as a beam, girder, or column, supports live and dead loads accumulated from a section of floor or roof called its *tributary area*. Various framing systems have alternate ways of accumulating loads and therefore have different configurations for tributary areas. Although there are many variations of framing systems, ultimately all loads must work their way to the ground. Let's analyze load tributary areas and the corresponding load distribution for three general types of framing systems: one-way systems, two-way slab and beam systems, and two-way slab/joist systems. We'll look at the same example of a 40 ft × 40 ft structure, supported by nine columns, for each type of framing system. The dead loads given will include the weight of the structure itself.

11.1 One-Way Systems

One-way systems have floors spanning perpendicular to their supporting beams. Wood and steel structures are generally designed as one-way systems, as are some concrete structures (Figures 11.1 and 11.2).

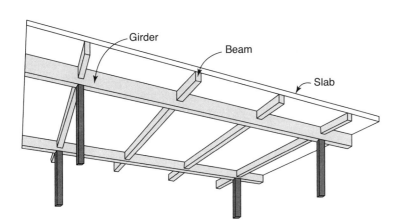

Figure 11.1 Slab, Beams, Girders, and Columns in a One-way System

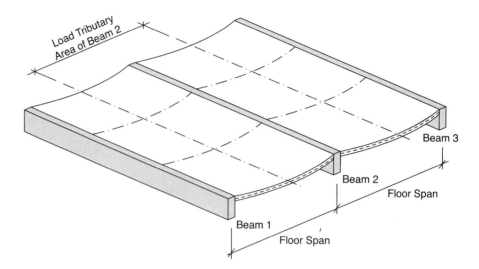

Figure 11.2 Span and Deflection in a One-way System

■ EXAMPLE 11a: Load Tributary Area/Load Path in a One-way System

The 40 ft × 40 ft one-way system in Figure 11.3 has a 100 psf dead load and a 50 psf live load, for a total load of 150 psf. What are the loads and reactions for Beam MN, Girder BE and Column E?

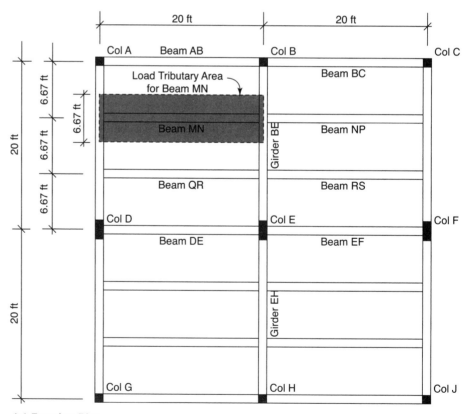

(a) Framing Plan

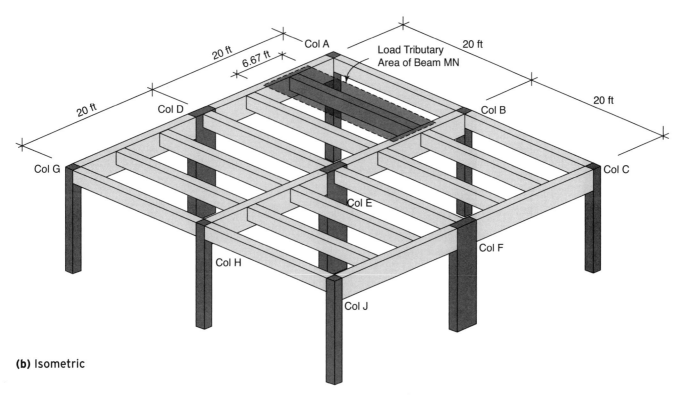

(b) Isometric

Figure 11.3 Load Tributary Area of Beam MN

Loads on Beam MN

The load tributary area for Beam MN is a section of floor 6.67 ft wide × 20 ft long (Figure 11.4). Each 1 ft wide strip of floor, running transversely to the beam, weighs 1000 lbs (6.67 ft × 150 psf), or 1 kip. In other words, the uniformly distributed load on Beam MN is 1 klf. The total load on Beam MN therefore is 20 kips (1 klf × 20 ft).

Since the loading condition of Beam MN is symmetrical, each end reaction, R_M and R_N, supports half of the 20 kip total load, and R_M and R_N therefore each equals 10 kips.

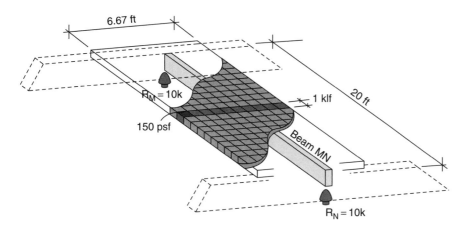

Figure 11.4 Loads on Beam MN

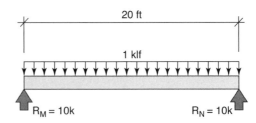

Figure 11.5 Free-body Diagram of Beam MN

Loads on Girders BE

Girder BE supports Beams MN, NP, QR, and RS (Figure 11.6). Since these beams all have the same loading conditions, we know that they all have reactions of 10 kips supported by the girder, for a total load on Girder BE of 40 kips (10 k + 10 k + 10 k + 10 k).

Since the loading condition of Girder BE is symmetrical, each end reaction, R_B and R_E, supports half the 40 kip total load, and R_B and R_E therefore each equals 20 kips.

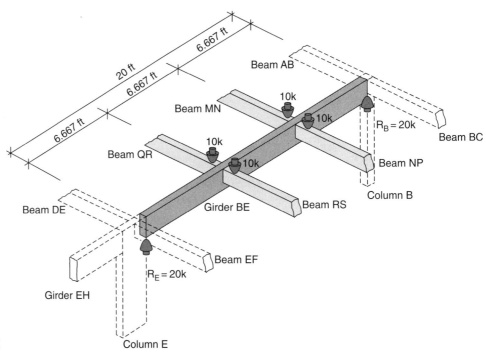

Figure 11.6 Loads on Girder BE

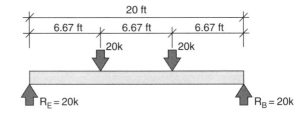

Figure 11.7 Free-body Diagram of Girder BE

Loads on Column E

Column E supports Girders BE and EH, as well as Beams DE and EF (Figure 11.8). Since each reaction from the girders is 20 kips and each reaction from the beams is 10 kips, the total load on Column E is therefore 60 kips (20 k + 20 k + 10 k + 10 k).

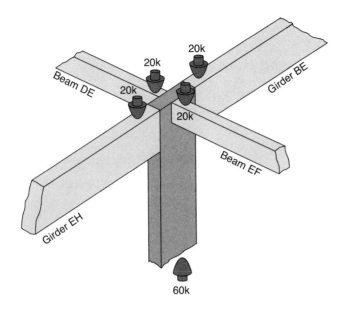

Figure 11.8 Loads on Columns E

11.2 Two-Way Slab and Beam Systems

Two-way slab and beam systems have floor slabs spanning in two directions, supported by beams at the edges (Figures 11.9 and 11.10).

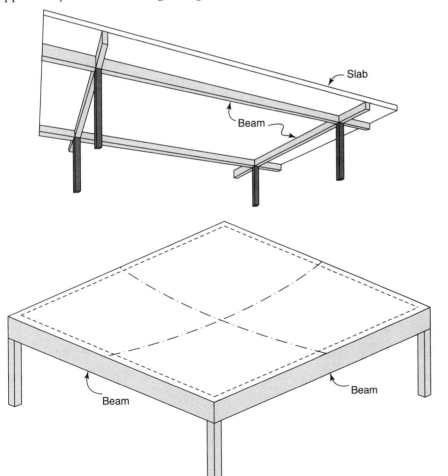

Figure 11.9 Slab, Beams, and Columns in a Two-way System

Figure 11.10 Span and Deflection in a Two-way System

■ EXAMPLE 11b: Load Tributary Area/Load Path in a Two-way Slab and Beam System

The 40 ft × 40 ft two-way slab and beam roof structure in Figure 11.11 has a 100 psf dead load and a 50 psf live load, for a total load of 150 psf. What are the loads and reactions for Beam BE and Column E?

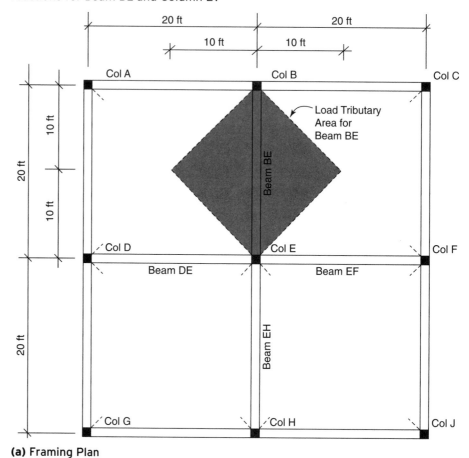

(a) Framing Plan

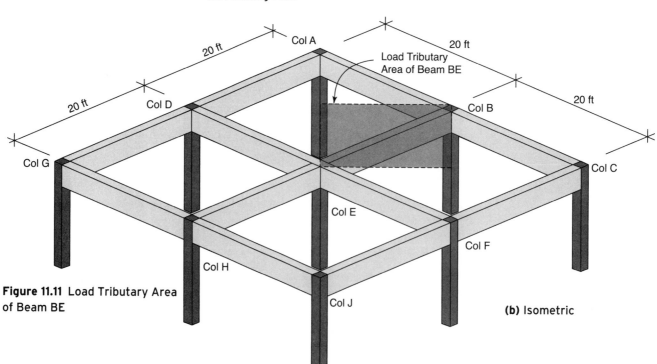

Figure 11.11 Load Tributary Area of Beam BE

(b) Isometric

Loads on Beam BE

The load tributary area for Beam BE is a triangular section of floor on each side of the beam (Figure 11.2). The triangular tributary areas produce loading that is non-uniform along the length of the beam.

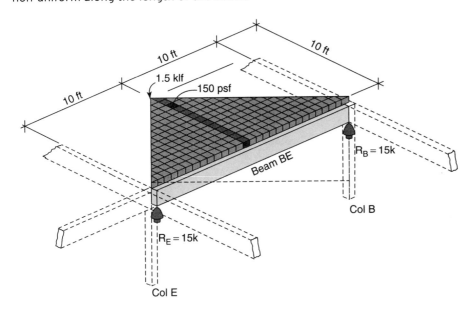

Figure 11.12 Loads on Beam BE

For each triangular section of tributary area on either side of Beam BE, the distributed load on the beam varies from zero at the ends to a maximum of 1500 plf (150 psf × 10 ft), or 1.5 klf, at the midspan. Combining the loading for the two triangular sections doubles the load at the midspan to 3 klf. The total load on Beam BE is therefore 30 kips ($\frac{1}{2}$ × 3 klf × 20 ft).

Since the loading condition of Beam BE is symmetrical, each end reaction, R_B and R_E, supports half of the 30 kip total load, and R_B and R_E therefore each equals 15 kips (Figure 11.13).

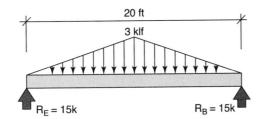

Figure 11.13 Free-body Diagram of Beam BE

Loads on Column E

Column E supports Beams BE, EF, EH and DE (Figure 11.14). Since each reaction from the beams is 15 kips, the total load on Column E is therefore 60 kips (15 k + 15 k + 15 k + 15 k).

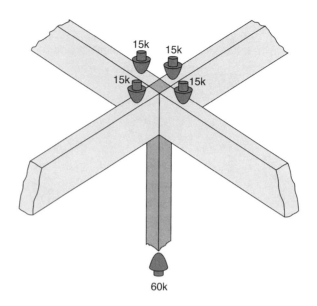

Figure 11.14 Loads on Column E

11.3 Two-Way Slab/Two-Way Joist Systems

Two-way slab and two-way joist systems have concrete floors spanning in two directions, directly supported by columns (Figures 11.15, 11.16 and 11.17).

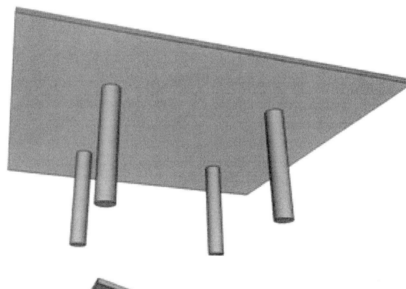

Figure 11.15 Concrete Floor and Columns in a Two-way Slab System

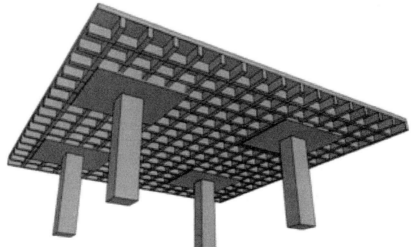

Figure 11.16 Concrete Floor and Columns in a Two-way Joist (Waffle Slab) System

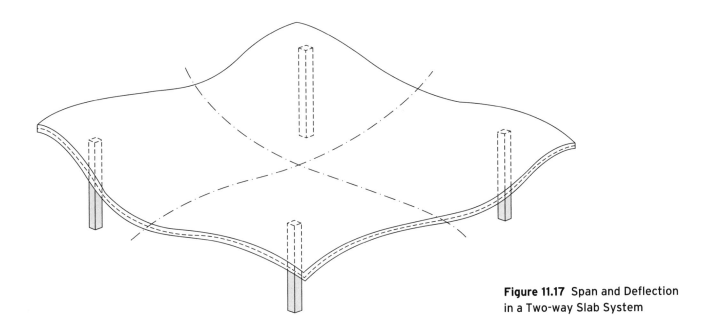

Figure 11.17 Span and Deflection in a Two-way Slab System

■ EXAMPLE 11c: Load Tributary Area/Load Path in a Two-way Slab System

The 40 ft x 40 ft two-way slab system in Figure 11.18 has a 100 psf dead load and a 50 psf live load, for a total load of 150 psf. What are the loads on Column E?

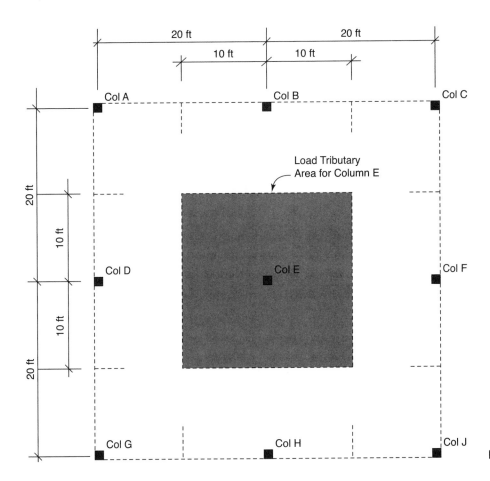

Figure 11.18 Framing Plan

Load Tributary Area of Column E

The load tributary area for Column E is a rectangular 20 ft × 20 ft section of floor centered on the column (Figure 11.19).

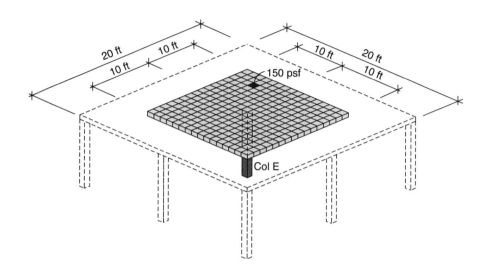

Figure 11.19 Load Tributary Area of Column E

Loads on Column E

Column E directly supports the load from the 20 ft × 20 ft floor area. The total load on Column E is therefore 60,000 lbs (150 psf x 20 ft × 20 ft), or 60 kips (Figure 11.20).

Figure 11.20 Loads on Column E

Discussion

You may have noticed that the load on Column E is the same 60 kips in each of the three examples. You should not place too much significance on this, since it is somewhat coincidental due to the symmetrical framing layouts with Column E at the center of each. It is more important to understand the nature of load tributary areas in order to analyze any variety of asymmetrical structural layouts.

CHAPTER 12

Shear and Moment Diagrams for Beams

Now that we're familiar with the external conditions (such as loads, reactions, and framing types) affecting the stability of a beam, let's turn our attention to the internal effect of these conditions on the beam. We'll begin our analysis with a study of shear and moment diagrams.

The two primary modes of failure for a beam are through (1) bending and (2) vertical shear. Shear and moment diagrams are simply graphic representations of the magnitude of the internal shear and bending moment to which a beam is subjected at every cross section along the beam's length. While shear and moment diagrams reflect the effects of external conditions on a beam, they are not related to beam material or cross-sectional shape, two other important considerations for design.

Shear and moment diagrams are useful for visualizing internal stresses placed on the beam and for determining the magnitude and location of maximum shear and moment that the beam must be designed to resist. A beam is typically designed (i.e., its material and cross sectional shape are selected) to resist moment and then checked to ensure that the shear, deflection, and resistance to lateral buckling are within acceptable limits.

Note that shear and moment "diagrams" are sometimes referred to as "curves," even though these curves may actually be straight lines.

12.1 Sign Conventions

For consistency in analysis, let's establish the following sign conventions.

For Shear

Upward forces are considered positive and downward forces are considered negative. The resulting shear is considered positive or negative as shown in Figure 12.1a. Keep in mind that whether the shear is positive or negative is irrelevant in terms of its magnitude or its effect on the beam. Positive and negative shear is only an indication (by convention) of which side of the beam is being pushed upward relative to the other side.

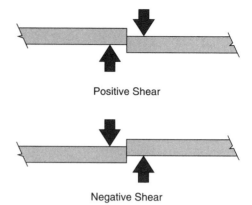

Figure 12.1a Shear Sign Conventions

For Moment

Clockwise moments are considered positive and counterclockwise moments are considered negative. Keep in mind that whether the moment is positive or negative is irrelevant in terms of its magnitude or effect on the beam. Positive and negative moment is only an indication (by convention) of the direction in which the force is tending to produce rotation.

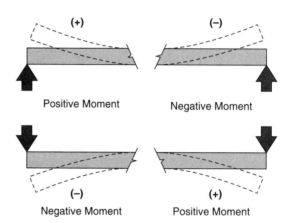

Figure 12.1b Moment Sign Conventions

12.2 Typical Shear and Moment Diagrams

Shear and moment diagrams can be created for any combination of beam types and loading conditions. However, the *AISC Steel Construction Manual* (see Appendix A2.3) gives examples of shear and moment diagrams, along with relevant formulae, for numerous more common beam support conditions and loading variations. Before we create a few simple shear and moment diagrams, let's take a look at several examples in the manual to get a sense of what they look like.

In the following examples and formulae, shear is represented by V, moment by M, point loads by P, support reactions by R, uniformly distributed loads by w, and lengths by l and a (Figures 12.2, 12.3, and 12.4)

For a Simply Supported Beam

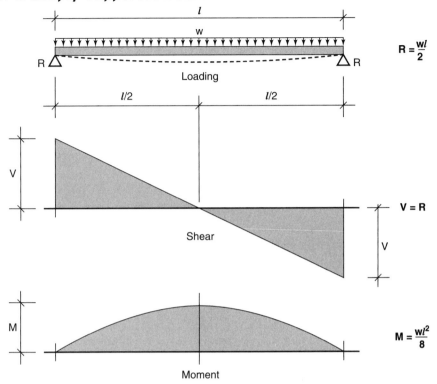

$R = \dfrac{wl}{2}$

$V = R$

$M = \dfrac{wl^2}{8}$

(a) A Uniformly Distributed Load

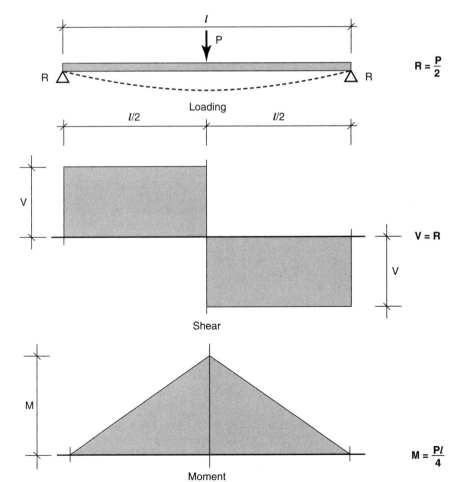

$R = \dfrac{P}{2}$

$V = R$

Figure 12.2 Shear and Moment Diagrams for a Simply Supported Beam

$M = \dfrac{Pl}{4}$

(b) A Concentrated Load at Midspan

For a Fixed-end Beam

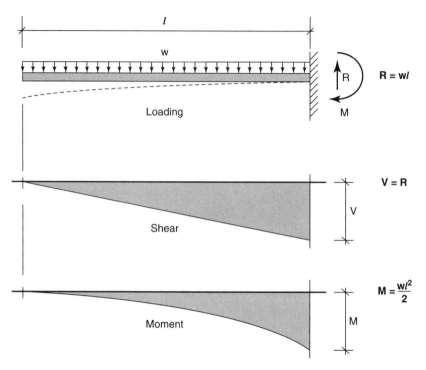

(a) A Uniformly Distributed Load

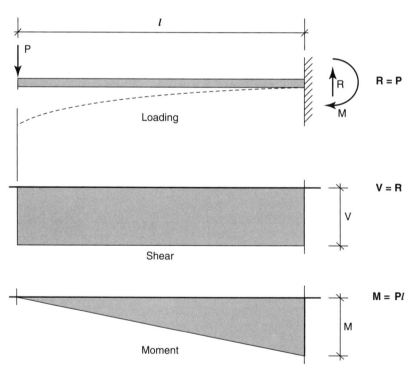

Figure 12.3 Shear and Moment Diagrams for a Fixed-end Beam

(b) A Concentrated Load at the Free End

For a Simply Supported Beam with a Single Overhang

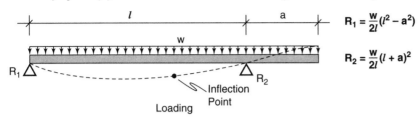

$$R_1 = \frac{w}{2l}(l^2 - a^2)$$

$$R_2 = \frac{w}{2l}(l + a)^2$$

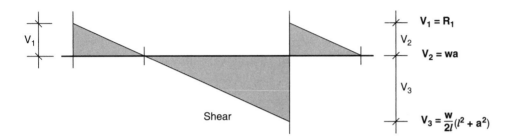

$$V_1 = R_1$$

$$V_2 = wa$$

$$V_3 = \frac{w}{2l}(l^2 + a^2)$$

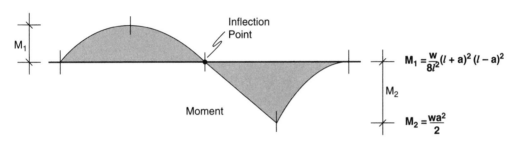

$$M_1 = \frac{w}{8l^2}(l + a)^2(l - a)^2$$

$$M_2 = \frac{wa^2}{2}$$

(a) A Uniformly Distributed Load

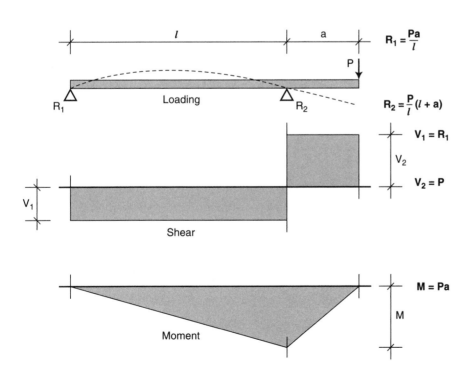

$$R_1 = \frac{Pa}{l}$$

$$R_2 = \frac{P}{l}(l + a)$$

$$V_1 = R_1$$

$$V_2 = P$$

$$M = Pa$$

(b) A Concentrated Load at End of Overhang

Figure 12.4 Shear and Moment Diagrams for a Simply Supported Beam with a Single Overhang

12.3 Creating Shear and Moment Diagrams

Although the *AISC Manual* has many examples, it is important to understand how shear and moment diagrams can be developed through analysis. Let's perform this analysis on two examples, 12a and 12b, each applying to a 20 ft long simply supported beam. The total load in both examples will be 20 kips.

In Example 12a, the load will be a 1 kip uniformly distributed load over the length of the beam. In Example 12b, the load will be a 20 kip concentrated load located at the midspan of the beam. We'll begin with free-body diagrams and deformation curves, and then create shear diagrams from which we'll develop moment diagrams. (As another exercise, you can compare the results from analysis with the results from using the formulae in Figures 12.2, 12.3 and 12.4.

■ EXAMPLE 12a: A Simply Supported Beam with a UDL Over Its Length

A 20 ft long simply supported beam has a 1 klf UDL along its length. To help understand the process, let's reference points A, B, C, D, and E, each at 5 ft intervals along the length of the beam.

Draw the Free-body Diagram and Deformation Curve

Step F1: Draw the free body diagram and calculate the reactions.

We can readily determine that $R_1 = R_2 = 10$ k (Figure 12.5).

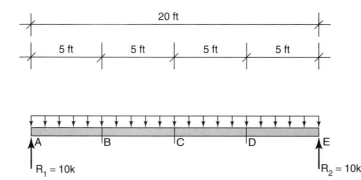

Figure 12.5 Free-body Diagram

Step F2: Based upon our understanding of how beams bend under loads (see Chapter 10), we can draw the approximate deformation curve for this beam (Figure 12.6). (Visualizing the beam's behavior and the location of any points of inflection helps us to understand and construct the shear and moment diagrams, especially under more complex support and loading conditions.)

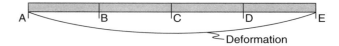

Figure 12.6 Deformation Curve

Create the Shear Diagram

Step V1: Begin by drawing the shear diagram first, starting at the left side. At A there is an upward shear force (R_1) of +10 k, resulting in a shear of +10 k (Figure 12.7a).

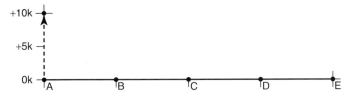

Figure 12.7a

Step V2: Between A and B, there is a downward uniform load of -1 klf, totaling -5 k (i.e., -1 klf × 5 ft) and resulting in a net shear force at B of +5 k (i.e., +10 k - 5 k) (Figure 12.7b).

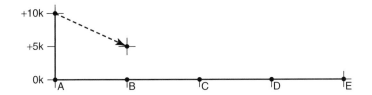

Figure 12.7b

Step V3: Between B and C, there is a downward uniform load of -1 klf, totaling -5 k (i.e., -1 klf × 5 ft) and resulting in a net shear force at C of 0 k (i.e., +5 k - 5 k) (Figure 12.7c).

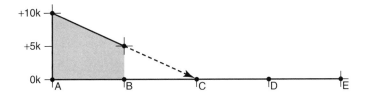

Figure 12.7c

Step V4: Between C and D, there is a downward uniform load of -1 klf, totaling -5 k and resulting in a net shear force at D of -5 k (i.e., +0 k - 5 k) (Figure 12.7d).

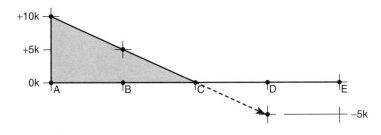

Figure 12.7d

Step V5: Between D and E, there is a downward uniform load of -1klf, totaling -5 k and resulting in a net shear force at E of -10 k (i.e., -5 k - 5 k) (Figure 12.7e).

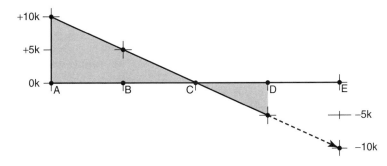

Figure 12.7e

Step V6: At E, there is an upward shear force (R_2) of +10 k, closing and completing the shear diagram (i.e., –10k + 10k) (Figure 12.7f).

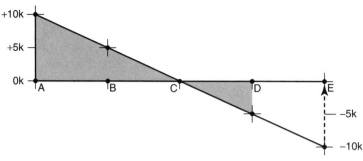

Figure 12.7f

Step V7: The completed shear diagram is shown in Figure 12.7g.

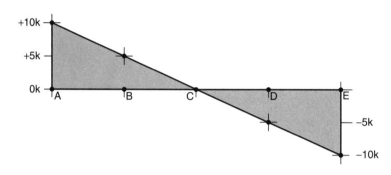

Figure 12.7g

Develop the Moment Diagram

With the shear diagram complete, begin drawing the moment diagram. Moment diagrams can be created by actually calculating the moments to either side of successive points along the length of the beam. However, another means, known as the *shear area method,* is usually an easier way to create moment diagrams. The shear area method stipulates that the magnitude of moment, at every successive point along the length of a beam, is equal to the area enclosed within the corresponding section of its shear diagram. We'll use the shear area method to create the moment diagram.

Step M1: Between A and B, the area within the shear diagram is +37.5 k-ft (i.e., + 7.5 k × 5 ft), resulting in a total moment of +37.5 k-ft at B (Figure 12.8a).

Figure 12.8a

Step M2: Between B and C, the area within the shear diagram is +12.5 k-ft (i.e., +2.5 k × 5 ft), resulting in a total moment of +50 k-ft (i.e., +37.5 k-ft +12.5 k-ft) at C (Figure 12.8b).

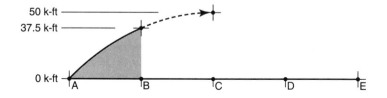

Figure 12.8b

Step M3: Between C and D, the area within the shear diagram is −12.5 k-ft (i.e., 2.5 k x 5 ft), resulting in a total moment of +37.5 k-ft at D (i.e., +50 k-ft −12.5 k-ft) (Figure 12.8c).

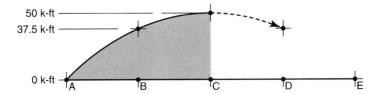

Figure 12.8c

Step M4: Between D and E, the area within the shear diagram is −37.5 k-ft (i.e., −7.5 k x 5 ft), resulting in a total moment of 0 k-ft at E (i.e., +37.5 k-ft −37.5 k-ft), closing and completing the moment diagram (Figure 12.8d).

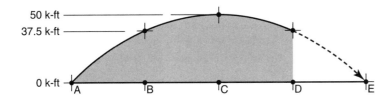

Figure 12.8d

Step M5: The completed moment diagram is shown in Figure 12.8e.

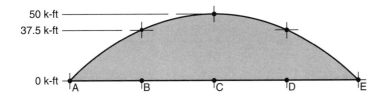

Figure 12.8e

■ EXAMPLE 12b: A Simply Supported Beam with a Point Load at the Midspan

A 20 ft long simply supported beam has a 20 kip concentrated load at the midspan.

Draw the Free-body Diagram and Deformation Curve

Step F1: Draw the free-body diagram and calculate the reactions.

We can readily determine that $R_1 = R_2 = 10$ k (Figure 12.9).

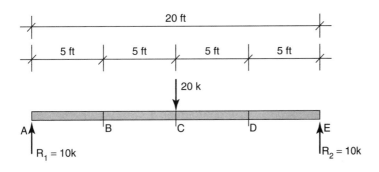

Figure 12.9

Step F2: Draw the approximate deformation curve (Figure 12.10).

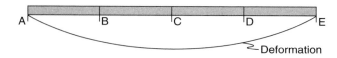

Figure 12.10 Deformation Curve

Create the Shear Diagram

Step V1: Begin the shear diagram by starting at the left side. At A there is an upward shear force (R_1) of +10 k, resulting in a shear of +10 k (Figure 12.11a).

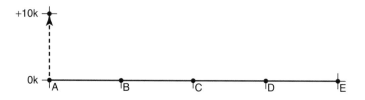

Figure 12.11a

Step V2: Since no other loads occur between A and C, the total shear remains constant at +10 k between these two points (Figure 12.11b).

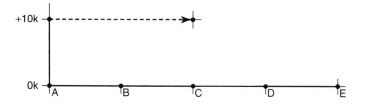

Figure 12.11b

Step V3: At C, there is a downward concentrated load of −20 k resulting in a net shear of 0 k (i.e., + 10 k −10 k) (Figure 12.11c).

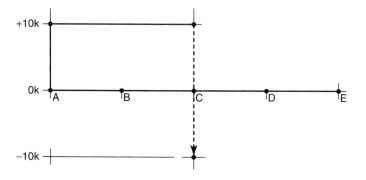

Figure 12.11c

Step V4: Since no other loads occur between C and E, the shear remains constant at −10 k between these two points (Figure 12.11d).

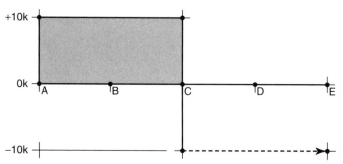

Figure 12.11d

Step V5: At E, there is an upward shear force (R_2) of +10 k, closing and completing the shear diagram (i.e., −10 k +10 k) (Figure 12.11e).

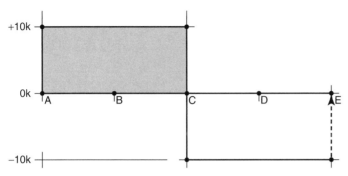

Figure 12.11e

Step V6: The completed shear diagram is shown in Figure 12.12f.

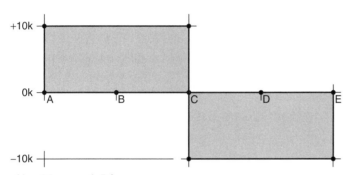

Figure 12.12f

Develop the Moment Diagram

Step M1: Between A and C, the area within the shear diagram is +100 k-ft (i.e., +10 k × 10 ft), resulting in a total moment of +100 k-ft at C (Figure 12.12a).

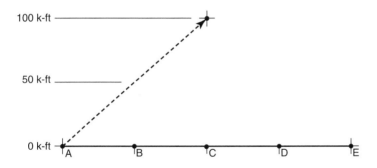

Figure 12.12a

Step M2: Between C and E, the area within the shear diagram is −100 k-ft (i.e., −10 k × 10 ft), resulting in a total moment of 0 k-ft at E (i.e., +100 k-ft −100 k-ft), closing and completing the moment diagram (Figure 12.12b).

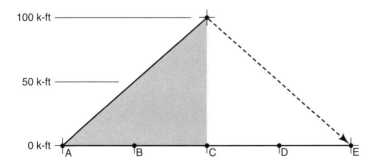

Figure 12.12b

Step M3: The completed moment diagram is shown in Figure 12.12c.

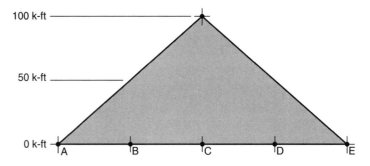

Figure 12.12c

12.4 Comparing V and M for Uniformly Distributed Versus Concentrated Loading

For the two conditions of the simple beam in Examples 12a and 12b, let's compare the free-body, deformation, shear, and moment diagrams, side by side, to visualize relationships and draw some general conclusions (Figures 12.13 through 12.16).

Free-body Diagram Comparison

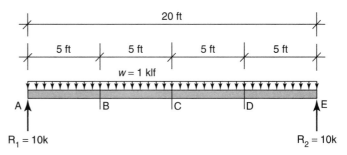

(a) Uniformly Distributed Loading

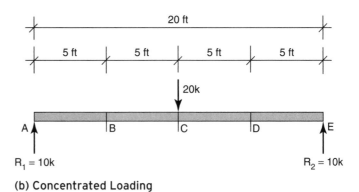

Figure 12.13 Free-body Diagram Comparison

(b) Concentrated Loading

DISCUSSION

- Since the total load in both examples is 20 kips, R_1 and R_2 in both cases is 10 kips.

Deformation Curve Comparison

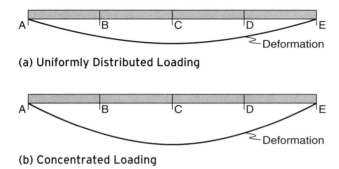

(a) Uniformly Distributed Loading

(b) Concentrated Loading

Figure 12.14 Deformation Curve Comparison

DISCUSSION

- Both deformation curves are similar, having maximum deflection at the midpoint, C. However, the deflection in Example 12b (from the concentrated load) is greater than the deflection in Example 12a (from the uniformly distributed load).

Shear Diagram Comparison

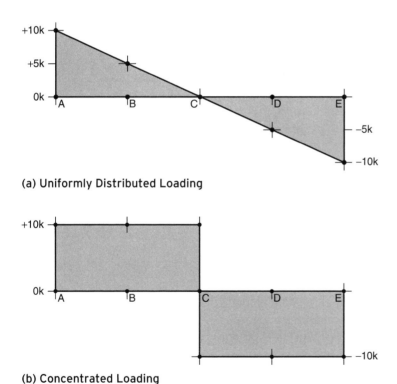

(a) Uniformly Distributed Loading

(b) Concentrated Loading

Figure 12.15 Shear Diagram Comparison

DISCUSSION

- Both examples have a maximum shear of 10 kips at reactions A and E.
- In Example 12a, there is a downward uniformly distributed load between the reactions at A and E, producing a straight-line, sloping shear diagram between these two points. There is zero shear at the midpoint C, and the shear increases gradually to the left or right of C.

- In Example 12b, there are no forces acting between the reaction at A and the concentrated load at C. Therefore, the shear diagram remains constant (horizontal) between these two points. At C, the concentrated load produces an abrupt vertical line change from +10 kips to –10 kips. There is zero shear at the exact midpoint C, but the shear increases abruptly to 10 kips immediately to the left or right of C. There are no forces acting between the concentrated load at C and the reaction at E, and therefore the shear diagram remains constant (horizontal) between these two points.
- Both shear diagrams "close" by beginning and ending at zero.

Moment Diagram Comparison

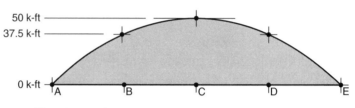

(a) Uniformly Distributed Loading

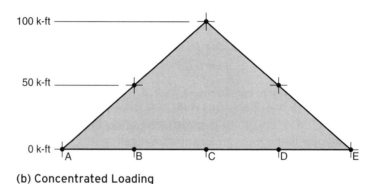

Figure 12.16 Moment Diagram Comparison

(b) Concentrated Loading

DISCUSSION
- Both examples have a maximum moment at the midpoint C, the point of zero shear.
- Both examples have zero moment at reactions A and E.
- The maximum moment in Example 12b (concentrated load) is double that of Example 12a (uniformly distributed load).
- In Example 12a, the clockwise moment resulting from the reaction A is immediately offset by the counterclockwise moment of the uniform load, so the moment diagram increases parabolically between A and C and then decreases parabolically between C and E.
- In Example 12b, the clockwise moment resulting from the reaction A has no clockwise moment to offset it until the concentrated load at C, so the moment diagram increases linearly (i.e., has a constant slope) between A and C and then decreases linearly between C and E.
- Both moment diagrams "close" by beginning and ending at zero.

12.5 Summary of Deformation, Shear, and Moment Relationships

Deformation Curves

A deformation curve is the shape in which a beam will deform under a given support and loading condition.

- An inflection point is a location at which the curvature of the deformation (i.e., the curvature of the bending) changes shape from concave to convex or vice versa, resulting in zero moment at that point.

Shear Diagrams

A shear diagram is the measure of internal vertical shear in a beam at every point along its length.

- The magnitude of vertical shear, at any cross section along the length of the beam, is equal to the algebraic sum of the vertical forces on either side of the section.
- A free-body diagram with a vertical reaction, and/or a vertical concentrated point load, produces an abrupt vertical line in the shear diagram at the point of the reaction and/or the concentrated load.
- A uniformly distributed load produces a straight-line, sloping shear diagram.
- Since the entire beam is in equilibrium, the summation of shear forces equals zero, and the shear diagram must begin and close at zero.

Moment Diagrams

A moment diagram is the measure of internal bending in a beam at every point along its length.

- The magnitude of bending moment, at any cross section along the length of the beam, is equal to the algebraic sum of the moments created by the forces (loads and reactions) on either side of the section under consideration.
- The change in moment value, between any two points on the moment diagram, is equal to the area within the shear diagram between the same two points, provided that no other external moment is applied (i.e., the shear area method of moment calculation).
- A straight-line, sloping shear diagram produces a parabolic moment diagram.
- A horizontal-line shear diagram (i.e., no slope) produces a straight-line, sloping moment diagram.
- A concentrated moment produces an abrupt vertical line in the moment diagram.
- Points at which the slope of the deflection curve is zero (i.e., where the tangent of the deformation curve is horizontal) are points of maximum moment.
- An inflection point is a point of zero moment.
- Points of zero shear are peaks on the moment diagram (i.e., points of maximum positive or maximum negative moment).
- Since the entire beam is in equilibrium, the summation of moments equals zero, and the moment diagram must begin and close at zero.

CHAPTER 13

Stress, Strain, and Properties of Materials

13.1 Stress

When a load (i.e., a force) is applied to a material, it creates one or more of the three basic states of stress within that material: compression, tension, or shear (see Chapter 4). For direct compression and tension, the stress typically acts perpendicular to the cross section of the material; for shear, the stress typically acts parallel to the cross section. All stress is expressed as force per unit of area and is determined by dividing the applied force by the total cross-sectional area on which the force is acting.

$$f = P/A$$

where:

    f = stress
    P = force
    A = cross-sectional area

■ EXAMPLE 13a: Stress on a Rod

A cylindrical rod having a cross-sectional area (A) of 5 sq in is subjected to a 10,000 lb force (P) in three different ways: (a) in compression perpendicular to the cross section, (b) in tension perpendicular to the cross section, and (c) in shear parallel to the cross section (Figure 13.1). What is the stress created in the rod under each of these three conditions?

DISCUSSION

The 10,000 lb force P creates the same 2000 psi stress on a cross section of the rod, regardless of the rod's material, whether P is perpendicular to the cross section (in compression or tension) or is parallel to the cross section (in shear). When P is perpendicular, the stress is the same for every cross section along the length of the rod; when P is parallel, the stress occurs on the cross section where P is applied. The rod's ability to resist the 2000 psi stress is, of course, very much dependent upon the material of which the rod is made.

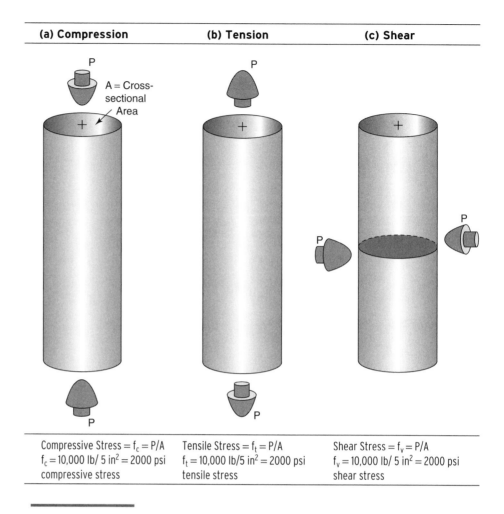

(a) Compression	(b) Tension	(c) Shear
Compressive Stress = f_c = P/A	Tensile Stress = f_t = P/A	Shear Stress = f_v = P/A
f_c = 10,000 lb/ 5 in^2 = 2000 psi compressive stress	f_t = 10,000 lb/5 in^2 = 2000 psi tensile stress	f_v = 10,000 lb/ 5 in^2 = 2000 psi shear stress

Figure 13.1 Stress on a Rod

13.2 Strain

As a result of the stress created in a material, the material will tend to change shape, or deform. Using the example of the rod in Figure 13.1, under compressive stress the rod will tend to shorten, while under tensile stress the rod will tend to lengthen. Proportionally the deformation is very small compared to the original length and is not visible to the eye. Nevertheless, it exists and is measurable by sensitive instruments called *strain gauges*.

The amount of shortening or lengthening (ignoring the minimal consideration of widening and narrowing), measured against the original unstressed length, is called the *strain*.

$$\textbf{strain} = \mathbf{\Delta L/L}$$

where:

      L = original unstressed length

      ΔL = change in length

■ EXAMPLE 13b: **Strain on a Rod**

The cylindrical rod in Example 13a is 10 in long (L). What is the strain created by the 2000 psi stress if the rod (a) shortens by .01 in (ΔL) under compression and (b) elongates by .01 in (ΔL) under tension (Figure 13.2)?

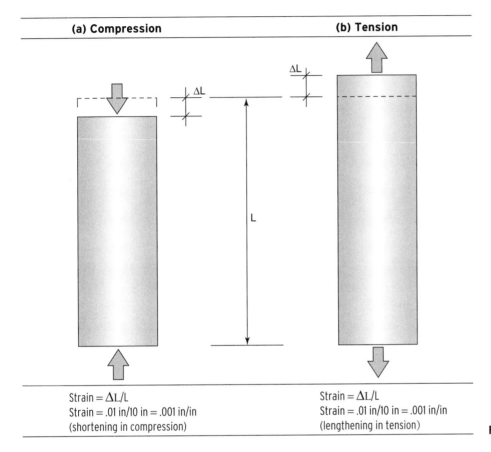

(a) Compression

(b) Tension

Strain = ΔL/L
Strain = .01 in/10 in = .001 in/in
(shortening in compression)

Strain = ΔL/L
Strain = .01 in/10 in = .001 in/in
(lengthening in tension)

Figure 13.2 Strain on a Rod

DISCUSSION

The elongation under tensile stress and the shortening under compressive stress create the same .001 strain in this example. This indicates that this rod's material has the same behavior in compression as in tension, which is not necessarily the case for all materials. Note also that since strain is a length divided by a length, strain is a ratio measured in inches/inch, or no unit at all.

13.3 Stress versus Strain

When any particular material is stressed, its resulting strain behavior (i.e., deformational behavior) is unique, not only for that material but also for the type of stress (compression or tension) to which the material is subjected. Steel, for example, behaves similarly in compression as in tension, while concrete behaves quite differently in compression than in tension.

A material's stress-strain relationship is graphically depicted in a *stress-strain curve* with stress plotted along the *y* axis and strain along the *x* axis. A stress-strain

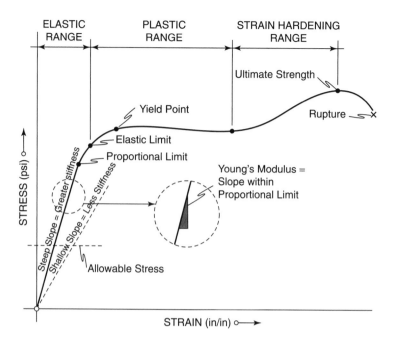

Figure 13.3 Stress-Strain Curve for a Hypothetical Ductile Material in Tension

curve is, in a sense, a material's signature behavior under stress. Although any particular material's stress-strain curve is unique, materials generally exhibit some (or all) of the strain behavior patterns broadly characterized as *elastic range*, *plastic range*, and *strain-hardening range* prior to rupture, the point at which the material actually breaks. The stress-strain curve in Figure 13.3 is for a hypothetical ductile material, such as steel, in tension. Table 13.1 describes the general characteristics of the three strain ranges.

TABLE 13.1 ELASTIC, PLASTIC, AND STRAIN-HARDENING RANGE CHARACTERISTICS

Range	Characteristics
Elastic Range	In this range, a force applied to a material causes it to become stressed, resulting in deformation (strain). When the force is removed, the material returns to its original unstressed shape.
Plastic Range	In this range, with relatively little increase in stress, the material behaves somewhat taffy-like and becomes permanently deformed.
Strain-Hardening Range	In this range, the material stabilizes somewhat and is able to take on additional stress with a corresponding increase in deformation (strain) until it reaches its ultimate strength and ruptures.

Stress-strain behavior for the variety of structural materials available is a complex field of study. The reader is referred to more technical sources for a detailed review of the topic. For a simplified comparison, however, the generalized stress-strain curves for steel, concrete (in compression), and wood are shown in Figure 13.4.

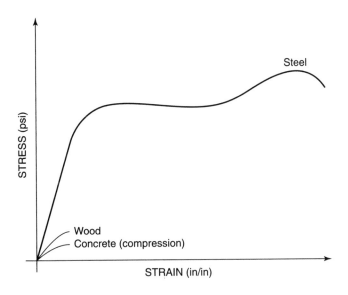

Figure 13.4 Stress-Strain Curve
Comparisons

13.4 Properties of Materials

Several other important terms that refer to the properties and characteristics of a material are given in Table 13.2.

TABLE 13.2 PROPERTIES AND CHARACTERISTICS OF MATERIALS

Term	Description
Yield Point	When stressed beyond its yield point, a deformed material will no longer return to its original unstressed shape when the stress is removed. This is a type of failure in the material.
Ductile Materials	Materials that exhibit plastic deformation when stressed beyond the yield point Ductile materials stretch, thereby "giving notice" before rupture. Steel is an example.
Brittle Materials	Materials that rupture suddenly with increasing stress, exhibiting no yield point and providing no "notice". Concrete and wrought iron are two examples.
Permanent Set	The permanent deformation that remains in a material, when stressed beyond the elastic limit, even when the stress is removed.
Ultimate Strength	The point at which a material ruptures (breaks).
Allowable (Working) Stress and Factor of Safety	The maximum permissible stress, to which a material may be safely subjected, reduced well below the material's limit of strength by a factor of safety. The following are generalized comparisons for average allowable stress for materials in compression: concrete (1000 psi), wood (1000 psi), steel (25,000 psi).
Stiffness	The ability of a material to resist deformation (strain) when stressed. Steel, for example, is stiffer than wood and therefore deforms substantially less under a given load.
Modulus of Elasticity (E) (Young's Modulus)	A measure of a material's stiffness. The modulus of elasticity is the ratio of stress divided by strain. The higher the modulus of elasticity, the stiffer the material. Steel, for example, has a higher modulus of elasticity than wood.
Fatigue	The tendency of a material to weaken or fail, at a stress below the yield point, when the stress is repeatedly applied and removed. A paper clip breaking after being bent back and forth several times is an example.
Creep	The tendency of a material to continue to deform over time (i.e., exhibit strain) when left under load for an extended period. Concrete is an example of a material that exhibits creep, albeit very slowly.
Malleability	The ability of a material to be shaped or formed by hammering or pressure. Wrought iron is an example.
Hardness	The ability of a material to resist indentation, penetration, and scratching.
Toughness	The ability of a material to absorb impact and not break or shatter when receiving a blow. A hard rubber block is an example.

13.5 Stress Distribution Diagrams

Stress distribution diagrams graphically show the relative stress in a cross section of a member at a particular location along the length of that member. For example, we know that a simple beam under load will exhibit compression along the upper part of the beam and tension along the lower part. If the cross section of the beam is symmetrical (such as a rectangle), then the neutral axis will be midway between the top and bottom edges, and the stress diagram would be symmetrical about the neutral axis (Figure 13.5).

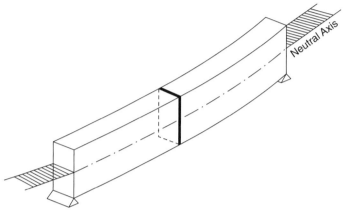

(a) A Simple Beam

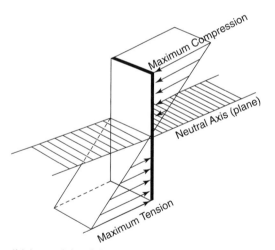

(b) Isometric of Cross Section

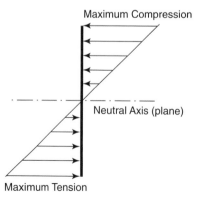

Figure 13.5 Stress Distribution Diagram at the Midspan of a Simple Beam

(c) Stress Distribution Diagram

Introduction to Columns

14.1 Columns, Compression, and Bending

Columns are vertical members that carry loads downward to foundations and the ground. Although the primary stress to which columns are subjected is compression (tending to cause failure by crushing—a failure of strength), columns can also be subjected to bending (tending to cause failure by buckling—a failure of stability) (Figure 14.1). A column is most efficient if designed for compressive strength, rather than buckling, to be its weakest link.

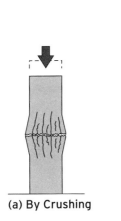 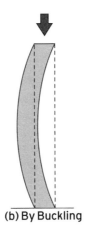

(a) By Crushing   (b) By Buckling

Figure 14.1 Column Failures

Columns are generally categorized as:
1. Short: thick and subject to failure by crushing rather than buckling
2. Tall: slender and subject to failure by buckling rather than crushing
3. Intermediate: where several formulae are used to predict how the column will fail

14.2 Column Loading

Columns are primarily subject to vertical loads, which can be axial or eccentric, and are also subject to lateral loads.

Axial loads are evenly distributed around the center of a column's longitudinal axis and cross section, and produce pure compressive stresses (Figure 14.2a).

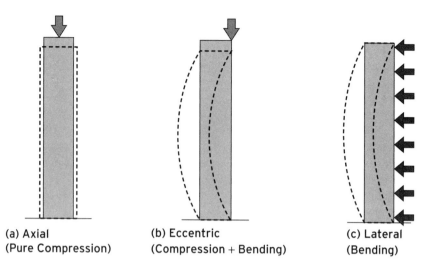

Figure 14.2 Loads on Columns

(a) Axial
(Pure Compression)

(b) Eccentric
(Compression + Bending)

(c) Lateral
(Bending)

Eccentric loads are unevenly distributed around a column's longitudinal axis and cross section and produce bending stresses in addition to compressive stresses (Figure 14.2b).

Lateral loads are perpendicular to a column's longitudinal axis and produce bending stresses (Figure 14.2c).

Axial, eccentric, and lateral loads can occur individually or in combination.

The eccentricity, e, of a vertical load is the distance between the line of action of the load and the geometric center of the column's cross section. Figure 14.3 shows the comparative stresses on a column's cross section for loads with varying eccentricities.

The greater the eccentricity, the greater the bending stresses and the greater the tendency for the column to buckle. Note that, an axial load has no eccentricity.

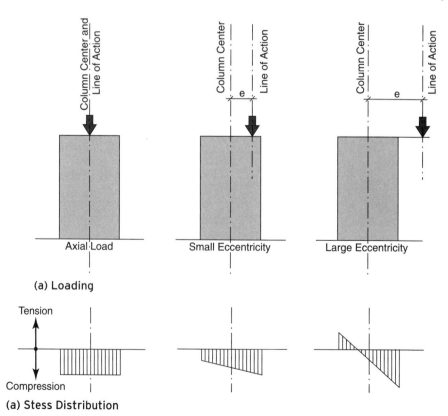

Figure 14.3 Comparative Stresses on a Column's Cross Section

To get a better intuitive sense of axial and eccentric loads, imagine yourself carrying a heavy basket loaded with fruit.

If you carry the basket on your head, the weight of the basket (i.e., the load) passes through the center of your body directly to the ground. This is an example of an axial load (Figure 14.4).

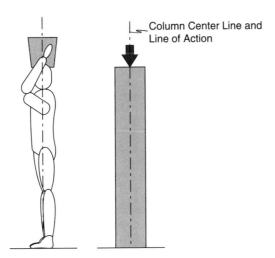

Figure 14.4 Axial Loading

If you carry the basket in front of you, away from the center of your body, you can easily imagine the weight of the basket tending to bend your body forward. This is an example of an eccentric load (Figure 14.5). The distance between the basket and the center of your body is the eccentricity.

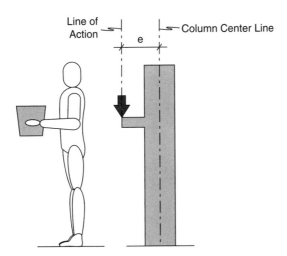

Figure 14.5 Eccentric Loading

14.3 Column Compression

For a column of a given material, resisting compressive stresses that tend to cause crushing is largely a matter of providing sufficient area in the column's cross section (Figure 14.6). This relationship is expressed by the formula:

$$f_a = P/A$$

where:

f_a = allowable stress of the column material
P = applied force on the column
A = cross-sectional area of the column

Depending upon the two givens, we can use this formula to solve for f_a, P, or A.

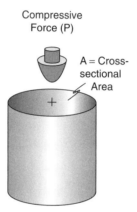

Compressive
Force (P)

A = Cross-
sectional
Area

Figure 14.6 Column Compression

■ EXAMPLE 14a: Compression on a Column

The short column in Figure 14.6:

1. Has a cross-sectional area (A) of 10 in² and is subjected to a load (P) of 10,000 lbs. What is the minimum allowable stress (f_a) that its material must be able to provide?

$$\text{min } f_a = P/A = 10{,}000 \text{ lb}/10 \text{ in}^2 = 1000 \text{ psi}$$

2. Is composed of wood having an allowable stress (f_a) of 1000 psi. If the column has a cross-sectional area (A) of 10 in², what is the maximum compressive force (P) that the column can support?

$$\text{max } P = f_a A = 1000 \text{ psi} \times 10 \text{ in}^2 = 10{,}000 \text{ lb}$$

3. Is composed of wood having an allowable stress (f_a) of 1000 psi. If the column is subjected to a compressive force (P) of 10,000 lbs, what minimum cross-sectional area (A) of wood is needed to resist this force?

$$\text{min } A = P/f_a = 10{,}000 \text{ lb}/1000 \text{ psi} = 10 \text{ in}^2$$

14.4 Column Bending

A column's resistance to buckling is largely dependent upon its *slenderness ratio*, a useful property describing column proportions. To understand the concept of slenderness ratio, we first have to understand the concepts of *effective length* and *radius of gyration*.

Effective Length

We can easily visualize that the greater a column's length, the greater its tendency to buckle. Similar to a beam, a column's top and bottom end restraints (supports) can be idealized as fixed, pinned, or free (i.e., unsupported) (see Chapter 8). The type of end restraint affects the column's tendency to bend. A column's end restraints are accounted for by an *effective length factor*, k, which differs according to the conditions of restraint. k is applied to a column's actual length, resulting in an effective length. This is expressed by the formula:

$$\mathbf{L_e = k} \times \mathbf{\mathit{l}_a}$$

where:

L_e = effective length of the column
k = the effective length factor
l_a = actual length of the column

Figure 14.7 shows several variations of column end restraints, their associated k factors, and their resulting effective lengths.

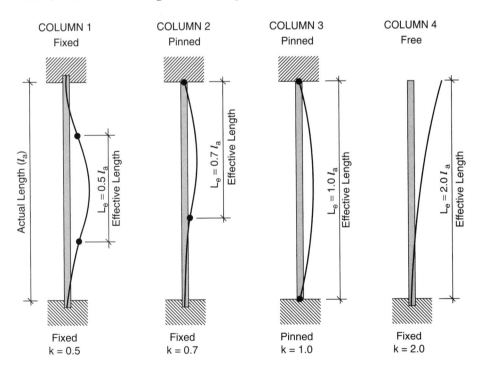

Figure 14.7 Various k Factors and Column Effective Lengths

As seen in Figure 14.7, depending upon the value of the k factor, a column's effective length can be greater than, less than, or equal to the column's actual length.

The larger the k factor is, the longer the effective length (L_e) and therefore the greater the tendency of the column to buckle.

■ EXAMPLE 14b: The Effective Lengths of Two 10 ft Columns

Column 1 in Figure 14.7, with fixed restraints at the top and bottom, has a k factor of 0.5. If the actual column length (l_a) is 10 ft, what is its effective length (L_e)?

$$L_e = k \times l_a$$
$$L_e = 0.5 \times 10 \text{ ft} = 5 \text{ ft}$$

Column 4, with a fixed restraint at the bottom and free at the top, has a k factor of 2.0. If the actual column length (l_a) is 10 ft, what is its effective length (L_e)?

$$L_e = k \times l_a$$
$$L_e = 2.0 \times 10 \text{ ft} = 20 \text{ ft}$$

DISCUSSION

Columns 1 and 4 both have the same 10 ft actual length. However, because of their different restraint conditions (as reflected by their k factors), Column 1 has an effective length that is half of its actual length, while Column 4 has an effective length that is twice its actual length.

Radius of Gyration

(See Appendix 5 and Table A5.1 for a review of moment of inertia, radius of gyration, and other properties of sections.)

In addition to a column's effective length, its resistance to bending is measured by a cross-sectional property called *radius of gyration*, which is derived from its moment of inertia. Just as moment of inertia is dependent upon a specific reference axis, so is radius of gyration. A column will tend to buckle about the axis having the least radius of gyration. Radius of gyration is expressed by the formula:

$$\mathbf{r = \sqrt{(I/A)}}$$

where:

    r = radius of gyration (in)
    I = moment of inertia (in^4)
    A = cross-sectional area (in^2)

For a given cross sectional area, the smaller the moment of inertia (I), the smaller the radius of gyration (r) and the greater the tendency of the column to buckle.

Slenderness Ratio

The slenderness ratio of a column is defined by the formula:

$$\text{Slenderness ratio} = L_e/r$$

where:

    L_e = effective length (in inches)
    r = radius of gyration (in inches)

Figure 14.8 shows the comparative slenderness ratios of three columns with varying effective lengths and radii of gyration.

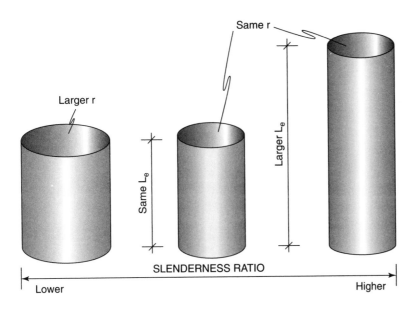

Figure 14.8 Comparative Slenderness Ratios

The larger the effective length (L_e), or the smaller the radius of gyration (r), the larger the slenderness ratio is and therefore the greater the tendency of the column to buckle.

A structural objective in efficient column design is to reduce the slenderness ratio by minimizing its effective length and/or maximizing its radius of gyration.

■ EXAMPLE 14c: The Slenderness Ratios of Two 10 ft Columns

Column 1 in Example 14b was calculated to have an effective length (L_e) of 5 ft (i.e., 60 in). If Column 1 has a 12 in radius circular cross section, what is its slenderness ratio (Figure 14.9)?

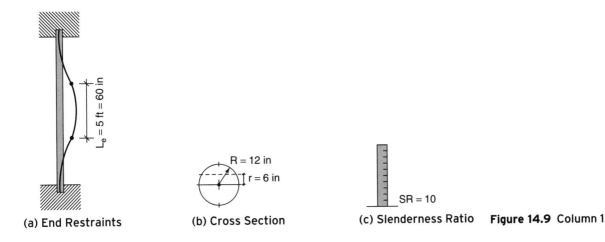

(a) End Restraints   **(b) Cross Section**   **(c) Slenderness Ratio**   **Figure 14.9** Column 1

$L_e = 60$ in
$r = R/2 = 12$ in$/2 = 6$ in
Slenderness ratio $= L_e/r = 60$ in$/6$ in $= 10$

Column 4 in Example 14b was calculated to have an effective length (L_e) of 20 ft (i.e., 240 in). If Column 4 has a 12 in radius circular cross section, what is its slenderness ratio (Figure 14.10)?

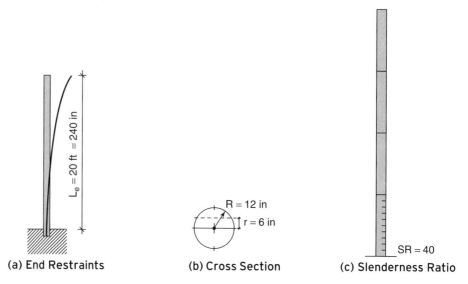

Figure 14.10 Column 4   **(a) End Restraints**   **(b) Cross Section**   **(c) Slenderness Ratio**

$L_e = 240$ in
$r = R/2 = 12$ in/$2 = 6$ in
Slenderness ratio $= L_e/r = 240$ in/6 in $= 40$

DISCUSSION

Although Columns 1 and 4 have the same 10 ft actual length and 24 in. diameter (12 in. radius) cross section, their differing end restraints result in the effective length and slenderness ratio of Column 4 being four times greater than those of Column 1.

What would be the required radius for Column 4 in order to make its slenderness ratio equal to that of Column 1 (i.e., 10) (Figure 14.11)?

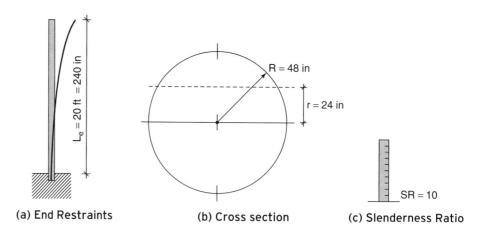

Figure 14.11 Column 4   **(a) End Restraints**   **(b) Cross section**   **(c) Slenderness Ratio**

$L_e = 240$ in

Slenderness ratio $= 10$

$r = R/2 = L_e/$slenderness ratio

$R = 2 \times (L_e/$slenderness ratio$)$

$\quad = 2 \times (240/10) = 48$ in

DISCUSSION

Since slenderness ratio is inversely proportional to radius of gyration, a fourfold increase in r produces a correspondingly proportional decrease in the slenderness ratio.

14.5 Leonhard Euler and Column Buckling

The eighteenth-century mathematician Leonhard Euler derived a formula defining the maximum axial load that an "ideal" slender column can support without buckling. An ideal column is one that is perfectly vertical, of constant cross section, of homogeneous material, and subject to no other stresses than a vertical axial load.

The formula relates load, column length, moment of inertia (a cross sectional property), and modulus of elasticity (a material property):

$$P = \Pi^2 EI / (kL_a)^2$$

where:

  $P =$ the maximum axial load the column can carry without buckling

  $E =$ the modulus of elasticity of the column's material

  $I =$ the moment of inertia of the column's cross section

  $k =$ the effective length factor

  $L_a =$ the actual length

The reader is referred to more advanced texts for the application of Euler's formula.

Frames, Rigidity, and Lateral Resistance Systems

Framed structures are the predominant structural form used throughout history to the present day. To begin to understand the behavior of frames, let's examine two basic shapes: triangular frames and rectangular frames.

15.1 Triangular Frames

Triangular frames are inherently stable (i.e., rigid).

Imagine any triangular frame with its legs connected by pins at the corners (Figure 15.1). No matter how you try, a triangular frame cannot be distorted.

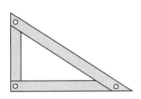 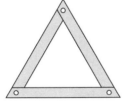 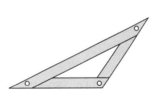

Figure 15.1 Rigid Triangular Frames

15.2 Rectangular Frames

Rectangular frames are inherently unstable.

Imagine a rectangular frame with its legs connected by pins at the corners (Figure 15.2a). If a lateral force is applied at corner A, for example, it's easy to see how the frame would distort, or "rack" (Figure 15.2b).

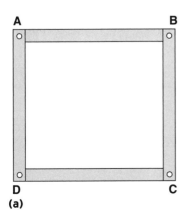 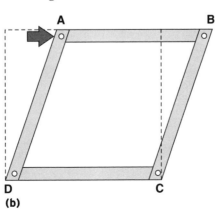

(a) **(b)**

Figure 15.2 Racking of a Rectangular Frame

141

15.3 Making Rectangular Frames Rigid

Although inherently unstable, rectangular frames can be made rigid by several methods:

- Triangulation
- Tensile member cross bracing
- Moment connections
- Shear Walls

Triangulation

By connecting two opposite corners with a diagonal member capable of resisting both tensile and compressive stress, a rectangular frame can be made rigid (Figure 15.3). When a building frame is made rigid using this method, it's called a *braced frame*.

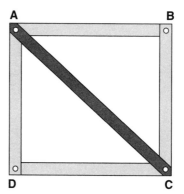

Figure 15.3 A Rectangular Frame Made Rigid by Triangulation

Tensile Member Cross Bracing

By connecting the four opposing corners with tensile member cross bracing (such as cables), each member sufficiently strong to resist only tensile stress, a rectangular frame can be made rigid (Figure 15.6). When a building frame is made rigid using this method, it's also called a *braced frame*.

Imagine a rectangular frame having its opposite corners connected with springs that could easily expand or contract, depending on the stress placed on them (Figure 15.4a). By applying a lateral force at corner A, we can see how the frame would rack and cause spring BD to expand under tension, and spring AC to shorten under compression (Figure 15.4b).

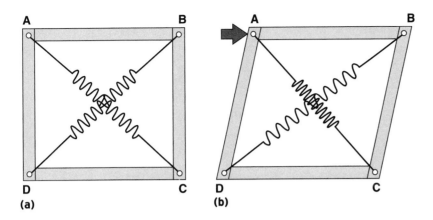

Figure 15.4 Tension and Compression of Diagonals in a Racked Rectangular Frame

If corners B and D were instead connected by a cable, the frame would be rigid for the force applied at corner A (Figure 15.5a), but not for the force applied at corner B (Figure 15.5b).

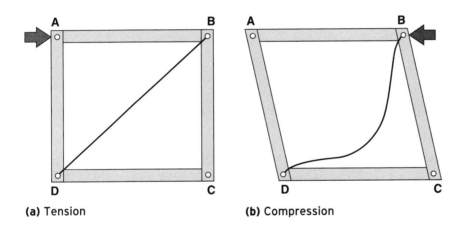

(a) Tension   **(b)** Compression

Figure 15.5 Tension and Compression on Cable BD.

If corners A and D were also connected by a cable, thereby creating tensile cross bracing, the frame would now be rigid (Figure 15.6).

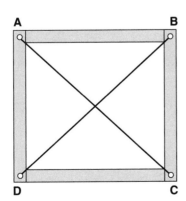

Figure 15.6 A Rectangular Frame Made Rigid by Tensile Member Cross Bracing

Moment Connections

By making one or more corners rigid connections, a rectangular frame can be made rigid (Figure 15.7). When a building frame is made rigid using this method, it's called a *moment frame*.

Triangulation and tensile member cross bracing are not always practical methods for making rectangular frames rigid. Another method frequently used in construction is to make the corners of the frame rigid.

By attaching large plates to the corners (gusset plates), the corners are prevented from rotating, thereby making them rigid. Gusset plates and other types of connections that make corners rigid are called *moment connections*.

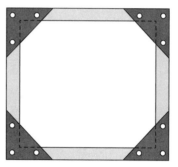

Figure 15.7 A Rectangular Frame Made Rigid by Moment Connections

Shear Walls

By infilling or sheathing the frame (e.g., plywood in wood frame light construction) with a solid material sufficiently strong to resist the shearing forces of racking, a rectangular frame can be made into a rigid *shear wall* (Figure 15.8). Shear walls can be used to make a building frame rigid.

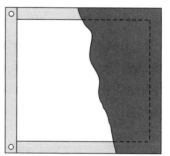

Figure 15.8 A Rectangular Frame Made Rigid by Sheathing

15.4 Lateral Resistance Systems

Lateral Resistance Methods

We see that a frame structure, often consisting of a series of rectangular frames, will tend to rack (i.e., deform) under lateral loads (Figure 15.9). All structures must have a proper lateral resistance system to prevent this.

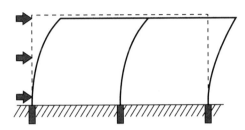

Figure 15.9 Deformation of Un braced Frame under Lateral Load

Braced frames, moment frames, and shear walls (or a combination thereof) are the common methods used to provide lateral resistance for framed structures (Figures 15.10, 15.11, 15.12, and 15.13).

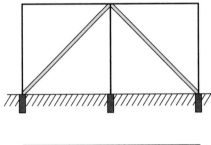

Figure 15.10 Braced Frame with a Single Brace in Each Bay

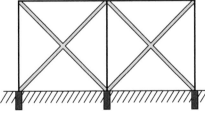

Figure 15.11 Braced Frame with Cross Bracing in Each Bay

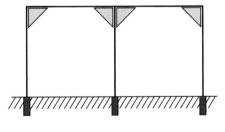

Figure 15.12 Moment Frame

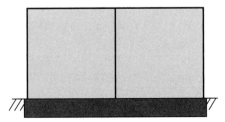

Figure 15.13 Shear Walls

Understanding Braced Frames

For the overall stability of a framed structure, it's not always necessary for each bay to be braced. The designer must decide between bracing more frames with lighter bracing members and bracing fewer frames with heavier bracing members (Figures 15.14 and 15.15).

The number, direction, and placement of bracing members in a frame are a matter of architectural considerations and economics, as well as the judgment and preferences of the designer. Equally important, bracing decisions are also a matter of resisting torsional stresses on the frame. Since torsional behavior and the variables involved in bracing-placement decisions are complex, we'll concentrate on the basic structural principles of bracing members.

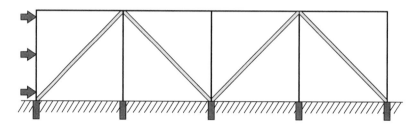

Figure 15.14 More Frames Braced with Lighter Members

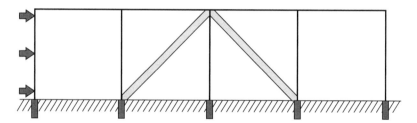

Figure 15.15 Fewer Frames Braced with Heavier Members

Let's analyze three bracing options, and the consequences thereof, for the simple two-bay frame structure in Figure 15.16. Although we'll separately examine stress in the diagonal bracing members when lateral forces are from (a) left to right and (b) right to left, it's understood that lateral forces are unpredictable and that any lateral bracing system must be capable of resisting forces from either direction.

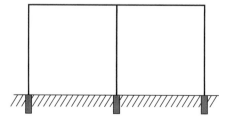

Figure 15.16 A Two-bay Frame Structure

**BRACING OPTION 1: LATERAL RESISTANCE WITH A SINGLE
DIAGONAL BRACE IN ONE BAY**

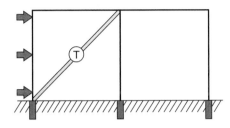

Figure 15.17a Lateral Forces from
Left to Right

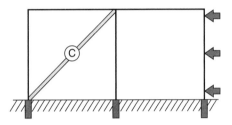

Figure 15.17b Lateral Forces from
Right to Left

DISCUSSION

When lateral forces are from left to right, the diagonal brace is in tension
(Figure 15.17a). Conversely, when lateral forces are from right to left, the diagonal
brace is in compression (Figure 15.17b). When in compression, the tendency of
the brace is to buckle. Designing the brace to resist buckling is inefficient, requiring a rigid, heavier member than if the brace were designed to resist only
tension. When braced in this manner, the diagonal brace must be designed to
resist compression as well as tension.

BRACING OPTION 2: LATERAL RESISTANCE WITH A SINGLE DIAGONAL BRACE IN EACH BAY

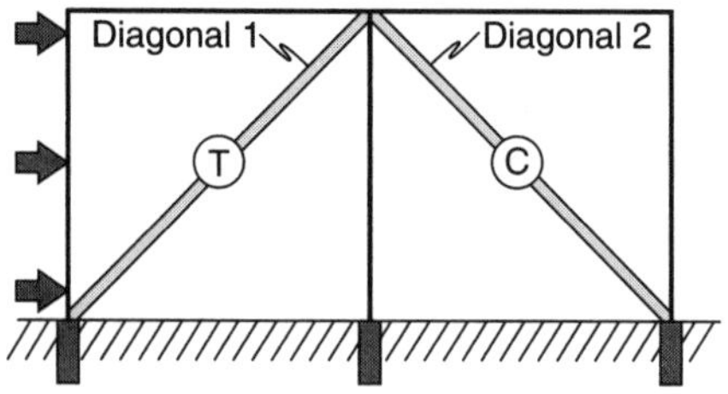

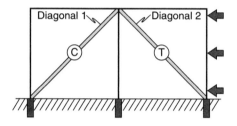

Figure 15.18a A Lateral Forces from Left to Right

Figure 15.18b Lateral Forces from Right to Left

DISCUSSION

When lateral forces are from left to right, Diagonal 1 is in tension and Diagonal 2 is in compression (Figure 15.18a). Conversely, when lateral forces are from right to left, Diagonal 1 is in compression and Diagonal 2 is in tension (Figure 15.18b). Since we know that it is inefficient to design a diagonal for compression, each diagonal can be designed to resist only tension for the frame to have lateral resistance. Instead of the rigid, heavier diagonals needed to resist compression, the diagonals could be lighter-weight cables or rods acting only in tension.

BRACING OPTION 3: LATERAL RESISTANCE WITH DIAGONAL CROSS BRACING IN ONE BAY

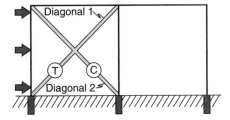

Figure 15.19a Lateral Forces from Left to Right

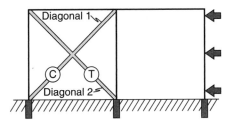

Figure 15.19b Lateral Forces from Right to Left

DISCUSSION

Instead of a single diagonal brace in each bay, the designer may choose, for architectural or other reasons, to place the two diagonals in a single bay. In this case, the bracing principles are exactly analogous to those in Option 2. When lateral forces are from left to right, Diagonal 1 is in tension and Diagonal 2 is in compression (Figure 15.19a). Conversely, when lateral forces are from right to left, Diagonal 1 is in compression and Diagonal 2 is in tension (Figure 15.19b). Since we know that it is inefficient to design a diagonal for compression, each diagonal can be designed to resist only tension for the frame to have lateral resistance. Instead of the rigid, heavier diagonals needed to resist compression, the diagonals could be lighter-weight cables or rods acting only in tension (Figure 15.20).

Lateral bracing of a framed building can be concealed or, if desired, exposed as part of a building's architectural expression (Figure 15.20).

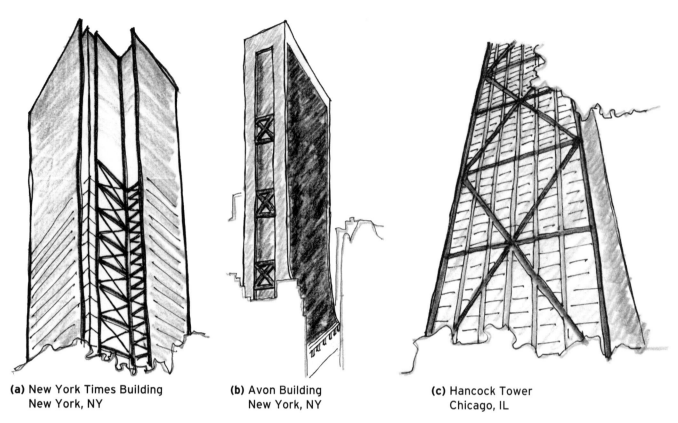

(a) New York Times Building
New York, NY

(b) Avon Building
New York, NY

(c) Hancock Tower
Chicago, IL

Figure 15.20 Exposed Lateral Bracing

Diaphragms

In a framed structure, just as a shear wall resists racking and provides lateral resistance in a vertical plane, a rigid diaphragm resists racking and provides lateral resistance in a horizontal plane (Figures 15.21 and 15.22). If they are designed as such, horizontal floors and roofs can act as diaphragms, transferring lateral forces to the vertical lateral resistance components of the structure (i.e., the braced frames, moment frames, or shear walls).

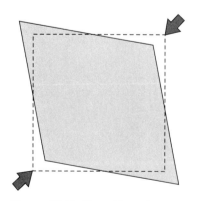

Figure 15.21 Floor Plan of Horizontal Racking

Figure 15.22 Floor Structure Acting as a Rigid Diaphragm Resisting Horizontal Racking

Introduction to Trusses

16.1 Introduction

A truss is an assembly of relatively lightweight structural elements, having an open framework of triangulated individual members in a single plane, generally used to span larger distances. The generally accepted terminology for truss members and components is shown in Figure 16.1.

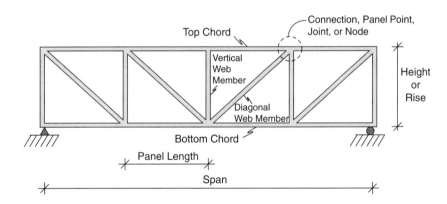

Figure 16.1 Truss Members and Components

Larger trusses are commonly used in bridges and long-span roofs (Figure 16.2). Smaller trusses are commonly used as floor and roof joists (Figure 16.3). Depending upon transport and erection considerations, trusses can be fabricated in the shop, in the field, or a combination of both, In the United States, trusses are typically made of steel or wood. Trusses have an inherent danger that is well known to firefighters, who are trained to use extra caution when entering trussed structures during a fire. Should any single truss member fail, there is potential for a sudden catastrophic collapse.

Figure 16.2 A Bridge Truss

Figure 16.3 Floor/Roof Truss Joists

16.2 Trusses As Beams

In general, a beam and a truss bend and behave similarly under load with compression along the top edge and tension along the bottom edge (Figures 16.4 and 16.5).

While a beam is an efficient structural member for short to medium spans, as spans increase the beam's weight increases disproportionately, thereby making it increasingly inefficient and uneconomical.

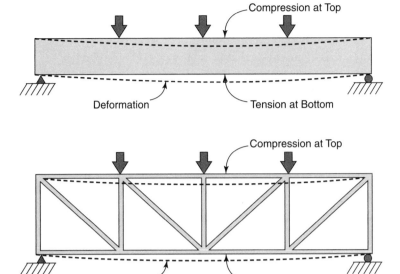

Figure 16.4 A Beam Bending under Load

Figure 16.5 A Truss Bending under Load

In a beam, the concentration of material at the top and bottom edges (away from the neutral axis) provides the majority of the beam's strength. The material and weight of the beam's solid web contribute little to its strength (Figure 16.6a).

In a truss, the concentration of material at the top and bottom chords (away from the neutral axis) similarly provides the majority of the truss's strength. However, unlike a beam, the lightness of the truss's open web does not add unnecessary weight (Figure 16.6b).

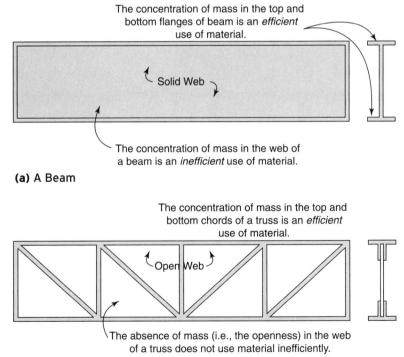

(a) A Beam

(b) A Truss

Figures 16.6 Comparing a Beam and a Truss

In essence, the concept of a truss is that of a deep beam with an open web and a concentration of material at the top and bottom edges.

16.3 Types of Trusses

Trusses can have innumerable configurations, with various names or combination of names. Some trusses are named after their shape (Figure 16.7).

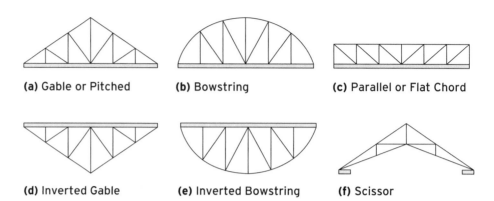

(a) Gable or Pitched   **(b)** Bowstring   **(c)** Parallel or Flat Chord

(d) Inverted Gable   **(e)** Inverted Bowstring   **(f)** Scissor

Figure 16.7 Trusses Named by Shape

Other trusses such as Warren, Pratt, and Howe, are named after the designers who developed and popularized them. These trusses are defined primarily by the configuration and/or type of stress in their diagonals:

- A Warren truss is characterized by the alternating direction of diagonals, with or without verticals. The stresses in the diagonal members generally alternate in tension and compression (Figure 16.8).

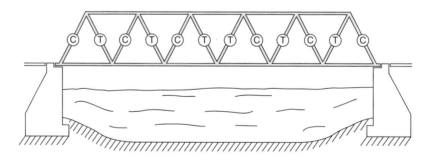

Figure 16.8 Parallel Chord Warren Truss

- A Pratt truss is characterized by diagonals in tension and verticals in compression (Figure 16.9).

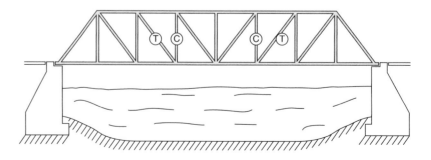

Figure 16.9 Parallel Chord Pratt Truss

- A Howe truss is characterized by diagonals in compression and verticals in tension (Figure 16.10).

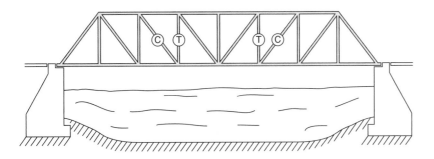

Figure 16.10 Parallel Chord Howe Truss

The Vierendeel "truss," named after its European designer at the beginning of the twentieth century, is a deep rectangular framework of members *without diagonals*. In order to support loads, it relies on rigid connections at its joints, which introduce very real bending stresses (i.e., moment) into its members. Having no diagonals, it is not really a truss and should not be called one. A more appropriate name is Vierendeel *"girder"* (Figure 16.11).

Unlike a true truss, a Vierendeel girder is an inefficient way to span large distances. It has value, however, when large, clear openings are desired within which diagonals would interfere. Vierendeel girders are not analyzed in the same manner as a true truss.

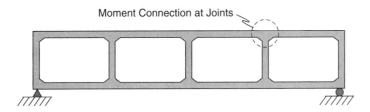

Figure 16.11 A Vierendeel Girder

Unfortunately, it's not always easy to immediately visualize the type of stress in a truss member without more detailed analysis. Therefore, it's best not to focus too much on a truss type or name but to concentrate, instead, on the principles of truss behavior and analysis. Regardless of how a truss is envisioned, shaped, or named, the principles of stability and equilibrium will always apply with respect to:

- The external forces acting on the truss as a whole
- The internal forces acting on the individual members within the truss

16.4 Design Considerations

Pitched, Arched, and Parallel Chord Trusses

The most efficient trusses are generally those that have pitched or arched chords and their longer members (i.e., the diagonals) in tension. As spans increase, however, the depth of pitched and arched chord trusses may make them impractical. While pitched and arched chord trusses may be appropriate for roofs, bridges, and other open-air structures, they may not be practical for interior spaces when horizontal upper and lower chords are needed. For these reasons, as well as for their simpler fabrication and erection requirements, parallel chord trusses find use in many truss applications.

Span-to-Depth Ratios

While the optimum span-to-depth ratio of a truss is dependent upon the loads that it is designed to carry, trusses of various types and materials have approximate span-to-depth ratios ranging from 4:1 to 12:1. The lower ratio of 4:1 (i.e., a deeper truss) is appropriate for heavier loads, while the upper ratio of 12:1 (i.e., a shallower truss) is appropriate for lighter loads.

A span-to-depth ratio of 8:1 is a good estimating average for a truss (Figure 16.12). For example, with this span-to-depth ratio, a truss having a 48 ft span would have a depth of 6 ft (i.e., 48 ft/8 = 6 ft).

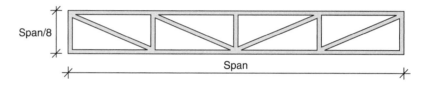

Figure 16.12 Average Span-to-Depth Ratio of a Truss

For any given span and loading condition, the optimum span-to-depth ratio is ultimately determined by the designer's evaluation of the variables of (a) the truss depth and (b) the weight of the members. The designer must decide between a deeper truss with lighter members or a shallower truss with heavier members (Figures 16.13 and 16.14).

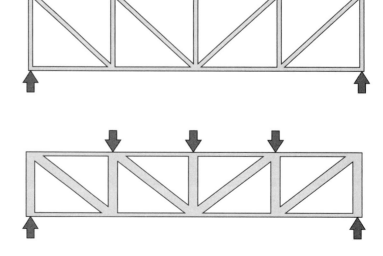

Figure 16.13 A Deeper Truss with Lighter Members

Figure 16.14 A Shallower Truss with Heavier Members

For long, spans such as those found on bridges, greater depth is often provided at the supports primarily to control the large shear forces at these locations (Figure 16.15).

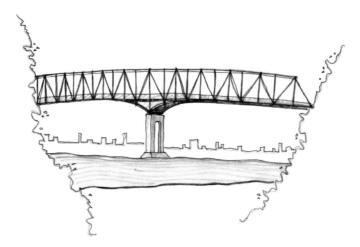

Figure 16.15 Greater Truss Depth at Supports of a Bridge

16.5 Truss Joints

For simplicity of analysis, trusses are idealized as consisting of *individual members* connected at each of their two ends by *pin connections*. As we know from Chapter 8, pin connections cannot restrain rotation at the joint (pin connections are free to rotate) and therefore cannot create bending within the member (Figure 16.16).

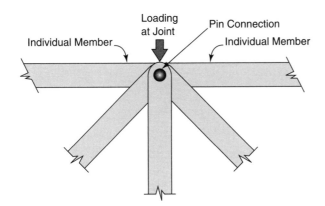

Figure 16.16 Idealized Truss Joint

By being so idealized with pin connections, and when loaded only at the joints, each truss member is either in pure axial tension or pure axial compression. There is no bending in the member itself (Figure 16.17).

(a) Member in Axial Compression

(b) Member in Axial Tension

Figure 16.17 Axial Loading of a Truss Member

In reality, most trusses consist of partially continuous top and bottom chords connected to their vertical and diagonal members by gusset plates (Figure 16.18). The continuous chords and rigid gusseted connections do indeed create some degree of bending stresses within the member. However, since these bending stresses are relatively minor compared to the much larger tensile and compressive axial stresses, they are generally ignored in truss analysis.

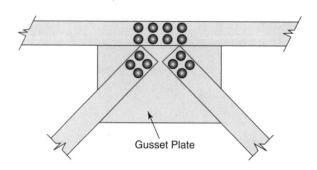

Figure 16.18 Gusset Plate Rigid Connection

16.6 Truss Loading

When supporting point loads from above, such as columns, trusses are typically designed so that the point loads coincide with joints on the top chord (Figure 16.19).

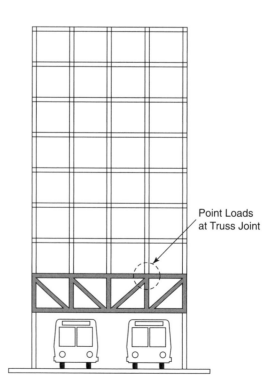

Figure 16.19 Point Loads Supported at Top Chord

When they are supporting uniform loads such as roadways, trusses can be designed to support the loads along either their top or bottom chords (Figures 16.20 and 16.21).

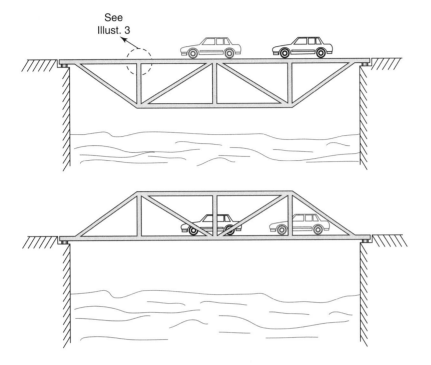

Figure 16.20 Uniform Loads Supported at Top Chord

Figure 16.21 Uniform Loads Supported at Bottom Chord

In either case, trusses are most efficiently designed to have uniform loads transferred as point loads at the joints (Figure 16.22).

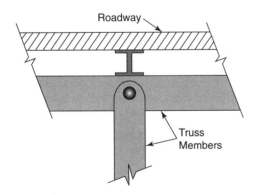

Figure 16.22 Uniform Load Transferred as a Point Load at a Truss Joint

16.7 Truss Analysis

Truss Determinancy

Before beginning an analysis of a truss, note that just as the equilibrium equations are useful only for the analysis of statically determinate beams, the equilibrium equations are similarly useful only for the analysis of statically determinate trusses. Generally speaking:

- Trusses with more than two external supports are said to be *externally indeterminate* (Figure 16.23).

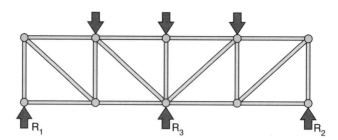

Figure 16.23 Externally Indeterminate Truss (more than two external support)

- Trusses with one or more redundant internal members (i.e., members not needed for its basic stability—see Chapter 15) are said to be *internally indeterminate* (Figure 16.24).

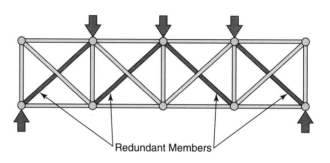

Figure 16.24 Internally Indeterminate Truss (one or more redundant internal members)

The following equation is used to determine the degree to which a simply supported truss is internally determinate. If the equation holds true, a truss is internally determinate.

$$\mathbf{m = 2j - 3}$$

where:

m = the number of members
j = the number of joints

Applying the equation to the truss example in Figure 16.25:

$$17 = (2 \times 10) - 3$$
$$17 = 17$$

The equation holds true; therefore, the truss is internally determinate.

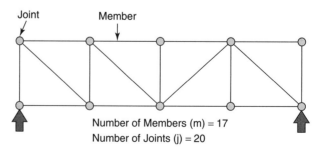

Figure 16.25 Truss Determinancy

The analysis of a statically indeterminate truss is significantly more complex and is beyond the scope of this text.

Assumptions and Conventions

Let's briefly review assumptions and conventions typically used in the analysis of statically determinate trusses:

- The truss has no more than two external supports and has no redundant internal members.
- The truss is composed of individual members connected at each of their two ends by pin connections.
- Loads are applied at the joints only and not at intermediate points along the members. Any member not loaded at its joint (i.e., loaded so as to experience bending) is assumed to transfer no moment to an adjacent member by virtue of its pinned connection.
- The weight of truss members is considered insignificant compared to the applied loads and is therefore ignored.
- An arrow away from a joint or cut section indicates tension in the member; an arrow toward a joint or cut section indicates compression in the member.
- In the absence of an educated guess, unknown forces are assumed to be in tension. If the result is negative, the assumption is wrong and the member is in compression.
- If a member is shown to have no internal forces acting on it, it is said to be a *zero force member*. A zero force member is not needed for the stability of the truss.

Let's now analyze the truss in the following example.

■ EXAMPLE 16: Analysis of a Statically Determinate Truss

A statically determinate, simply supported truss, 48 ft long and 12 ft deep, is symmetrically configured and loaded. 10 kip vertical loads (P_1 and P_2) are at joints B and C, and a 5 kip vertical load (P_3) is at joint E (Figure 16.26). Determine:

- The external reactions R_1 and R_2
- The internal forces within all truss members

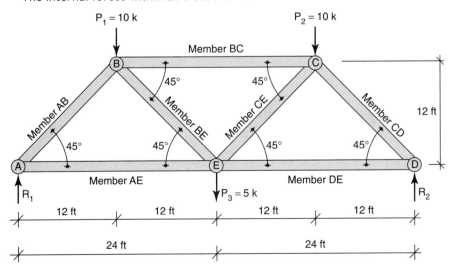

Figure 16.26 A Symmetrically Configured and Loaded Truss

Determining External Reactions R_1 and R_2

To determine the reactions R_1 and R_2, ignore the internal configuration of truss members, envision the truss as a deep beam, and apply the equilibrium equations (Figure 16.27).

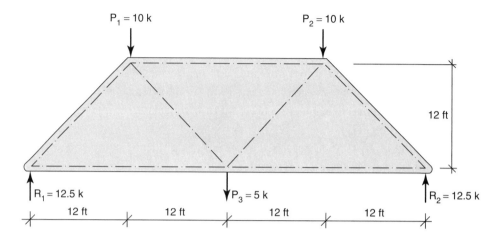

Figure 16.27 Determining Truss Reactions

Although we could apply the equilibrium equations, since our truss is symmetrically loaded and supported, we can readily determine that each reaction, R_1 and R_2, carries half the 25 kip (10 k + 10 k + 5 k) total load or 12.5 kips.

Determining Internal Forces within Truss Members

With all external forces (i.e., loads and reactions) known, there are two analytical methods for determining the internal forces acting on individual members within the truss. These two methods "cut" the truss in different ways to create free-body diagrams. The "cut away" part of any member is then replaced by an internal force that is acting along a line of action coincident with the longitudinal axis of the member. The equilibrium equations are then applied to determine the force's magnitude.

a. The Method of Joints (also called The Method of Joint Equilibrium)

This method successively cuts around each individual joint, creating a free-body diagram of it. Each isolated joint is then treated as a set of concurrent forces, to which the equilibrium equations $\Sigma F_x = 0$ and $\Sigma F_y = 0$ are applied to determine the unknown internal forces within the members.

b. The Method of Sections

This method cuts through the truss across no more than three members, creating a free-body diagram of one side of the cut truss. The equilibrium equation $\Sigma M = 0$ is then successively applied about selected points to determine the unknown internal forces within the members.

In general, the method of joints is used for shorter trusses, whereas the method of sections is used on longer trusses when solving for stresses in members that are closer to the center of the span. However, once you are familiar with these two methods, you can choose to use them in combination as you see fit.

A third graphical method, utilizing what is known as a *Maxwell Diagram*, is also available for truss analysis but it is seldom used and beyond the scope of this text.

Understanding Internal Forces

Before we start our truss analysis, let's take a closer look at how external and internal forces are transmitted within any particular truss member that has theoretical pinned joints at each end.

Envision a truss member, MN, with pinned connections at joints M and N at each end. Remember that, with pinned connections, the member experiences no bending—only either axial compression or axial tension. If we apply an external compressive force of 1 kip at joint M, we know an equal and opposite external compressive force of 1 kip must also be applied at joint N for the member to be in equilibrium (Figure 16.28).

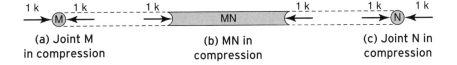

Figure 16.28 Free-body Diagram of a Member under Axial Compression

Let's now examine the internal forces within the membera to envision how they are transmitted. We'll break our member apart into three free-body diagrams—joint M, MN, and joint N (Figure 16.29).

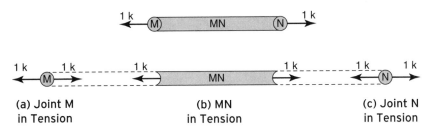

(a) Joint M in compression

(b) MN in compression

(c) Joint N in compression

Figure 16.29 Free-body Diagram of Internal Forces within the Member

From the free-body diagrams of joints M and N, we see that MN must "push" against both joints with an (internal) force of 1 kip for the joints to be in equilibrium. This compressive "push" is represented by a force arrow acting toward the joint. We also see that joints M and N must "push" against MN with an (internal) force of 1 kip for MN to be in equilibrium. This compressive "push" is represented by a force arrow acting toward MN.

Similarly, with member MN under a 1 kip tensile force, we see that MN must "pull" against each joint with an (internal) force of 1 kip for the joints to be in equilibrium. This tensile "pull" is represented by a force arrow acting away from the joint. We also see that joints M and N must "pull" against MN with an (internal) force of 1 kip for MN to be in equilibrium. This compressive "pull" is represented by a force arrow acting away from MN (Figures 16.30 and 16.31).

Figure 16.30 Free-body Diagram of a Member under Axial Tension

(a) Joint M in Tension

(b) MN in Tension

(c) Joint N in Tension

Figure 16.31 Free-body Diagram of Internal Forces within the Member

We're now ready to apply the method of joints and the method of sections to analyze our truss and determine the internal forces within the truss' members.

Truss Analysis by the Method of Joints

With external reactions R_1 and R_2 determined to be 12.5 kips, we'll begin by isolating and analyzing joint A, since it has only two unknown internal forces (AB and AE) acting on it and we can solve for both. We'll then proceed to joint B and then to joint E. Since the truss configuration and loading conditions are symmetrical, we know that the analysis of joint C will be analogous to joint B and that the analysis of joint D will be analogous to joint A.

ANALYSIS OF JOINT A

Step 1: Draw the free-body diagram isolating joint A (Figure 16.32).

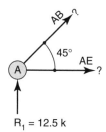

Figure 16.32 Free-body Diagram of Joint A

From the free-body diagram, we observe three forces acting at joint A:
- R_1 acting vertically upward with a magnitude of 12.5 kips
- Force AB of unknown magnitude and direction, acting along the axis of member AB
- Force AE of unknown magnitude and direction, acting along the axis of member AE

The experienced reader can often assess the direction of unknown forces and should do so when able. However, for our purposes, we'll assume unknown forces to be tension, represented by an arrow acting away from the joint. A negative result will indicate that the assumption was wrong, and the force acting on the joint is actually compression.

Step 2: Resolve all forces into their x and y components, and apply the equilibrium equations $\Sigma F_y = 0$ and $\Sigma F_x = 0$ to solve for unknown forces AB and AE (Figure 16.33).

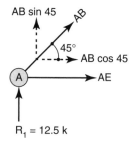

Figure 16.33 Resolution of Forces into x and y Components

$$\Sigma F_y = 0$$
$$+ (R_1) + (AB \sin 45°) = 0$$
$$+ (12.5) + (AB \times 0.7071) = 0$$
$$+ (AB) = - (12.5 / 0.7071)$$

AB = (−) 17.7 k

Force AB is (−) 17.7 kips, the (−) sign indicating that our assumption of tension was incorrect and that member AB is actually in compression.

$$\Sigma F_x = 0$$
$$+ (AE) + (AB \cos 45°) = 0$$
$$+ (AE) + (-17.7 \times 0.7071) = 0$$
$$\mathbf{AE = (+) \ 12.5 \ k}$$

Force AE is (+) 12.5 kips, the (+) sign indicating that our assumption of tension in member AE was correct.

The final free-body diagram of joint A is shown in Figure 16.34.

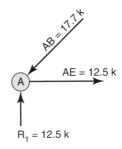

Figure 16.34 Final Free-body Diagram of Joint A

ANALYSIS OF JOINT B

Step 1: Draw the free-body diagram isolating joint B (Figure 16.35).

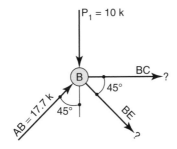

Figure 16.35 Free-body Diagram of Joint B

From the free-body diagram, we observe four forces acting at joint B:

- P_1 acting vertically downward with a magnitude of 10 kips
- Force AB, known to be 17.7 kips compression from our analysis of joint A, represented by an arrow acting towards joint B along the axis of member AB
- Force BC of unknown magnitude and direction, acting along the axis of member BC
- Force BE of unknown magnitude and direction, acting along the axis of member BE

As in joint A, we'll assume unknown forces BC and BE to be tension.

Step 2: Resolve all forces into their x and y components, and apply the equilibrium equations $\Sigma F_y = 0$ and $\Sigma F_x = 0$ to solve for unknown forces BC and BE (Figure 16.36).

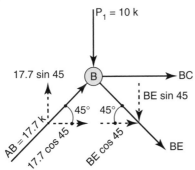

Figure 16.36 Resolution of Forces into x and y Components

$$\Sigma F_y = 0$$
$$- (P_1) + (17.7 \sin 45) - (BE \sin 45°) = 0$$
$$- (10\ k) + (17.7 \times 0.7071) - (BE \times 0.7071) = 0$$
$$- (10) + (12.51) - (BE \times 0.7071) + 0$$
$$+ (BE \times 0.7071) = + (2.51)$$
$$+ (BE) = + (2.51 / 0.7071)$$
$$\textbf{BE} = \textbf{(+) 3.5 k}$$

Force BE is (+) 3.5 kips, the (+) sign indicating that our assumption of tension in member BE was correct.

$$\Sigma F_x = 0$$
$$+ (BC) + (17.7 \cos 45°) + (BE \cos 45°) = 0$$
$$+ (BC) + (17.7 \times 0.7071) + (3.5 \times 0.7071) = 0$$
$$+ (BC) + (12.51) + (2.47) = 0$$
$$\textbf{BC} = \textbf{(-) 15.0 k}$$

Force BC is (–) 15.0 kips, the (–) sign indicating that our assumption of tension was incorrect and that member BC is actually in compression.

The final free-body diagram of joint B is shown in Figure 16.37.

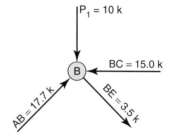

Figure 16.37 Final Free-body Diagram of Joint B

ANALYSIS OF JOINT E

Step 1: Draw the free-body diagram isolating joint E (Figure 16.38).

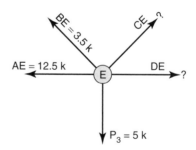

Figure 16.38 Free-body Diagram of Joint E

From the free-body diagram, we observe five forces acting at joint E:

- P_3 acting vertically downward with a magnitude of 5 kips.
- Force AE, known to be 12.5 kips tension from our analysis of joint A, represented by an arrow acting away from joint E along the axis of member AE.
- Force BE, known to be 3.5 kips tension from our analysis of joint B, represented by an arrow acting away from joint E along the axis of member BE.

- Force CE of unknown magnitude and direction, acting along the axis of member CE.
- Force DE of unknown magnitude and direction, acting along the axis of member DE.

Although we could do the Step 2 mathematical analyses to determine the magnitude and direction of unknown forces CE and DE, we can readily observe that since both the truss configuration and loading conditions are symmetrical:

- Force CE will be the same magnitude and stress as force BE (i.e., 3.5 kips tension) acting along the axis of member CE.
- Force DE will be the same magnitude and stress as member AE (i.e., 12.5 kips tension) acting along the axis of member DE.

The final free-body diagram of joint E is shown in Figure 16.39.

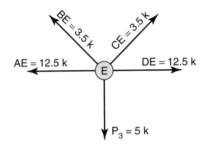

Figure 16.39 Final Free-body Diagram of Joint E

ANALYSIS OF JOINTS C AND D

Given the symmetrical truss configuration and loading conditions, we know that:

- The forces at joint C are analogous to those at joint B.
- The forces at joint D are analogous to those at joint A.

The final free-body diagrams of joints C and D are shown in Figures 16.40 and 16.41.

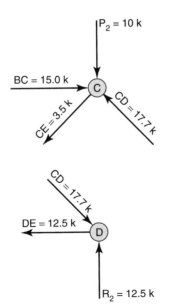

Figure 16.40 Final Free-body Diagram of Joint C

Figure 16.41 Final Free-body Diagram of Joint D

The stresses in all members are now fully determined and shown in Figure 16.42.

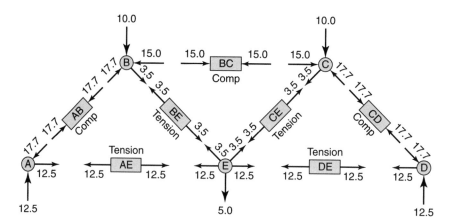

Figure 16.42 Stresses at all Truss Joints and Members

Truss Analysis by the Method of Sections

Although we could apply the method of sections to solve for stresses in all truss members, we'll use it as an example to simply determine unknown forces through a single cut.

With external reactions R_1 and R_2 established as 12.5 kips, let's cut a section through the truss across members BC, AE, and BE to create a free-body diagram of the left side, showing the internal forces acting along the lines of action of members BC, AE, and BE (Figure 16.43). We'll then apply the equilibrium equation $\Sigma M = 0$ about successive joints to determine unknown internal forces BC, AE, and BE.

As was done for the method of joints, we'll assume unknown forces to be tension represented by an arrow acting away from the cut member, understanding that a negative result will indicate an incorrect assumption.

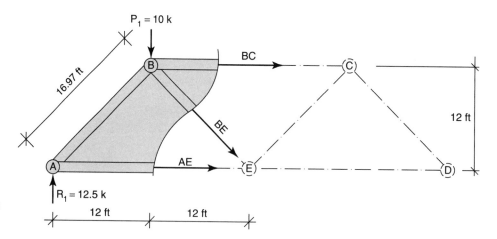

Figure 16.43 Free-body Diagram of Left Side of Truss

We'll start by taking moments about joint E. Since forces AE and BE will not contribute to moment about this joint, we can solve for force BC directly. We'll then similarly take moments about joint B to solve for force AE. Finally we'll take moments about joint A to solve for force BE.

Taking moments about joint E to solve for force BC:

$\Sigma M_E = 0$

$+ (R_1 \times 24) - (P_1 \times 12) + (BC \times 12) = 0$

$+ (12.5 \times 24) - (10 \times 12) + (BC \times 12) = 0$

$+ (300) - (120) + (12BC) = 0$

$+ (12BC) = - (300) + (120) = - (180)$

$+ (BC) = - (180 / 12)$

BC = (–) 15.0 k

Force BC is (–) 15.0 kips, the (–) sign indicating that our assumption of tension was incorrect and member BC is actually 15.0 kips compression.

Taking moments about joint B to solve for force AE:

$\Sigma M_B = 0$

$+ (R_1 \times 12) - (AE \times 12) = 0$

$+ (12.5 \times 12) - (AE \times 12) = 0$

$+ (150) - (12AE) = 0$

$+ (AE) = + (150 / 12)$

AE = (+) 12.5k

Force AE is (+) 12.5 kips, the (+) sign indicating that our assumption of tension in member AB was correct.

Taking moments about joint A to solve for force BE: (by trigonometry, the perpendicular distance between force BE and joint A is determined to be 16.97 ft)

$\Sigma M_A = 0$

$+ (P_1 \times 12) + (BC \times 12) + (BE \times 16.97) = 0$

$+ (10 \times 12) + (-15.0 \times 12) + (BE \times 16.97) = 0$

$+ (120) + (-180) + (16.97BE) = 0$

$+ (16.97BE) = - (120) + (180) = + (60)$

$+ (BE) = + (60/16.97)$

BE = (+) 3.5k

Force BE is (+) 3.5 kips, the (+) sign indicating that our assumption of tension in member BE was correct.

Comparing the results for stresses in members BC, AE, and BE by the method of sections with the method of joints, we see that they are the same (Figure 16.44).

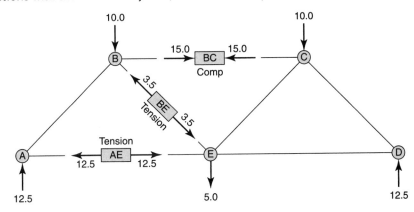

Figure 16.44 Stresses in Members BC, AE, and BE

Structural Walls

Walls are used to enclose space, to provide support for other structural members, or to resist elements such as earth, water, wind, and fire. There are many ways to classify walls. However, since our concern is the structural behavior of walls, let's focus instead on the types of load to which a wall can be subjected, and the stresses those loads produce.

A wall can be subjected to three general types of load (Figure 17.1):

- Vertical gravity loads
- Horizontal lateral loads perpendicular to the plane of the wall
- Horizontal loads parallel to the plane of the wall

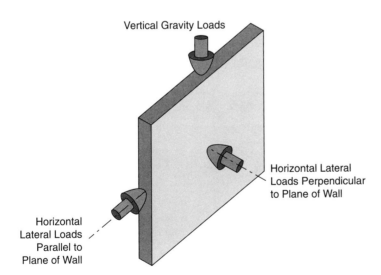

Figure 17.1 Loads on a Wall

17.1 Loads and Deformational Stresses

Vertical Gravity Loads

Vertical gravity loads produce simple compression. Walls that primarily resist gravity loads are called *bearing walls* (Figure 17.2).

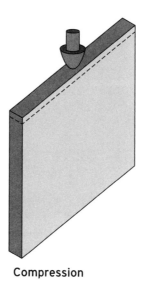

Figure 17.2 Compression under Gravity Load

Compression

Horizontal Lateral Loads

Horizontal lateral loads (such as those from wind and earthquake) produce different deformations and stresses, depending upon their direction relative to the plane of the wall.

PERPENDICULAR TO THE PLANE OF A WALL

Lateral loads perpendicular to the plane of a wall produce bending and bowing (Figures 17.3a and 17.3b).

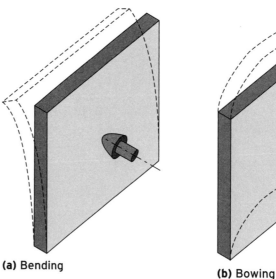
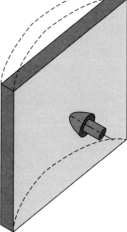

Figure 17.3 Lateral Load Perpendicular to Plane of a Wall

(a) Bending

(b) Bowing

PARALLEL TO THE PLANE OF A WALL

Lateral loads parallel to the plane of a wall produce shear. Walls that primarily resist shear are called *shear walls* (Figure 17.4). Shear walls can play an important role in the lateral bracing system of a building (see Chapter 15).

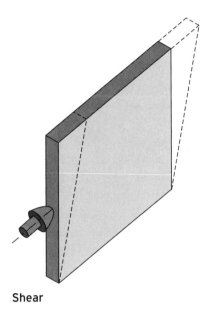

Shear

Figure 17.4 Lateral Load Parallel to Plane of a Wall

17.2 Stresses and Wall Construction

In steel and concrete construction, structural walls are typically reinforced concrete and reinforced masonry. In wood light frame construction, plywood sheathing over studs typically serve as structural walls. Let's examine the stresses to which a structural wall is subjected.

Concrete and Masonry Walls

The concept behind reinforced concrete and masonry wall construction is that the concrete and the masonry primarily resist compressive stresses, while the steel reinforcing primarily resists tensile stresses. For a wall subjected to pure compression, this concept is simple enough, but let's take a closer look at the stresses resulting from the bending and bowing of a wall.

Figures 17.5a and b show a concrete wall with steel reinforcing placed to resist tensile stresses resulting from the bending and bowing due to forces from one direction. Steel reinforcing must, of course, also be placed on the other side of the wall, if forces are anticipated from the other direction as well.

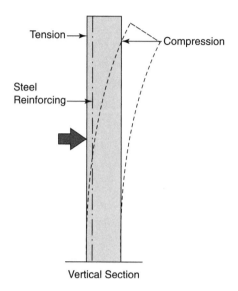

Figure 17.5a Bending Stresses in a Wall

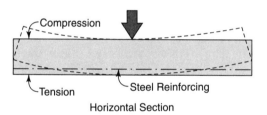

Figure 17.5b Bowing Stresses in a Wall

In a masonry wall, it is impractical to place horizontal steel reinforcing bars at an edge. Figure 17.6 shows the truss-type horizontal joint reinforcement that is used in masonry construction as a means to resist the bowing of a wall in either direction.

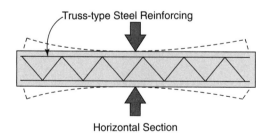

Figure 17.6 Truss-type Masonry Reinforcement

Wood Stud Walls

The concept behind stud wall construction is that individual closely spaced vertical wood studs act as small columns that resist compression When sheathed with a structural material such as plywood, the row of studs forms a structural wall that can also resist shear (Figure 17.7).

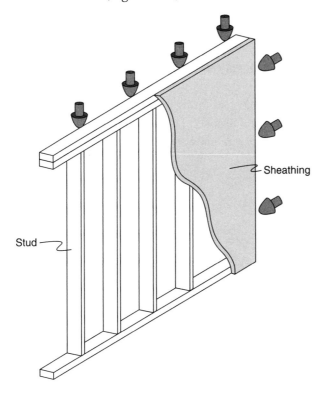

Figure 17.7 Stud Wall Construction

17.3 Retaining Walls

Retaining walls are site structures that hold back (retain) earth in order to create usable, relatively flat land. Retaining walls are used to create abrupt grade changes (Figure 17.8).

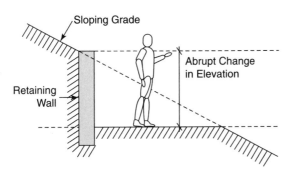

Figure 17.8 Retaining Wall Holding Back Earth

Site Slopes and Grades

All sites generally have some degree of slope to the land.

If the slope is relatively shallow, existing grades may remain (with only minor recontouring for proper drainage) for the land to be usable (Figure 17.9).

Figure 17.9 Shallow Sloping Grade

If the slope is relatively steep, existing grades may have to be changed for the land to be reasonably level and usable). This is often accomplished by the *cut and fill* of grades and by the use of retaining walls (Figure 17.10).

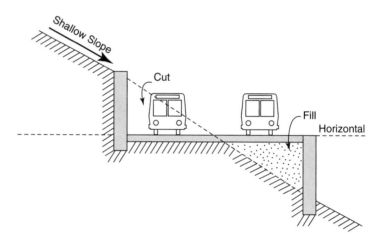

Figure 17.10 Steeply Sloping Grade

Angle of Repose of a Soil

The decision on whether or not to use a retaining wall in a grading design is dependent on many factors, including the stability of the sloping soil, as measured by its *angle of repose*. The angle of repose is dependent upon the characteristics of the particular type of soil but is generally about 30 degrees. Proper landscaping and vegetation on a sloping soil can increase its angle of repose.

A soil sloping less than its angle of repose will be stable (Figure 17.11).

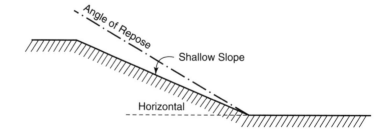

Figure 17.11 Shallow Sloping Stable Soil

A soil that slopes more than its angle of repose will be unstable and tumble of its own accord (Figure 17.12).

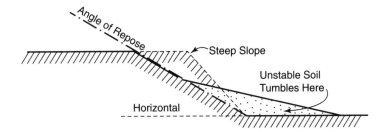

Figure 17.12 Steeply Sloping Unstable Soil

Soil Pressure

Just as water pressure increases at greater depths below the surface of bodies of water, soil pressure increases at greater depths below grade. Any groundwater that may be contained in the earth tends to increase the soil pressure.

Imagine yourself swimming on the surface of a lake; your ears would feel normal. But if you dive down, you would notice increasing pressure on your ears. This is caused by the increasing accumulated weight of the water above. This pressure acts not only downward but sideways (laterally) as well.

Let's use the example of a swimming pool to get a better sense of lateral soil pressure.

If the pool is above ground, we can easily envision the water pressure acting vertically downward against the ground, and laterally outward against the walls (Figure 17.13).

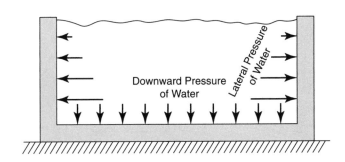

Figure 17.13 Vertical and Lateral Water Pressure in an Aboveground Pool

The walls of the pool must be designed to resist the lateral pressure of the water so as not to break apart outwardly (Figure 17.14).

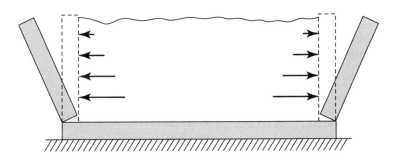

Figure 17.14 Effect of Lateral Water Pressure in an Aboveground Pool

Let's now suppose that the pool is below ground but emptied of water for maintenance. Just as water pressure exerts outward lateral pressure on the pool walls, soil pressure exerts an inward lateral force on the pool walls. Under normal circumstances, with water in the pool, the outward lateral pressure of the water opposes the inward lateral pressure of the soil. But because the pool is sometimes emptied, the walls must be designed to resist the lateral pressure of the soil so as not to break apart inwardly (Figure 17.15)

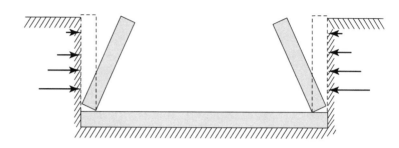

Figure 17.15 Effect of Lateral Soil Pressure in an Empty Belowground Pool

Design Principles for Retaining Walls

Retaining walls are typically constructed of concrete, masonry, or treated wood timbers. Regardless of the material used, the principles for the design of retaining walls are the same.

Retaining walls are susceptible to failure by settling, sliding, overturning, and bending (Figure 17.16).

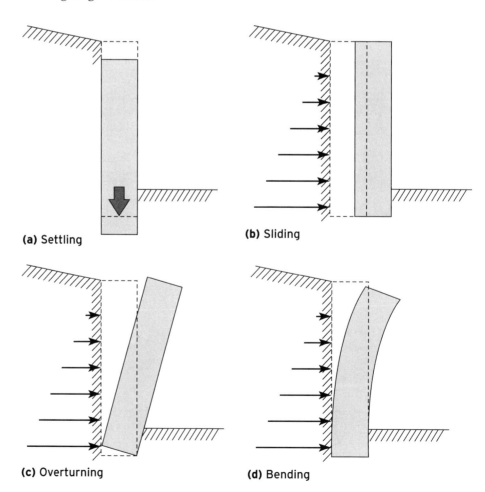

(a) Settling

(b) Sliding

(c) Overturning

(d) Bending

Figure 17.16 Retaining Wall Failures

Retaining walls are designed to resist these effects by providing sufficient:

- Soil bearing to prevent settling
- Frictional resistance to prevent sliding
- Downward weight and/or reinforcing to prevent overturning and bending

Retaining walls fall into two general categories, gravity and cantilever.

Gravity Retaining Walls

Gravity retaining walls rely on their own mass and weight to resist sliding, bending, and overturning. They often have a slight *batter* (i.e., slope) to improve stability on the vertical side that retains the soil (Figure 17.17).

For large grade differentials, gravity walls may become too massive and impractical.

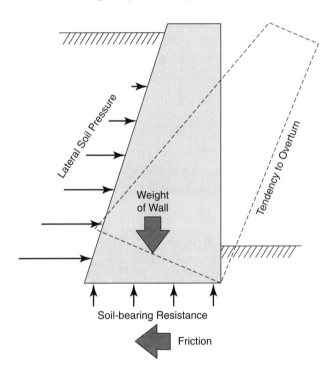

Figure 17.17 Forces on a Gravity Retaining Wall

Cantilever Retaining Walls

Cantilever retaining walls are constructed of reinforced concrete, generally using less material than gravity walls. Cantilever retaining walls consist of a stem and a footing (Figure 17.18). The stem acts as a vertical cantilever projecting up from the footing. (The heel is the portion of the footing below the retained soil, while the toe is the portion on the opposite side.) If the frictional resistance between the footing and soil is insufficient to prevent sliding, a shear key is provided. If the retaining wall is constructed on a property line, the toe is omitted and the cantilever footing takes on an L shape.

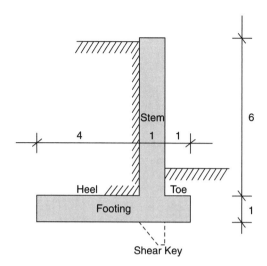

Figure 17.18 Parts of a Cantilever Retaining Wall

RESISTANCE TO SETTLING, SLIDING, AND OVERTURNING IN A CANTILEVER RETAINING WALL

By spreading out the weight on the stem, the footing resists the tendency to settle.

By its own weight and the weight of soil above the heel, the footing provides the friction to resist the tendency to slide.

By its own weight and the weight of soil above the heel, the footing and stem work monolithically together to resist the tendency to overturn (Figure 17.19).

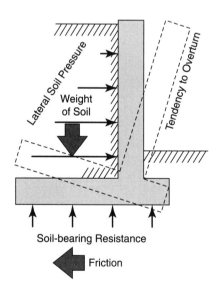

Figure 17.19 Forces on a Cantilever Retaining Wall

RESISTANCE TO BENDING IN A CANTILEVER RETAINING WALL

Soil pressure tends to create deformation and bending stresses in the stem and footing of a cantilever retaining wall. Steel reinforcing must be appropriately placed where the bending creates tensile stress (Figure 17.20).

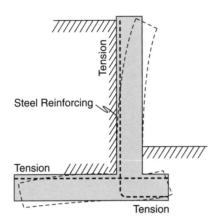

Figure 17.20 Bending Stresses and Reinforcing in a Cantilever Retaining Wall

COUNTERFORT BRACING IN A CANTILEVER RETAINING WALL

As the height of a cantilever retaining wall increases, so does the tendency of the stem to bend and bow. *Counterforts*, wedge-shaped concrete braces at spaced intervals, can provide additional bracing of the stem to resist bending and bowing (Figure 17.21).

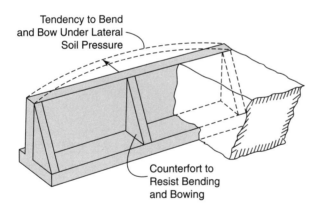

Figure 17.21 Counterfort Bracing in a Cantilever Retaining Wall

Soils and Rock

All loads must eventually work their way down through a structure to its foundation and ultimately to the ground, meaning soil or rock. The ground, in turn, must be capable of exerting resisting forces sufficient to oppose the loads and keep the structure stable. Although the ground may be under a body of water, such as a river, lake, or ocean, the principles of foundation support remain the same. Let's take a closer look at what is meant by "ground".

18.1 The Earth's Interior

The Earth was formed approximately 4.6 billion years ago. At its center, 4000 miles beneath the surface, is a superheated solid inner core covered by a molten outer core. A decreasingly viscous mantle overlies the core, extending to a relatively thin solid crust at the outer surface (Figure 18.1).

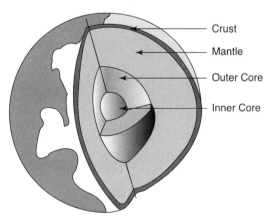

— Crust

— Mantle

— Outer Core

— Inner Core

Figure 18.1 Cross Section of the Earth

18.2 The Earth's Crust

The Earth's crust, approximately 5 to 25 miles thick, is composed of rock broadly classified as igneous, sedimentary, or metamorphic. The Earth's crust has been in a constant state of change over geologic periods of time so great as to dwarf the time of human existence by comparison.

Igneous Rock

Igneous rock, comprising the majority of the Earth's crust, is geologically ancient rock crystallized from cooling molten material (magma) in the outerlying regions of the mantle. Granite is one commonly known type of igneous rock (Figure 18.2).

Figure 18.2 Granite Outcropping

Sedimentary Rock

Sedimentary rocks are younger rocks that were generally formed in shallow coastal waters or marshes from the layered deposition of sediment produced from the land erosion of mineral matter and/or the decaying of organic matter. As a result of geologic processes occurring over millions of years, the sediment became solidified into rock. Limestone, sandstone, and shale are commonly known types of sedimentary rocks (Figure 18.3).

Figure 18.3 Horizontally Layered Sedimentary Rock

Metamorphic Rock

Metamorphic rock is igneous or sedimentary rock that, over long periods of geologic time, has been subsumed deep below the Earth's surface and subjected to heat and pressure so intense that its mineral composition has been partially or totally altered. Marble and slate are commonly known types of metamorphic rocks recrystallized from what was originally limestone and shale (Figure 18.4).

Figure 18.4 Metamorphic Rock

Rock Formations

Rock formations can be any combination of igneous, sedimentary, and metamorphic rock that may be layered, inclined, or folded into undulating valleys and ridges known as *synclines* and *anticlines* (Figures 18.5 and 18.6). These rock formations, often visible in surface outcroppings, are referred to as *bedrock* and are the base upon which natural soils may have been formed.

Figure 18.5 Rock Folded into a Syncline

Figure 18.6 Rock Folded into an Anticline

18.3 Natural Soils

Natural soils are generally a loose mixture of mineral matter (rock) and decayed organic matter (plants and animals), accumulated above bedrock over geologically recent periods of time ranging from hundreds to thousands of years. Soils are broadly characterized as coarse-grained (gravels and sands), fine-grained (clays and silts), or organic (peat and topsoil) and are often found deposited over time in different layers called *strata*. Total soil profiles may range in thickness from a few feet to hundreds of feet (Figure 18.7). The composition and compaction of a soil determine its structural ability to support load and is expressed as its *soil bearing capacity*. The study of the engineering properties and behavior of soils is known as *soil mechanics*.

Figure 18.7 Natural Soil Profile

18.4 Groundwater

Water that collects beneath the land's surface is known as *groundwater* (Figure 18.8). Groundwater collects in soils and porous areas of rock formations. In general, the greater the distance is beneath the surface, the greater the concentration of groundwater in the soil. The elevation at which the ground becomes saturated with water is known as the *water table*. Groundwater is an important factor in the structural behavior of soils. For example, clays tend to retain water and expand when significantly saturated. Groundwater, and its effects on soils, must be carefully considered in the design of foundations.

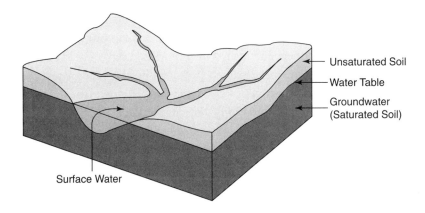

Figure 18.8 Groundwater

18.5 Engineered Fill

When upper areas of soil upon which a foundation will rest consist of structurally unacceptable material, these areas must be excavated and replaced with engineered fill. *Engineered fill* is crushed and graded mineral material placed and compacted in relatively thin layers (generally 6 to 12 in.), to a total specified depth under controlled conditions, in order to achieve a specified soil-bearing capacity.

18.6 Foundation Settlement

All new foundations initially settle to some degree when loads are applied. Foundations on bedrock settle negligibly. Foundations on soil cause compression of the soil accompanied by minor settlement measured in fractions of an inch. If a structure's underlying soil or material is the same over its expanse, uniform settlement will occur with little or no harmful effect. Frequently, however, a structure's underlying material is not the same at different foundation locations. This tends to produce differential settlement, which will indeed have harmful effects on the structure. Accordingly, a major consideration in foundation design is to minimize the potential for differential settlement (Figure 18.9).

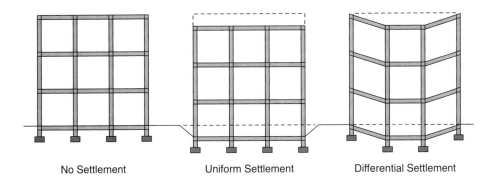

| No Settlement | Uniform Settlement | Differential Settlement |

Figure 18.9 Foundation Settlement

18.7 Soil Bearing Capacity and Subsurface Conditions

Guidelines and recommendations on various soil bearing capacities and other design characteristics of various types of soil are given in building codes. Soils information from codes may be generally adequate for the foundation design of a small structure, but for a large or complex structure, a detailed soils investigation is required to assess existing subsurface conditions. For this purpose, a *soils report* is prepared by a geotechnical engineer. This report is based on field observations and laboratory analyses of soils obtained from soil borings and/or test pits. The report presents recommendations to the structural engineer for allowable soil bearing capacities, types of foundations systems, and special construction techniques (such as excavating, backfill, compaction, and dewatering), as well as other pertinent design criteria needed for the proper design and construction of the structure's foundation. Table 18.1 shows the approximate allowable soil bearing capacity for a few generalized soil and rock types.

TABLE 18.1 SOIL BEARING CAPACITIES

Material	Allowable Soil Bearing Capacity
Organic soils (peat and topsoil)	Not suitable
Fine-grained soils (silts and clays)	2,000 psf
Coarse-grained soils (sands and gravel)	4,000 psf
Sedimentary rock	6,000 psf
Crystalline bedrock	12,000 psf

Foundations

The foundation of a building is its lowermost section, partly or wholly below ground, consisting of structural elements that transmit loads from the superstructure above (columns, walls, etc.) to the ground.

Although there are many variations of foundations, they fall into two broad categories: *shallow* and *deep*. Rather than having precise meanings, shallow and deep foundations are relative terms having more to do with the type of foundation construction than with the actual foundation depth below grade (Figure 19.1).

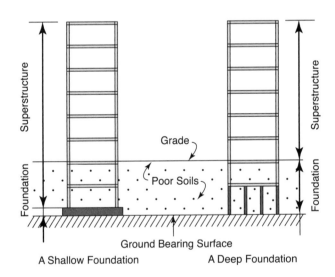

Figure 19.1 Shallow and Deep Foundations

19.1 Shallow Foundations

Spread Footings

Shallow foundations are typically concrete *spread footings* that do what their name implies: spread loads placed on them so as not to exceed the bearing capacity of the ground (Figure 19.2).

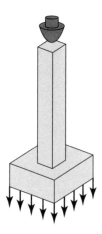

Figure 19.2 A Spread Footing Distributing Load

Just as your foot helps to spread the weight of your body over a larger surface area, a spread footing serves the same purpose in a building foundation (Figure 19.3).

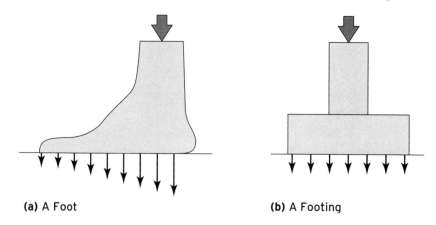

Figure 19.3

(a) A Foot

(b) A Footing

Symmetrical and Asymmetrical Footing Loads

The objective in designing a spread footing is to have its superimposed loads distributed as evenly as possible onto the ground below. This is accomplished by making the footing as symmetrical as possible about its load. Your foot has been ingeniously designed for both spreading your weight and keeping you balanced when you walk, run, or bend. If you were a stationery object, however, your foot would probably have been more symmetrically designed to more evenly distribute your weight.

In a column footing, the effect of asymmetrical loading, and the resulting uneven distribution of pressure onto the ground, is shown in Figure 19.4.

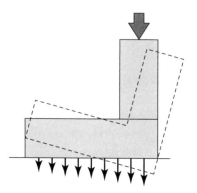

Figure 19.4 Uneven Footing Settlement below an Asymmetrical Load

While the effect of asymmetrical loading may be easily visualized in a footing for a single column, if site conditions dictate an asymmetrical column and footing arrangement as shown in Figure 19.5, the effect would be more difficult to envision and to design for.

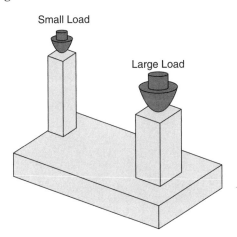

Figure 19.5 Asymmetrical Loads on a Footing

To the extent possible, the following principle for footing design should be followed:

- The center of gravity of a spread footing should coincide with the line of action of the resultant of the superimposed loads so that pressure exerted on the underlying soil is distributed as uniformly as possible (Figure 19.6).

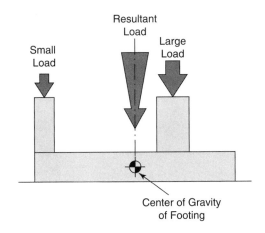

Figure 19.6 Principle of Footing Design

Placement of Spread Footings

Mostly due to moisture content, soils expand when frozen and then contract when thawed. Placing a spread footing on soil that expands and contracts would obviously have a harmful effect on any structure supported above. Spread footings must therefore be placed at a depth that not only has structurally suitable soils, but also at a depth below the soil's frost line—that is, the depth below which the ground is protected from the freeze/thaw cycle (Figure 19.7). Minimum depths for frost lines are dictated by building codes and vary according to geographic location. In the continental United States, the frost line can vary from zero in southern Florida to almost 8 ft below grade in northern Minnesota. In the New York City area, the frost line is 4 ft below grade.

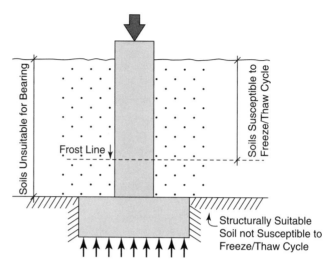

Figure 19.7 Placement of a Spread Footing

While the width and thickness of individual footings in a foundation may vary, depending on their loading and strength requirements, common practice is to generally keep the bottom surfaces of footings at the same elevation for ease of construction. (In other circumstances, however, such as when footing thicknesses vary, it may be more practical to keep the top surfaces of footings at the same elevation in order to simplify the masonry or formwork being placed upon them.) When the bottom surfaces of footings are not at the same elevation, it's important to ensure that the distributed weight from one footing does not bear on another. The *soil bearing prism*, underlying a footing and reflecting the clearance required below it, is somewhat soil dependent but is generally accepted to be 45 degrees (Figure 19.8).

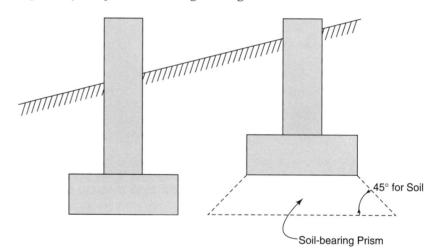

Figure 19.8 Soil Bearing Prism Below a Footing

Variations of Spread Footings

Depending upon their conditions of loading, numerous variations and combinations of spread footings are used. For convenience, these variations are given generally accepted names that sometimes overlap in meaning. However, whatever its name or variation, the concept behind a spread footing remains the same:

- *To uniformly distribute and disperse concentrated loads from above so as not to exceed the allowable bearing capacity of the ground below.*

An *isolated footing* (also called an *independent* or *column footing*) is placed directly below an individual column. The footing should be symmetrically placed below the column so that loads on the underlying soil are evenly distributed (Figure 19.9).

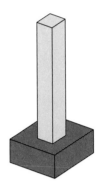

Figure 19.9 An Isolated Footing

A *combined footing* is placed below two closely-spaced individual columns whose footings would overlap if placed as two isolated footings (Figure 19.10).

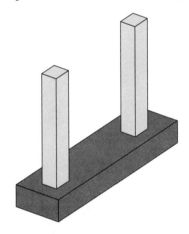

Figure 19.10 A Combined Footing

A *cantilever footing* is a type of combined footing most often used when a column occurs at the edge of a building along a property line. Since a footing cannot project beyond a property line, an isolated footing placed there would be asymmetrically loaded since the column would be at its edge. To help balance this asymmetrical loading, a cantilever footing generally ties back to an adjacent interior column (Figure 19.11).

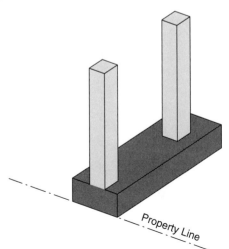

Figure 19.11 A Cantilever Footing

A *continuous footing* (also called a *strip footing*) is placed below three or more closely-spaced columns (Figure 19.12).

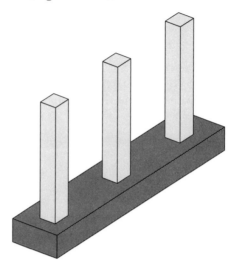

Figure 19.12 A Continuous Footing

A *strap footing* is simply a term for two footings that are connected to help balance their loads. Combined and cantilever footings are types of strap footings (Figure 19.13).

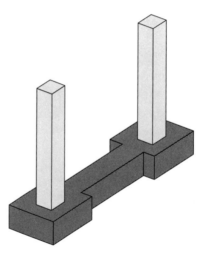

Figure 19.13 A Strap Footing

A *wall footing* is a continuous footing placed below a bearing wall (Figure 19.14).

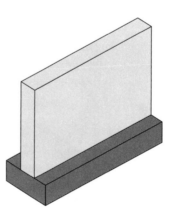

Figure 19.14 A Wall Footing

A *mat foundation* (also called a *raft foundation*) is one large footing placed under the entire superstructure (Figure 19.15).

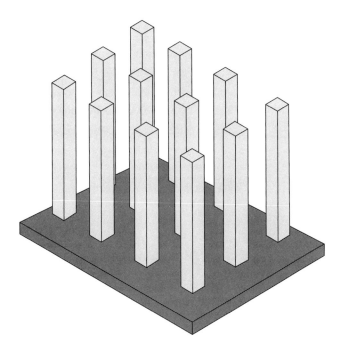

Figure 19.15 A Mat Foundation

A *ribbed foundation* is a mat foundation reinforced by ribs (i.e., beams and/or girders) placed above, or below, the mat slab (Figure 19.16).

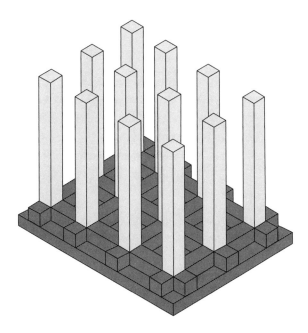

Figure 19.16 A Ribbed Foundation

A *floating foundation* is a mat foundation placed at a sufficient depth beneath a building so that the weight of the soil removed is greater than the weight of the building loads above. The resulting stress on the underlying soils therefore remains same (or less) after construction as before construction (Figure 19.17).

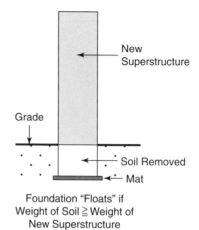

New
Superstructure

Grade

Soil Removed

Mat

Foundation "Floats" if
Weight of Soil ≥ Weight of
New Superstructure

Figure 19.17 A Floating Foundation

General Design of Spread Footings

A spread footing is subject to a variety of stresses and is therefore susceptible to the following types of failure: settlement, beam shear, punching shear, and bending (Figure 19.18).

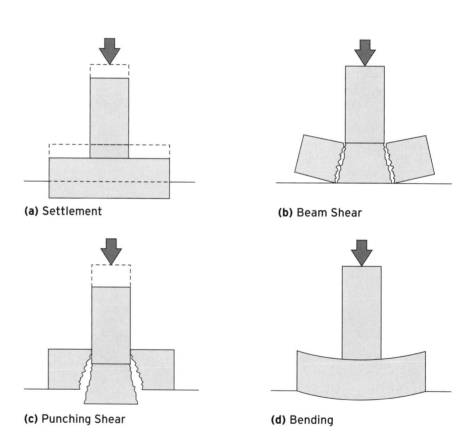

(a) Settlement

(b) Beam Shear

(c) Punching Shear

(d) Bending

Figure 19.18 Types of Footing Failure

To resist these failures, concrete spread footings must always be designed with (Figure 19.19):

- *Sufficient bearing area surface to resist settlement*
- *Sufficient thickness to resist beam shear and punching shear*

- *Steel reinforcing properly placed to resist tensile, compressive, and shear stresses*

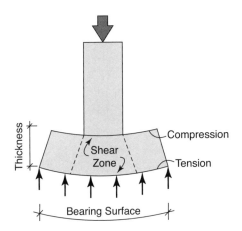

Figure 19.19 Stresses in a Concrete Footing

19.2. Deep Foundations

Deep Foundations and Load Resistance

The purpose of all types of deep foundations is to penetrate through the upper layers of unsuitable soils to obtain proper load resistance by (Figure 19.20):

- *End-bearing on an underlying stratum of more stable soil or bedrock*
- *Frictional resistance along the length of the deep foundation*
- *A combination of end-bearing and frictional resistance*

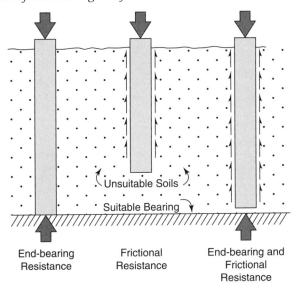

Figure 19.20 Load Resistance from Deep Foundations

Piles and Drilled Piers

Depending on soil conditions and desired construction methods, deep foundations can consist of the following:

- *Driven piles* that are driven into the soil by a pile driver. Types of driven piles include treated timber, steel, concrete-filled steel pipes, precast concrete, or a composite of these materials.
- *Drilled piles* (also called *drilled piers, caissons, mini-piles,* or *auger cast piles,* depending upon their diameter and construction) are cast-in-place concrete piles formed by boring a shaft with an auger (a large screw) and filling the shaft

with concrete. Drilled piers are sometimes belled at the bottom to increase their bearing surface (Figure 19.21).

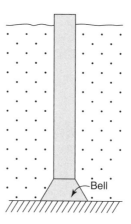

Figure 19.21 A Belled Pier

Both driven and drilled piles are usually placed in clusters that act together as one in providing the required load resistance.

Pile Caps, Grade Beams, and Structural Slabs

With a cluster of piles in place, concrete *pile caps* and *grade beams* are then formed and placed on top of them. The pile caps and grade beams create the surface onto which columns and bearing walls are then placed (Figure 19.22).

Although the pile caps and grade beams may be temporarily formed on the ground's surface, once they cure, they rely entirely on the piles (not the ground) for structural support. Similarly, a *structural slab* at grade, although temporarily formed on the ground, relies entirely on the deep foundation system (not the ground) for its support. A structural slab should never be confused with a *slab-on-grade*, which is indeed supported by the ground on which it rests.

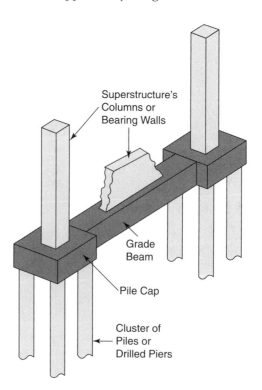

Figure 19.22 Pile Caps and Grade Beam Supporting a Superstructure

Summing Up

The focus of this book has been on the presentation of structural fundamentals in a straightforward and intuitive way. The intent has been to help prepare students for more advanced studies in structural systems and the integration of those systems into architectural form. In summing up, let us simply emphasize that the complexity of any particular topic in structural engineering always can be reduced to the following basic essentials: creation of stress, states of stress, and resistance to stress.

Creation of Stress

Loads create stress on a structure and its individual members and components. Loads accumulate within tributary areas and follow a load path through a structure, ultimately to the ground. By understanding the principles of stability, the forces and reactions created by the loads can be determined, and the resulting stresses identified, located, quantified, and designed for.

States of Stress

Whether induced axially or by bending, a structural member can only be subjected to the three basic states of stress: tension, compression, and shear, or some combination thereof.

Resistance to Stress

With stability established and the stresses on an individual member known, the designer essentially has two considerations for providing the strength to resist the stresses: (1) the selection of material resistance and (2) the selection of cross sectional resistance. Selecting a stronger material allows a weaker cross section, while selecting a stronger cross section allows a weaker material.

Simply put:

LOADS CREATE STRESS, MATERIAL AND CROSS SECTION RESIST STRESS.

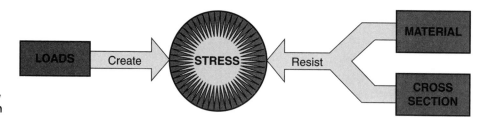

Figure 20.1 Relationship of Loads, Stress, Material, and Cross Section

With a firm grasp of the structural fundamentals presented in this book, the reader is now ready to use the principles learned in more advanced applications.

Structural Forms

APPENDIX **1**

Buildings and other structures can take any of several structural forms, either alone or in combination, to enable them to stand up and resist forces. The term *member* refers to any individual piece of a structural form. For example, a column, a girder, or a beam is an individual member of a frame building. The structural designer analyzes the structural behavior of the building as a whole, as well as that of each member within the building, to ensure the building's stability and to properly size its structural components. A description of some structural forms and members follows.

A1.1. *Frames* are structures that generally consist of vertical and horizontal structural members (Figure A1.1).

Figure A1.1 The Steel Frame of a Building

Columns are vertical structural members that primarily resist compression. *Pillar* and *post* are two other terms for columns, usually implying shorter height.

Beams are horizontal structural members that primarily resist bending.

Girders are larger beams that support other smaller beams (Figure A1.2).

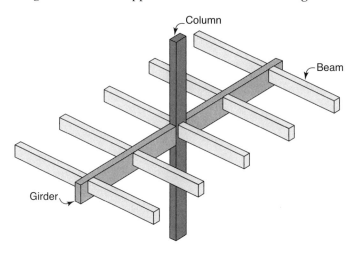

Figure A1.2 Column, Beams, and Girders

Transfer girders support offset columns and transfer the load to supports below (Figure A1.3).

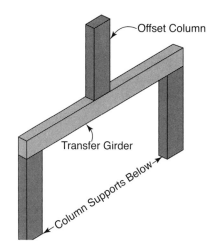

Figure A1.3 Transfer Girder

Joists are relatively light parallel beams, closely spaced (Figure A1.4).

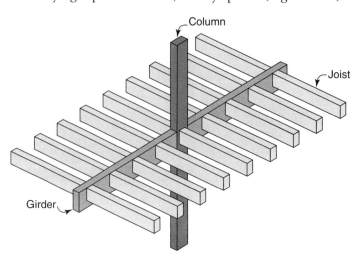

Figure A1.4 Wood Floor Joists

A *cantilever* (or overhang) is a section of a structural member, such as a beam, extending beyond its point of support. The *backspan* is the section between the supports (Figure A1.5).

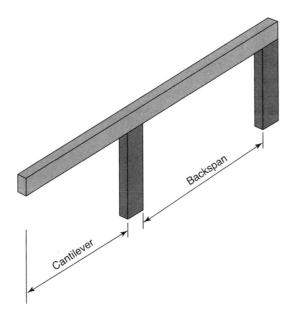

Figure A1.5 Cantilever

A1.2. *Bearing walls* carry loads by supporting structural members such as girders, beams, joists, and columns (Figure A1.6).

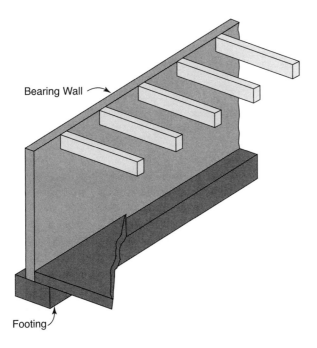

Figure A1.6 Foundation Bearing Wall

A1.3. *Trusses* are frameworks of individual structural members, triangulated and in a single plane, used to span relatively large distances (Figure A1.7).

Figure A1.7 Truss

A1.4. *Space frames* are three-dimensional trusslike frameworks (Figure A1.8).

Figure A1.8 Space Frame Canopy

A1.5. *Arches* are curved structural forms whose strength derives from compression (Figure A1.9). The base of an arch has to resist outward lateral forces called *thrust* (Figure A1.10).

Figure A1.9 Arches of Ancient Ruins

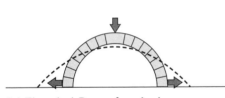

(a) Thrust at Base of an Arch

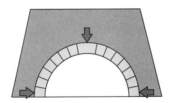

(b) Thrust Resisted by Heavy Abutment

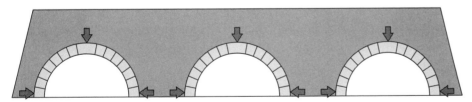

(c) Thrust Resisted by Other Arches

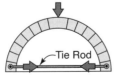

Tie Rod

(d) Thrust Resisted by a Tie Rod

Figure A1.10 The Outward Thrust of an Arch

A1.6. *Vaults* are continuous arched structures. Like an arch, a vault has to resist thrust, but along the entire length of its base (Figure A1.11).

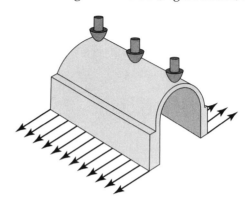

Figure A1.11 Barrel Vault

A1.7. *Domes* are sphere-like structures whose strength, like that of an arch, derives from compression. Like an arch, the base of a dome has to resist thrust, but in all directions (Figure A1.12).

Figure A1.12 Domed Structure

Geodesic domes, best known from Buckminster Fuller's work in the 1950s and 1960s, are dome-shaped frames in which the geometry of a triangle is inscribed in the geometry of a hexagon, with individual members of the frames being of equal dimensions (Figure A1.13).

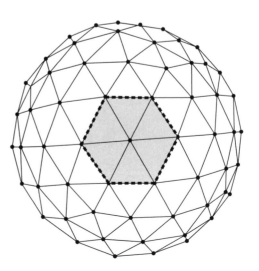

Figure A1.13 Geodesic Sphere

A1.8. *Form-resistant structures* are relatively thin, curved or planar surfaces (or a combination of both), usually constructed of reinforced concrete, that derive strength from their shape (Figure A1.14). Curved form-resistant structures are generally called *shells*, while planar form-resistant structures are generally called *folded plates* (Figure A1.15).

Figure A1.14 Form-Resistant Structures Derive Strength from Their Shape

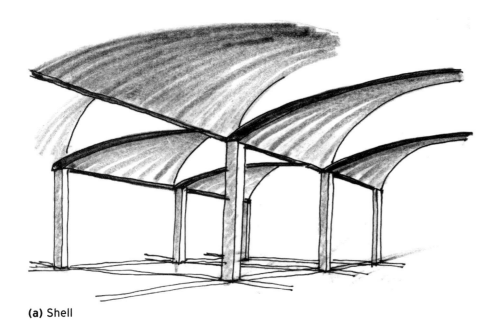

(a) Shell

(b) Folded plate

Figure A1.15 Form-Resistant Structures

A1.9. *Cable structures*, such as suspension bridges or buildings with cable roofs, use cables in tension as their principal means of support (Figure A1.16).

Figure A1.16 Cable Structure (Brooklyn Bridge)

Madison Square Garden in New York city is an example of a cable roof with an inner tension ring and an outer compression ring connected by cables (Figure A1.17).

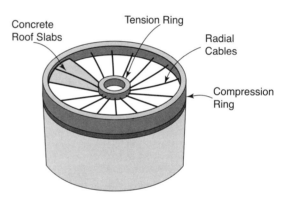

Figure A1.17 Madison Square Garden's Cable-Supported Roof

Although external loads are applied differently, Madison Square Garden's roof is similar in principle to a bicycle wheel with a hub (inner tension ring) and a rim (outer compression ring) connected by spokes. For this cable roof, external loads (such as snow) are generally applied transverse to the tension and compression rings. For a bicycle wheel, external loads (such as the weight of a rider) are generally applied parallel to the rings (Figure A1.18).

Figure A1.18 Bicycle Wheel

A1.10. *Membrane structures* have thin, flexible, stretched fabric surfaces supported by masts (Figure A1.19).

Figure A1.19 Fabric Membrane Structure

A1.11. *Air-supported structures* consist of a fabric membrane securely anchored along its perimeter and held aloft by air pressure (Figure A1.20).

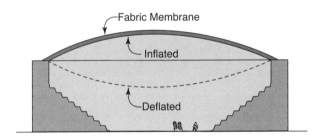

Figure A1.20 Air-supported Structure

A1.12. *Long span construction* is a general term for any number of structural forms, alone or in combination, covering large areas of column-free space. Long spans are generally considered to be over 60 ft in length and have special design concerns for such factors as temperature expansion and contraction, deflection, and others (Figure A1.21).

Figure A1.21 Hell's Gate Bridge

Structural Materials– Steel

APPENDIX 2

A2.1 Composition and Manufacture

Steel is a range of alloys of iron and carbon, containing between approximately 0.2% and 2.0% carbon. Iron, the predominant ingredient in steel, is a basic element naturally present in certain rock formations (ore). Iron is extracted from the ore by the blast furnace process and cast into pigs (i.e., large iron bricks) prior to being further processed. Controlling the carbon content alloyed with the iron, as well alloying with various other metallic elements, is a major factor in determining iron's and steel's qualities. Too much carbon produces a hard, brittle metal, while too little carbon produces a relatively soft, weak metal.

- Wrought iron has a carbon content of approximately 0.2% and is relatively soft, ductile, and malleable (easily shaped).
- Cast iron has a carbon content of approximately 2.0 to 4.0% and is hard, brittle, and nonmalleable.
- Steel is iron with a carbon content between those of wrought iron and cast iron, whose properties have been optimized for hardness, elasticity, and especially strength. *Structural steel* is the term for steel used in a load-bearing capacity.

A2.2 Characteristics and Properties

Steel is one of the most popular and most widely used structural materials employed today.

Advantages of Steel

- It has an extremely high strength-to-weight ratio in both compression and tension.
- Its ductile (opposite of brittle) property allows it to withstand high deformations (and hence high tensile stresses) and enables it to "stretch" before failing. Ductility is an extremely useful property when designing structures for earthquake and wind forces.
- Its high modulus of elasticity makes it very stiff, and its high strength-to-weight ratio allows the construction of buildings with smaller dead loads and cost-efficient structural designs.

- It is incombustible, resistant to fungi and insects, and dimensionally stable.
- It is recyclable during demolition.
- The manufacture, fabrication, and erection of steel have evolved into a very efficient process, resulting in a high level of quality control and speedy erection.

Disadvantages of Steel

- It is dramatically weakened by fire and generally requires fire protection by any of several methods, such as enclosure, spray-on, or intumescent paint.
- Its manufacture is energy intensive.
- It tends to corrode and expand in the presence of moisture, requiring protection by alloying or protective coatings.

A2.3 The American Institute of Steel Construction

The American Institute of Steel Construction (AISC) is a trade association representing the structural steel industry. It publishes the *Steel Construction Manual*, the standard reference for steel design and construction adopted by various codes in the United States. Among many other things, the manual contains information and specifications on the manufacture, grades and properties, design, detailing, and fabrication of structural steel. It has numerous tables and charts of structural shapes, organized in several ways to assist the designer in performing the task at hand. For example, there are several different tables on steel shapes, depending upon whether the designer is primarily interested in the shape's dimensions, the shape's design properties, selection by the shape's section modulus Z (see Section A5.3), or selection by the shape's ability to support load.

A2.4 Grades of Structural Steel

Several grades of structural steel are available, each with its own properties and strengths for selection by the designer. The most common grades for structural steel are given by the ASTM designations A36 and A992 (Table A2.1).

TABLE A2.1 GRADES OF STRUCTURAL STEEL

Grade	Yield Strength (F_y)	Availability
A36	36 ksi	All hot-rolled shapes
A992	50 ksi	W shapes

Steel of higher yield strengths are also available, though they are less common.

A2.5 Shapes and Forms
Hot-Rolled Structural Steel Sections

Structural steel is produced in a variety of *shapes*, also referred to as *sections*. In the mill, hot steel bars are passed through a succession of rollers that progressively squeeze the steel into the desired shapes, called *hot-rolled* sections (Figure A2.1). Common steel sections are shown in Table A2.2 at the end of this chapter.

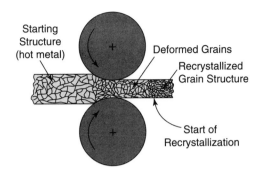

Figure A2.1 Hot-Rolling Steel

Compact Steel Sections

We know that there is a tendency for the compression edge of a beam to buckle. This tendency can be resisted by providing lateral bracing using any of several methods reviewed in Chapter 10. Steel sections are also classified as compact or non-compact, depending upon the yield stress of the grade of steel and the width-to-thickness ratios of the web and flanges.

If a section is considered compact, its web and flange width-to-thickness ratios are sufficiently heavy so that the section can achieve its upper limit of flexural strength without limitation for lateral buckling (Figure A2.2).

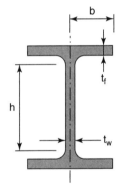

Flange Width-to-thickness Ratio = b/t_f
Web Width-to-thickness Ratio = h/t_w

Figure A2.2 A Wide Flange Compact Steel Section

Open Web Steel Joists

Open web steel joists are basically lightweight trusses, fabricated from steel angles and bars, which can be used to support floor and roof decks (Figure A2.3).

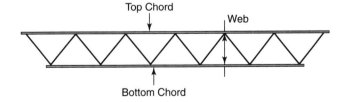

Figure A2.3 Open Web Steel Joist

Open web joists are produced in three series:

- K series for spans up to 60 ft
- LH series for spans up to 96 ft (called *longspan* joists)
- DLH series for spans up to 144 ft (called *deep longspan* joists)

A2.6 Joining Steel

The three commonly found steel-to-steel connections are bolts, welds, and rivets.

Bolts

- Bolts were developed in the1950s to replace rivets for structural steel connections. Although there are many variations, the typical bolt consists of the head, the shank, threads, a washer, and a nut (Figure A2.4).
- Bolts can be installed relatively quickly and easily, which is especially important for field connections.
- The most commonly used bolts for connecting structural steel are high strength (ASTM) A325 and A490, which are heat treated during their manufacture.
- So-called common bolts, used in less demanding structural applications, are (ASTM) A307.

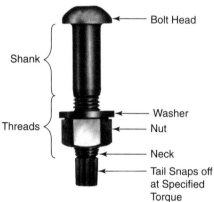

Figure A2.4 Parts of a Typical High Strength Bolt

STRESSES ON BOLTS

STRESSES DUE TO TIGHTENING

When the nut on a bolt is tightened (also called *tensioned* or *torqued*), the bolt is stressed in tension (Figure A2.5). Structural bolts require verification for the proper amount of tensioning, neither too little nor too much.

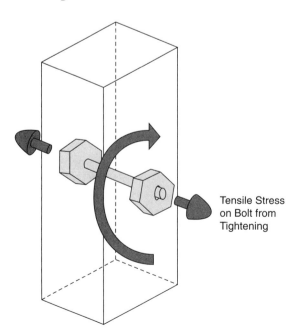

Figure A2.5 Tension on a Bolt

STRESSES DUE TO CONNECTIONS

Aside from tensile stress resulting from tightening, bolts can be subject to shear or additional tensile stress, depending on their actual connection.

Bolts in Shear

The most common type of stress to which bolts are subjected is shear (Figure A2.6). Shearing stresses can occur on one or more bolt planes, depending on the connection.

For a given force, the greater the number of shear planes, the less the stress on each plane.

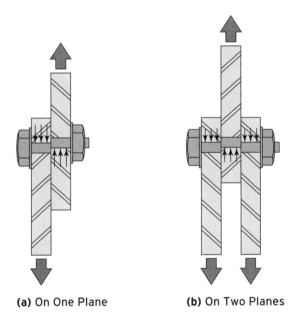

(a) On One Plane   **(b)** On Two Planes

Figure A2.6 A Bolt in Shear

Bolts in Tension

When connecting suspended members, bolts are stressed in tension (Figure A2.7).

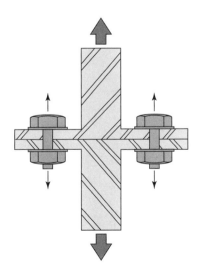

Figure A2.7 Bolts in Tension

STRESSES ON MEMBERS

In addition to the stresses placed on bolts, bolts place bearing stress on the members being attached. Sufficient bearing depth must be considered in these members to account for this bearing stress (Figure A2.8).

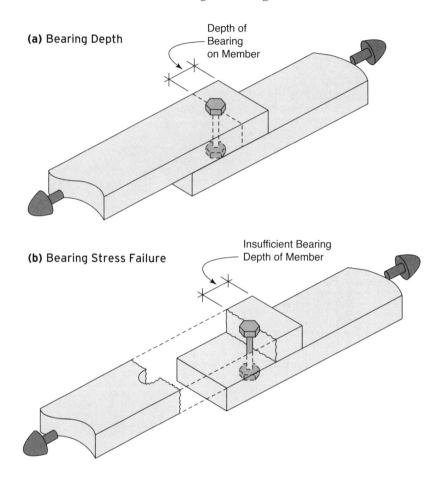

(a) Bearing Depth

Depth of Bearing on Member

(b) Bearing Stress Failure

Insufficient Bearing Depth of Member

Figure A2.8 Bearing Stress on a Member

SLIP-CRITICAL BOLTED CONNECTIONS

The resistance from this type of connection results from the friction between the surfaces of the members being bolted together. Essentially, the members are clamped tightly together to achieve the high degree of frictional resistance. Slip-critical connections are exacting and labor-intensive, requiring surfaces to be carefully prepared and the bolts highly tensioned (Figure A2.9).

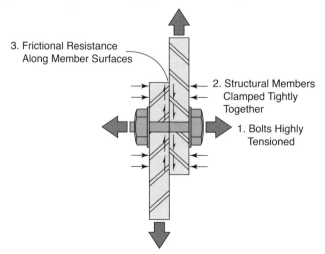

3. Frictional Resistance Along Member Surfaces

2. Structural Members Clamped Tightly Together

1. Bolts Highly Tensioned

Figure A2.9 Slip-Critical Bolted Connection

Welds

Welding is a highly technical and labor-intensive method of joining steel, requiring the skills of trained workers. As such, welding is expensive and best suited to the controlled and automated conditions of a shop. Field welding is difficult and should be used only when required. All critical shop and field welds must be tested using sophisticated techniques such as radiographic ultrasonic testing. Many steel connections combine bolts and welds.

THE ELECTRIC ARC WELDING PROCESS

The most common method of welding is the electric arc process. This involves establishing an electrical potential between the steel members being joined and a metal electrode (steel rod) held by the welder. When the electrode is brought close to the steel members, an electric arc is formed by the flow of current, creating intense heat. The heat melts the members and the tip of the electrode into a small molten puddle at the point of the weld. When the puddle cools it solidifies, creating an extremely strong, homogeneous mass (Figure A2.10).

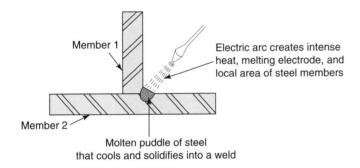

Figure A2.10 Electric Arc Welding Process

Weld lengths can be spot, intermittent, or full-length (continuous) (Figure A2.11). For welds other than spot welds, the electrode is slowly drawn across the line of the weld, leaving behind a continuous welded seam of the desired length between the members.

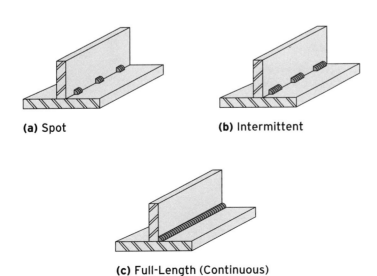

(a) Spot

(b) Intermittent

(c) Full-Length (Continuous)

Figure A2.11 Weld Lengths

TYPES OF WELDS

Although there are many variations, welds fall into three broad categories: fillet, groove, and plug & slot.

- *Fillet* welds are triangular and are typically used for T, lap, and corner joints where the two surfaces to be joined are at right angles to each other (Figure A2.12).

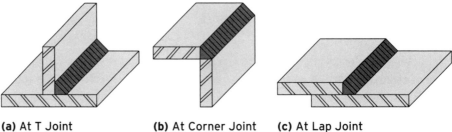

Figure A2.12 Fillet Welds

(a) At T Joint   **(b)** At Corner Joint   **(c)** At Lap Joint

- *Groove* welds are typically used for edge-to-edge (butt) joints. These welds can have many different shapes, such as the more common single V weld shown in Figure A2.13. Groove welds are classified as partial penetration (pen) and full penetration.

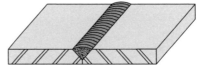

Figure A2.13 Single V Groove Weld

- Partial *pen* welds have the weld and base material fused to only a partial depth of the joint (Figure A2.14a).
- *Full pen* welds are extremely strong and have the weld and base material fused throughout the full depth of the joint. Full pen welds may sometimes use a backer rod to keep the weld material in place while it solidifies (Figure A2.14b).

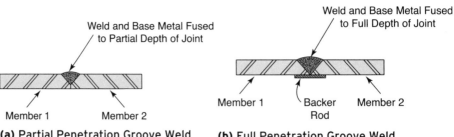

Figure A2.14

(a) Partial Penetration Groove Weld   **(b)** Full Penetration Groove Weld

Full pen welds are more difficult to do, but are extremely strong and are used for moment and other connections where the strength of the connection and the weld are critical (Figure A2.15).

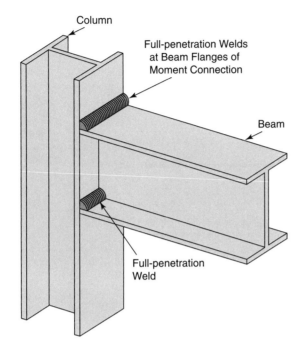

Figure A2.15 Full Pen Weld at a Moment Connection

Plug and *slot* welds are typically used for lap joints. Round (plug) or elongated (slot) holes are created in the top member and welded at these points to the bottom member (Figure A2.16).

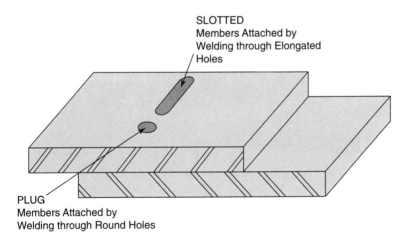

Figure A2.16 Plug and Slot Welds

WELD SYMBOLS

Weld symbols can look like hieroglyphics to the untrained eye, but with a brief explanation the basics are not difficult to understand. However, although the basics are relatively simple, the symbols can become complicated. For a more detailed description of welding symbols, the reader is referred to more technical sources.

The three basic components of a weld symbol are the reference line, the arrow, and the tail (Figure A2.17).

- The reference line is the heart of the symbol, giving basic instructions about the weld such as type and size.
- The arrow points to the location of the weld.
- The tail (if needed) contains supplementary information or details about the weld not described in the reference line.

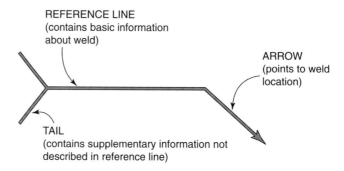

Figure A2.17 Weld Symbol

Examples of the basic symbols for the three common types of welds are shown in Figure A2.18.

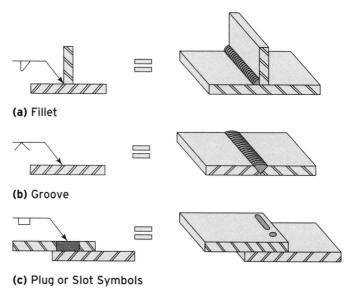

(a) Fillet

(b) Groove

(c) Plug or Slot Symbols

Figure A2.18 Typical Weld Symbols

Other common weld symbols are shown in Figure A2.19 and A2.20.

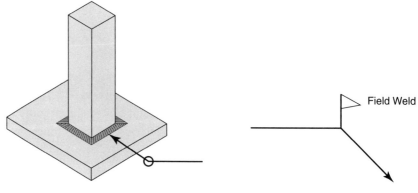

Figure A2.19 Weld All Around   **Figure A2.20** Field Weld

Rivets

Riveting was the method commonly used for steel connections prior to the 1950s. Riveting is labor-intensive and rivets, though rarely used today, are commonly found in the steel connections of older structures (Figure A2.21).

Figure A2.21 Rivet Connections in an Older Structure

A rivet is a cylindrical steel shank with a formed head on one side (Figure A2.22).

Figure A2.22 Rivets

The rivet is brought to a white heat and inserted into prepared holes in the steel members being attached. With the rivet hot, a pneumatic hammer forms another head opposite to the first. As the rivet cools, it shrinks, forming a tight joint (Figure A2.23). The stresses to which a rivet is subjected are similar to those on a bolt.

(a) A Formed Rivet

(b) A Riveted Joint

(c) A Riveted Member

Figure A2.23 Riveted Connections

A2.7 Decking

Floor and roof decking is placed atop structural steel beams or joists in steel frame buildings. The decking can be either metal or concrete.

Metal Decking

Metal decking is corrugated (to increase stiffness), galvanized, and available in numerous types and profiles (shapes). Its strength and its ability to span distances are determined by its gauge (thickness), depth, and spacing of corrugations (Figure A2.24).

There are three major types of metal decking:

- Form decking—serves as permanent formwork for a reinforced concrete slab until the concrete cures and can support itself and its live load.
- Composite decking—serves as tensile reinforcement for the concrete slab to which it is bonded. Composite action between the concrete slab and the beams or joists below can be achieved by welding shear studs through the decking to the supporting beam below.
- Cellular decking—manufactured by welding a flat sheet to a corrugated sheet, thereby creating cells that can be used for raceways for electrical and communications cabling.

Figure A2.24 Various Types of Metal Decking

Concrete Decking

There are two common types of concrete decking:

- Concrete reinforced slab, poured in place over temporary formwork
- Precast hollow core or solid slabs with a thin concrete topping (to produce a smooth floor) (Figure A2.25).

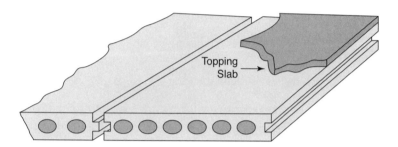

Figure A2.25 Precast Hollow Core Slab

A2.8 The Design/Fabrication/Erection Process

Steel construction requires considerable preplanning and detailing, but once it is delivered to the site, erection is quick. If the process is properly planned, steel is an excellent choice for fast-track projects because of its speed of on-site erection. The entire process of design, fabrication, and erection is typically as follows:

- The architect and structural engineer collaborate on an appropriate structural system and structural expression for the building.
- The engineer calculates loads, then designs and draws structural floor plans and generalized details.
- Once a contractor is on board, the steel subcontractor prepares shop drawings (based on the engineer's design) that show precise details (lengths, bolt holes, welds, etc.) for each piece of steel.
- After the shop drawings are approved by the engineer, the steel is fabricated, delivered to the site, and erected.

A2.9 Related Terms

- *Topping out*—Term used when the last steel member is put in place.
- *Pre-engineered steel buildings*—Buildings manufactured by companies that specialize in industrial-type buildings, usually with larger spans, that are relatively quick and economical to build; they are generally characterized by repetitive bays created by rigid frames and steel siding. Butler is one well-known manufacturer.
- *Fillet*—The rounded concave area between flanges and webs on W and C sections, and between legs on L sections (see Table A2.2).
- *Gusset plate*—A flat plate used to attach structural members that meet in a single plane, as in a truss.
- *Girt*—A horizontal member spanning between exterior columns to support wall sheathing or cladding.
- *Purlin*—General term for a small beam running above and at right angles to a main roof rafter (or beam) to support roof decking.

TABLE A2.2 STEEL SHAPES

Section	Designation	Cross Section	Explanation of Designation	Remarks
Wide Flange	W 12×19	Flange, Fillet, Web, Depth	W indicates a Wide Flange section 12 indicates the depth (inches) 19 indicates the weight (pounds per linear foot)	W sections have top and bottom flanges connected by a web, with parallel inner and outer flange surfaces. Tall and narrow W sections are generally used as beams, while more square W sections are generally used as columns.
Bearing Pile	HP 14×73	Flange, Web, Depth	HP indicates a Wide Flange Bearing Pile section 14 indicates the depth (inches) 73 indicates the weight (pounds per linear foot)	HP sections are similar to W sections but have equal flange and web thicknesses. HP sections are heavy members commonly used in foundations and shoring, and sometimes as columns.
American Standard Beam	S 24×100	Flange, Web, Depth	S indicates an American Standard Beam section 24 indicates the depth (inches) 100 indicates the weight (pounds per linear foot)	S sections have top and bottom flanges connected by a web, with sloped inner flange surfaces. S sections, still commonly referred to as *I-beams*, are older and perform less efficiently as beams than W sections. Although infrequently used today, they are commonly found in older buildings.
American Standard Channel	C 12×20.7	Flange, Web, Depth	C indicates an American Standard Channel section 12 indicates the depth (inches) 20.7 indicates the weight (pounds per linear foot)	C sections have top and bottom flanges, on one side only of a connecting web, with sloped inner flange surfaces. C sections are commonly used as stair stringers, as lintels, in trusses, and as short beams where the wide flanges of W sections may interfere with detailing.

(continued)

225

TABLE A2.2 (Continued)

Section	Designation	Cross Section	Explanation of Designation	Remarks
Structural Tee	WT 7×13		WT indicates a Structural Tee section (cut from W section) 7 indicates the depth (inches) 13 indicates the weight (pounds per linear foot)	WT, ST, and MT sections are created by cutting along the neutral axis of the webs of W, S, or M sections, respectively, thereby splitting the original section into two new T-shaped sections of equal size.
Angle	L 4×3×3/8		L indicates an Angle section 4 and 3 indicate the lengths (inches) of each of the two legs, 3/8 indicates the thickness (inches)	L sections can be equal leg or unequal leg. L sections are versatile, commonly used as lintels, diagonal bracing for frames and trusses, and many types of connections.
Hollow Structural Section (rectangular or square)	HSS 6×4×3/8		HSS indicates a Hollow Structural section 6 and 4 indicate the lengths (inches) of each of the two sides 3/8 indicates the wall thickness (inches)	HSS sections can be square, rectangular, or circular. These sections are especially useful as columns where torsional stresses are encountered. They may be hot rolled or cold formed.
Hollow Structural Section (circular)	HSS 5×1/2		HSS indicates a Hollow Structural section 5 indicates the diameter (inches) 1/2 indicates the wall thickness (inches)	HSS circular sections are sometimes referred to as *pipe* sections corresponding to their former designation.
Bar	Bar 2×6 ½ inch Round Bar		A rectangular bar, 2 in thick by 6 in wide in cross section A circular bar with a 2 in diameter	Bar sections are available in numerous rectangular, square, and round cross-sectional dimensions.
Plate	PL ½×18		A plate, ½ inch thick x 18 inches wide in cross section	Plate sections are available in numerous rectangular cross-sectional dimensions.

Miscellaneous	M 8×6.5	Similar to W section	M indicates a Miscellaneous section Other number notations similar to a W section	M sections are light W sections, with other variations so as to create a separate category. M sections are sometimes referred to as *Junior beams*.
Miscellaneous Channel	MC 8×6.5	Similar to C section	MC indicates a Miscellaneous Channel section Other number notations similar to a C section	MC sections are light C sections.
Built-up	Not applicable	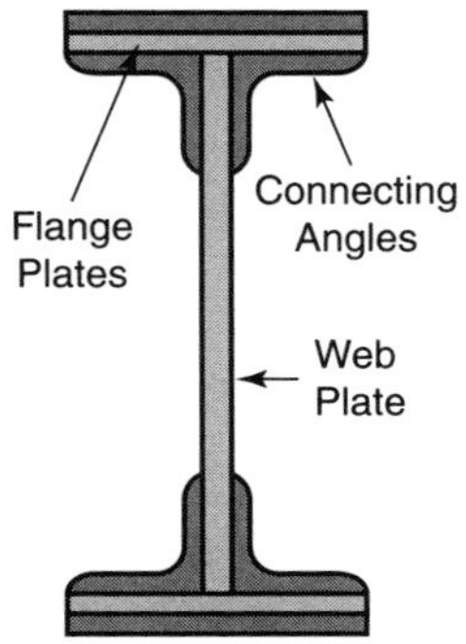	Illustration shows a web plate and flange plates attached by angles	Built-up sections consist of various steel sections and plates combined into a single member for strength and/or detailing. Plate girders are one such example.

Structural Materials– Reinforced Concrete

APPENDIX **3**

A3.1 Composition and Manufacture

Concrete is an artificial stone-like material made by mixing cement, mineral aggregate, and water, which causes the cement to set and bind the entire mass. Concrete's structural usefulness derives from its compressive strength. Since concrete has virtually no tensile strength, steel reinforcing bars are combined with concrete to resist tensile stresses, resulting in reinforced concrete, a formidable structural material. Concrete can be produced on-site (variously referred to as *site-cast, cast-in-place,* or *in situ*), or produced off-site (referred to as *precast*) in sophisticated plants and shipped to the construction site. Either way, the manufacture of structural concrete is a carefully controlled process in which the proportions and quality of its ingredients are balanced for the optimum combination of desired physical properties, workability, and acceptable cost.

Basic Ingredients

Concrete is a universal construction material whose basic ingredients, portland cement, aggregate, and water, are available worldwide:

- *Portland cement* is a manufactured product consisting primarily of lime, iron, silica, and alumina obtained from any number of raw materials. It was invented in the early 1800s and soon replaced naturally occurring cement, which had been used until then. There are several types of portland cement in use today, such as normal, high early strength (hardens quickly), low heat of hydration (produces less heat when curing), air entraining (lightweight), sulfate resisting (retards setting time), white (for precast), and insulating.
- *Aggregate* consists of hard, inert, clean gravel and sand mineral material, properly graded to eliminate voids in the concrete mix. Aggregate material constitutes approximately 75% of the volume of concrete and can vary according to the types of minerals available in any particular locale.
- *Water* is essential to mix the ingredients and activate the setting process of the cement. Water should be potable and free of organic material, clay,

and salts. The compressive strength of concrete is inversely proportional to the ratio of water to cement in any particular concrete mix. In other words, the smaller the amount of water, the stronger the concrete (but the greater the amount of water, the easier it is to work). The water-cement ratio represents the proportion, by weight, of water to cement and should generally be 0.6 or less. A water-cement ratio of 0.6 means that there are 6 parts water to 10 parts cement in that mix.

Admixtures

Admixtures are additives that also affect the properties of concrete:

- *Air-entraining agents* increase workability, improve resistance to cracking, and produce lightweight insulating concrete.
- *Accelerators* reduce the setting time and speed strength development.
- *Retarders* reduce the setting time and allow more time for placing and working the concrete.
- *Water-reducing agents* (superplasticizers) allow water content to be reduced, increasing concrete strength while maintaining workability.
- *Corrosion inhibitors* inhibit the rusting of steel reinforcing embedded in the concrete.
- *Coloring agents* (pigments or dyes) produce a desired color.

Steel Reinforcing

Steel reinforcing bars (commonly called rebar) are used to resist tensile forces in concrete:

- Standard cross-sectional diameters range from $3/8$ in to 1 in, in increments of $1/8$ in Bar thickness is identified simply by a number that corresponds to its cross-sectional diameter. For example, a #3 bar has a $3/8$ in diameter; a #7 bar has a $7/8$ in diameter.
- Standard available grades of steel are A40, A50, and A60, corresponding to different steel yield strengths of 40,000, 50,000 and 60,000 psi (pounds per square inch).
- Surface deformations on the bar help it bond with concrete.
- Epoxy-coated or galvanized bars are used for surface resistance to corrosion. Stainless steel and carbon fiber are rebar materials in the experimental stage.
- Concrete cover, usually 2 in minimum, is required to protect the bars against fire and corrosion.

A3.2 Curing

Curing (setting) is the process whereby the water in a concrete mix evaporates and the ingredients harden into a rock-hard mass. Proper curing is vital to quality concrete. During curing, considerable heat (called *heat of hydration*) is given off and the concrete mass shrinks slightly. Concrete that is curing should be kept moist and protected from freezing while allowing heat to dissipate. Concrete sets in one day, and as it cures, its strength continues to increase over a long period of time. Concrete is designed on the basis of its 28-day strength, developing approximately 75% of this strength after seven days.

A3.3 Characteristics and Properties

- Concrete itself is useful in compression, but without steel reinforcing, it is virtually useless in tension.
- Concrete does not rot or burn, but it can deteriorate under adverse conditions.
- The manufacture of portland cement is energy-intensive. However, fly ash, a waste material from power generation, and slag, a waste material from steel blast furnaces, are being increasingly used, in limited proportions, as a cement substitute. Thus, the amount of portland cement in a mix can be reduced, making it more environmentally friendly. Fly ash and slag, classified as pozzolans, have limitations, most notably increased curing time.
- Concrete is designed and specified as a function of its compressive strength, such as 4000 psi. Concrete up to 22,000 psi can be specified, but generally speaking, the stronger the concrete, the greater the proportion of cement and the greater the cost.

A3.4 Related Terms

- *Prestressed concrete*—Involves the application of initial compressive stresses to the concrete prior to actual loading. The concrete is prestressed (precompressioned, so to speak) so that when actual loads are applied, the resulting tensile forces in the concrete are "balanced" by the initial built-in compression. Prestressing uses high-strength steel strands placed in tension by one of two basic methods:

    Pretensioning—Steel strands are tensioned before concrete is cast; this method is used mostly for precast concrete.

    Posttensioning—Steel strands are tensioned after concrete is cast; this method is used mostly for site-cast concrete.

- *Welded wire fabric* (also called *welded wire mesh*)—A grid of steel wires, welded at the intersections, used as reinforcement in concrete slabs to prevent cracking due to temperature variations. Strands of steel or synthetic fibers, proportioned into a mix, are sometimes used in place of wire mesh for temperature reinforcement.
- *Microsilica concrete* (also called *silica fume*)—A type of dense concrete with low permeability (i.e., high resistance to water penetration).
- *Mix design*—A term for the specification of the exact properties and proportions of ingredients and admixtures in a particular mix. The concrete supplier prepares the mix design in response to the engineer's more general specification.

Structural Materials– Wood

APPENDIX **4**

A4.1 Source and Manufacture

Wood is one of the most common construction and structural materials in use today, as well as throughout history, largely due to its availability and ease of use. Natural wood is generally classified into two types, *hardwoods* and *softwoods*, depending upon the type of tree from which it was derived. These terms are somewhat misleading since they do not actually refer to the hardness of the wood (some hardwoods are actually softer than certain softwoods). However, in general, hardwoods are derived from deciduous trees and softwoods from coniferous trees.

- Deciduous trees are broad-leaf trees that shed their leaves annually. Mahogany, walnut, oak, cherry, rosewood, teak, and maple are some examples.
- Coniferous trees are cone-bearing evergreen trees that do not shed their needles. Pine, fir, cedar, spruce, redwood, and hemlock are some examples.

Wood for structural purposes is derived mainly from coniferous trees.

Lumber is the general term used for squared lengths of wood used for construction. The production of lumber involves:

- *Sawing*: Trees are felled (cut) and the resulting logs transported to mills, where they are sawn and squared into lengths of rough lumber.
- *Seasoning*: Living trees contain substantial amounts of water that begins to evaporate slowly once the tree is felled. Seasoning, the term used for the drying of wood, can be natural by air or mechanical by kiln. As water evaporates, the wood shrinks and becomes stronger and stiffer. Lumber suitable for structural purposes is considered to be seasoned when its moisture content is between approximately 15% and 19%. However, even seasoned wood is *hygroscopic*, meaning that it will take on or give off moisture (swelling or shrinking accordingly) with the varying moisture content in air.
- *Surfacing*: Rough lumber, surfaced with a planing machine to attain smooth and more dimensionally precise surfaces, is called *dressed lumber*. Seasoned, dressed lumber is used for construction framing.

- *Grading*: The load-carrying capacity of lumber is dependent on properties such as size, defects, direction of grain, and others. The grading of lumber, done under strict industry guidelines, is an important factor in establishing allowable design stresses for any particular wood species and grade.

A4.2 Products

Wood for structural purposes is either sawn and used naturally or manufactured in a variety of materials and shapes.

Sawn Lumber

Wood derived and processed directly from logs is called *sawn lumber* and is generally produced in two structural forms:

- *Dimensional lumber* is nominally 2 to 4 in thick (2×3, 2×4, 2×6, 2×8, etc.; 4×4, 4×6, etc.). However, after surfacing and drying, the actual size is less. The properties used for design are dependent upon the actual finished dimensions of the lumber.
- *Timbers* are wood members (sawn or manufactured) 5 in or more in the least dimension. Heavy timber construction is a specific construction classification type having heavy timber structural members.

Manufactured Lumber

Manufactured lumber, also known as *engineered wood*, generally refers to wood products made by bonding together wood strands, veneers, lumber, or other forms of wood fiber to produce a larger composite material with consistent structural and other properties. The use of manufactured lumber has grown rapidly in recent years due to its strength, predictable qualities, ease of use, environmental friendliness, and cost effectiveness. The Engineered Wood Association develops and maintains industry standards for engineered wood products, which are classified into four groups:

1. *Structural composite lumber* (SCL) is a family of engineered wood products in which the grains of small strands of wood are oriented parallel and glued into blocks of material known as *billets*, which are then cut to size. Types of SCL include laminated veneer lumber (LVL), parallel strand lumber (PSL), and oriented strand lumber (OSL). SCL's main structural uses are LVL headers, beams, and other primary load-carrying members. Microlam is a commonly used trade name referring to LVL beams (Figure A4.1).

Figure A4.1 LVL Beams

2. *Prefabricated wood I-joists* are extensively used for floors in residential and light commercial construction (Figure A4.2). I-joists were first introduced by the Trus Joist Corporation around 1970 and have since replaced sawn dimensional lumber as the standard for floor joists in wood light frame construction. As in steel wide flange sections, the "I" configuration provides efficient placement of material for stiffness and resistance to bending, allowing longer spans. Flange material is typically dimensional lumber or SCL; web material is typically LVL, plywood, or oriented strand board (OSB). I-joists are available in lengths of up to 60 ft, but because they are relatively light, they are easily handled.

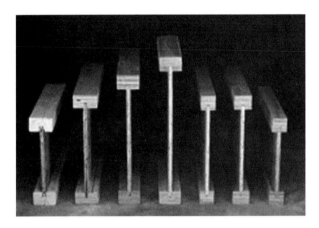

Figure A4.2 Wood I-joists

3. *Glued laminated timber (glulam)* is made by bonding together individual layers of lumber 2 in thick or less, creating an extremely versatile product that can be formed into any size or shape, including curves (Figure A4.3). The individual pieces of lumber in the layers are finger-jointed to create long lengths, referred to as laminations, which are then face-bonded together to form the finished product. Depending on the finish, glulam is generally classified as industrial, architectural, or premium. The use of synthetics and LVL as materials in glulam is in the developmental stage.

Figure A4.3 Curved Glulam Beams

4. *Structural wood panels*, most commonly used as floor, wall, and roof sheathing, provide lateral resistance in light frame construction. Plywood

and oriented strand board 4 ft × 8 ft panels are the two most commonly used types (Figure A4.4).

Figure A4.4 OSB in Wall Sheathing

A4.3 Characteristics and Properties

Engineered wood has changed the traditional way of thinking about wood as a structural material. Many of the defects and inconsistencies of natural wood have been largely eliminated from these products. Generally speaking, however, wood has certain advantages and disadvantages.

Advantages of Wood

- Wood has versatility and ease of construction in the field.
- It is readily available and relatively economical.
- It has good insulating qualities.
- It provides resistance to corrosive and salty environments.
- As a renewable resource, wood is a sustainable structural material. With the advent of engineered wood products, the wood industry now efficiently uses what was formerly waste from the lumber manufacturing process to create new products.

Disadvantages of Wood

- Wood is susceptible to swelling and shrinkage with changes in moisture content.
- It is susceptible to rot, insect infestation, and fire if left untreated.
- Sawn lumber contains defects and a high degree of variation.
- Wood I-joists are vulnerable to more rapid failure in a fire than dimensional lumber due to the ½ in thickness of their web.

A4.4 Structural Considerations

- Wood is useful for structural members in tension or compression. Pound for pound, it is strong, having a favorable strength-to-weight ratio.
- Sawn lumber is stronger when loaded parallel, rather than perpendicular, to the grain.
- The structural design of sawn lumber is dependent upon its species, grade, the direction of the grain, and availability, generally requiring conservative calculations to account for these uncertainties.
- Sawn lumber has an average allowable tensile strength of 700 psi and an allowable compressive strength of 1100 psi. Engineered wood manufacturers prepare design tables listing the properties and performance criteria for their products.

A4.5 Related Terms

- *Board lumber*—This is 1 in nominally thick sawn wood (1×3, 1×4, 1×6, 1×8, etc.).
- *Board foot*—Measuring 12 in × 12 in × 1 in, this is the basic unit of measurement for lumber. Panels, on the other hand, are measured in more familiar square feet.
- *Manufactured roof trusses*—These are prefabricated in plants and shipped to the construction site, saving on-site labor where repetitive trusses are needed (Figure A4.5).

Figure A4.5 Manufactured Roof Trusses

- *Flitch beams*—Beams consisting of built up sections of wood and plate steel bolted together, as in a sandwich (Figure A4.6). The steel plates are called *flitch plates*. Flitch beams are used in residential and wood light frame construction when additional strength is needed without having to resort to structural steel sections. The advantages of flitch beams are as:
  - They are significantly stronger than wood alone, requiring less depth than all-wood beams.
  - They are much lighter than steel beams of the same depth.
  - They provide easy attachments for wood frame construction.
  - They can be created with existing in situ joists or beams, facilitating alteration work.

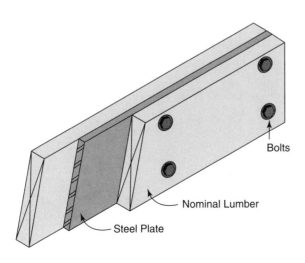

Bolts

Nominal Lumber

Steel Plate

Figure A4.6 A Flitch Beam

Properties of Sections

A5.1 Center of Gravity and Centroids

In addition to the material of which it is made, the ability of a structural member to resist stress is heavily dependent upon the geometric properties of its cross section. Descriptions of several important properties of cross sections follow.

Center of Gravity

All solid three-dimensional bodies have a point at which the mass of that body can be considered to be concentrated. That point is called the *center of gravity* (Figure A5.1).

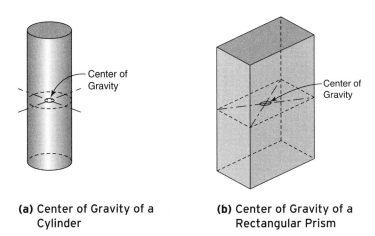

(a) Center of Gravity of a Cylinder

(b) Center of Gravity of a Rectangular Prism

Figure A5.1

Centroid

Flat two-dimensional bodies (such as cross sections through a member) have no depth and therefore no mass. Thus, a different term, *centroid*, is used, which corresponds to the center of gravity. The centroid is the point at which the area of a section is considered to be concentrated. In symmetrical sections, such as those

239

taken through a circular column or a rectangular beam, the centroid is located at the geometric center of the section area (Figure A5.2).

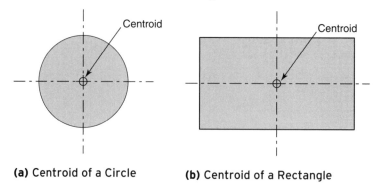

Figure A5.2

(a) Centroid of a Circle   **(b)** Centroid of a Rectangle

The center of gravity of a three-dimensional body, or the centroid of a two-dimensional section, can also be a point in space and does not necessarily have to fall within the mass of the body or the area of the section (Figure A5.3).

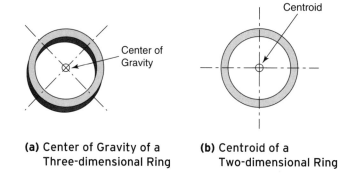

Figure A5.3

(a) Center of Gravity of a   **(b)** Centroid of a
Three-dimensional Ring   Two-dimensional Ring

Although beyond the scope of this book, centroid locations can be calculated for simple composite cross sections that are asymmetrical. For our purposes, let's use the examples in Figure A5.4 to simply visualize the approximate effect of asymmetry on centroid locations.

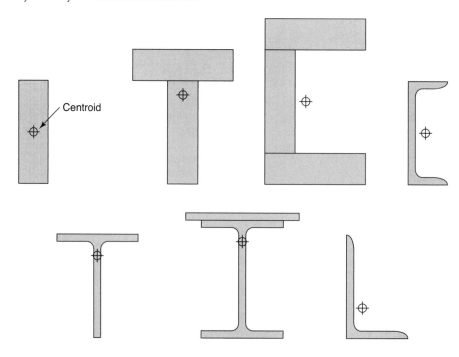

Figure A5.4 Centroids of
Asymmetrical Sections

Centroidal (Neutral) Axes

An axis passing through the centroid of a section is called a *centroidal axis* or *neutral axis*. Although there are an infinite number of centroidal axes, the two most commonly used in engineering analyses are the *xx* and *yy* centroidal axes (Figure A5.5).

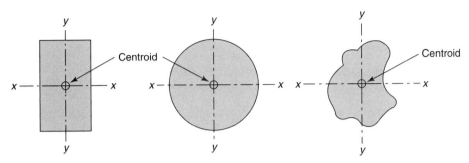

Figure A5.5 Centroidal (Neutral) Axes of Various Sections

The neutral axes of three common steel sections are shown in Figure A5.6. Neutral axes and other section properties, such as moment of inertia, section modulus, and radius of gyration (see Articles A5.2, A5.3, and A5.4), are published by manufacturers of structural members.

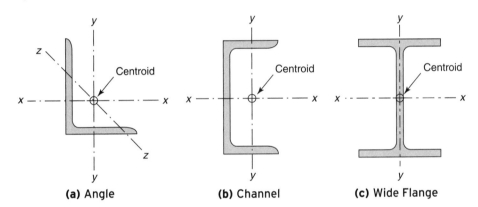

(a) Angle   **(b)** Channel   **(c)** Wide Flange

Figure A5.6 Centroidal (Neutral) Axes of Common Steel Sections

The centroid, the *xx* neutral axis passing through it, and other important section properties of three basic geometric sections, are shown in Table A5.1.

TABLE A5.1 PROPERTIES OF BASIC GEOMETRIC SECTIONS

	Rectangular Section	Circular Section	Right Triangular Section
Centroid @	Geometric Center	Geometric Center	b/3, d/3
A (Area) =	bd	πR^2	bd/2
I_{xx} (Moment of Inertia) =	$bd^3/12$	$\pi R^4/4$	$bd^3/12$
S_{xx} (Section Modulus) =	$bd^2/6$	$\pi R^3/4$	$bd^2/12$
r_{xx} (Radius of Gyration) =	$d/\sqrt{12} = 0.289d$	R/2	$d/\sqrt{18} = 0.236d$

A5.2 Moment of Inertia

Moment of inertia, denoted by I, is a basic and fundamental property of a cross section used to describe its ability to resist bending. Other important cross-sectional properties, such as section modulus and radius of gyration (see Articles A5.3 and A5.4), are derived from moment of inertia. Just as modulus of elasticity is a measure of the stiffness of a material (see Chapter 13), moment of inertia is a measure of the stiffness of a cross section.

Moment of inertia is always determined about a specific reference axis, usually (but not always) the *xx* or *yy* neutral axis. A section's moment of inertia can therefore have more than one value, depending upon the chosen reference axis. Unless stated otherwise, moment of inertia is assumed to be about a neutral axis.

The basic concept of moment of inertia is that the greater the distance of a section's area from a reference axis, the greater the moment of inertia and the greater the section's resistance to bending about that reference axis.

Note that the moment of inertia of a cross section of a *homogeneous* material is not affected by the material of which that cross section is made. In other words the moment of inertia of a 1 in × 6 in cross section of wood, about a specific reference axis, is exactly the same as 1 in × 6 in cross section of steel about the same reference axis. However, the moment of incrtia of a cross section of a *non-homogeneous* material is indeed affected by the differing materials of which that cross section is made. In such a non-homogeneous section, the relative densities and locations of the differing materials do have an effect on its moments of inertia. The reader is referred to more advanced sources for the study of moment of inertia of non-homogeneous sections.

Moment of Inertia for Rectangular Cross Sections

(See Table A5.1 for the moment of inertia of other basic geometric cross sections.)

Perhaps the best way to begin to understand the concept of moment of inertia is to use an example of a rectangular cross section and its xx neutral axis (Figure A5.7).

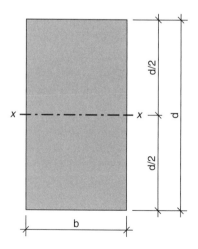

Figure A5.7 Moment of Inertia of a Rectangular Cross Section about xx Neutral Axis

The moment of inertia for a rectangular cross section about its xx neutral axis is given by the formula:

$$\mathbf{I_{xx} = bd^3/12 \ \ or \ \ I_{xx} = Ad^2/12}$$

where:

I$_{xx}$ = moment of inertia about its xx neutral (reference) axis
b = width of the cross section
d = depth of the cross section
A = area of the cross section

As seen from the formula, if b and d are expressed in inches, moment of inertia is expressed in inches to the fourth power (i.e., in^4).

■ EXAMPLE A5.1: Moment of Inertia of a Rectangular Cross Section

MOMENT OF INERTIA OF A RECTANGULAR CROSS SECTION ABOUT ITS XX NEUTRAL AXIS

To gain a better intuitive sense of moment of inertia, let's go back to the situation in Chapter 6 of a man crossing a stream.

Suppose that the man is crossing on a heavy timber beam having a rectangular 6 in x 12 in cross section.

We can readily visualize that the beam will deform differently under the man's weight, depending upon which cross-sectional dimension is oriented vertically. The beam will have significantly greater resistance to bending, and will deflect less, if the 12 in dimension is oriented vertically than if the 6 in dimension is oriented vertically (Figure A5.8).

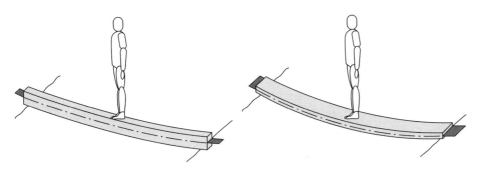

(a) With 12 in Side Placed Vertically   **(b)** With 6 in Side Placed Vertically   **Figure A5.8** A Man on a Beam

Let's see why this is true, using our conceptual understanding of moment of inertia and applying the above formula.

With the 12 in side oriented vertically, the majority of the beam's cross-sectional area is relatively far from the xx neutral axis, thereby creating a larger moment of inertia about this axis and providing greater resistance to bending (Figure A5.9a).

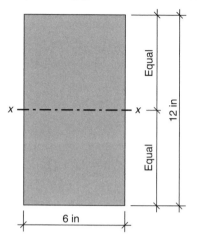

(a) With 12 in Side Placed Vertically

The moment of inertia about the xx axis for this orientation is:

$$\mathbf{I_{xx} = bd^3/12} = (6 \times 12^3)/12 = \mathbf{864\ in^4}$$

With the 6 in side oriented vertically, the majority of the beam's cross-sectional area is relatively close to the xx neutral axis, thereby creating a smaller moment of inertia about this axis and providing less resistance to bending (Figure A5.9b).

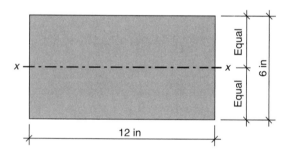

Figure A5.9 Cross Section of the Beam

(b) With 6 in Side Placed Vertically

The moment of inertia about the *xx* axis for this orientation is:

$$\mathbf{I_{xx} = (bd^3/12)} = (12 \times 6^3)/12 = \mathbf{216\ in^4}$$

DISCUSSION

Since the moment of inertia with the 12 in side oriented vertically (864 in⁴) is four times higher than the moment of inertia with the 6 in side oriented vertically (216 in⁴), we can say that the beam's cross section is four times more resistant to bending with the 12 in side oriented vertically.

MOMENT OF INERTIA OF A RECTANGULAR CROSS SECTION ABOUT AN AXIS THROUGH ITS BASE

Sometimes it's desirable for a section's moment of inertia to be taken about a reference axis through its base.

For a rectangular cross section (Figure A5.10) this is expressed by the formula:

$$\mathbf{I_{ff} = bd^3/3} \quad (or\ \mathbf{I_{ff} = Ad^2/3})$$

where:

    I_{ff} = moment of inertia about the ff reference axis through the base

    b = width of the cross section

    d = depth of the cross section

    A = area of the cross section

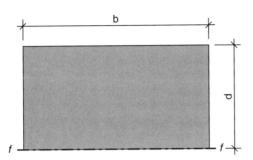

Figure A5.10 Moment of Inertia of a Rectangular Cross Section about an Axis through its Base

Let's calculate I_{ff} with b = 12 in and d = 6 in:

$$I_{ff} = bd^3/3 = (12 \times 6^3)/3 = \textbf{864 in}^4$$

DISCUSSION

We see that the moment of inertia of a rectangular cross section about an axis through its base is four times higher than the moment of inertia about its parallel neutral axis.

MOMENT OF INERTIA OF A RECTANGULAR CROSS SECTION ABOUT A REMOTE PARALLEL AXIS

Sometimes it's desirable for a section's moment of inertia to be taken about a remote reference axis parallel to a neutral axis. Then the section's moment of inertia is the sum of the moment of inertia about its neutral axis, plus the section's area times the square of the distance from the neutral axis to the reference axis.

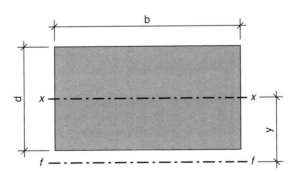

Figure A5.11 Moment of Inertia of a Rectangular Cross Section about a Remote Parallel Axis

For a rectangular cross section (Figure A5.11) (as well as for any other cross-sectional shape), this is expressed by the formula (known as the *transfer formula*):

$$I_{ff} = I_{xx} + Ay^2$$

where:

    I_{ff} = moment of inertia about a remote ff reference axis

    I_{xx} = moment of inertia about the section's xx neutral axis

    A = area of the cross section

    y = distance from the xx neutral axis to the ff reference axis

Let's calculate I_{ff} about a remote parallel axis 9 in from the xx neutral axis (i.e., y = 9 in), with b = 12 in, d = 6 in (i.e., A = 72 in²), and I_{xx} known to be 216 in⁴:

$$I_{ff} = I_{xx} + Ay^2 = 216 + (72)(9^2) = 216 + (72 \times 81) = 216 + 5832 = \mathbf{6048 \ in^4}$$

DISCUSSION

Of the total moment of inertia about the remote ff axis (6048 in⁴), we see that there is relatively little contribution from I_{xx} (i.e., 216 in⁴). The majority of the contribution to the moment of inertia comes from Ay^2 (i.e., 5832 in⁴). We can therefore readily observe that, when taken about a remote axis, a section's moment of inertia increases exponentially due to the *square* of the distance (i.e., y^2) between its neutral axis and the remote axis.

MOMENT OF INERTIA FOR COMPOSITE RECTANGULAR CROSS SECTIONS

Sometimes a section is composed of different shapes, securely attached and acting together as one piece. The moment of inertia of the resulting total composite section about a reference axis is then the sum of each shape's moment of inertia about its own neutral axis plus the shape's area times the square of the distance from its neutral axis to the reference axis.

For any composite section (including, of course, our examples of rectangular sections) this is expressed by the formula:

$$I_{ff} = \Sigma(I_{xx} + Ay^2)$$

where:

I_{ff} = moment of inertia about the ff reference axis for the combined shapes of the entire section

I_{xx} = each shape's moment of inertia about its own xx neutral axis

A = each shape's area

y = distance from each shape's xx neutral axis to the ff reference axis

Let's calculate the moment of inertia (I_{ff}) about the x_{ff} neutral axis for the composite symmetrical section in Figure A5.12 consisting of rectangular Shapes a, b, and c. The calculations are shown in Table A5.2.

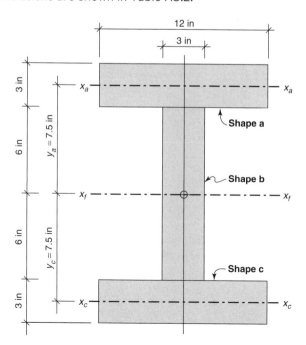

Figure A5.12 Moment of Inertia for a Composite Rectangular Cross Section

TABLE A5.2 MOMENT OF INERTIA CALCULATIONS

	$I_{xx} = Ad^2/12$	$A = (b \times d)$	y^2	$I_{xx} + Ay^2$
Shape a	$I_{xx} = (36 \times 3^2)/12$ $I_{xx} = 27$ in^4	$A = (3 \times 12) = 36$ in^2	$y^2 = 7.5^2 = 56.25$ in^2	$= 27 + (36 \times 56.25)$ $= 2052$ in^4
Shape b	$I_{xx} = (36 \times 12^2)/12$ $I_{xx} = 432$ in^4	$A = (12 \times 3) = 36$ in^2	$y^2 = 0$	$= 432 + (36 \times 0)$ $= 432$ in^4
Shape c (same as Shape a)	$I_{xx} = 27$ in^4	$A = 36$ in^2	$y^2 = 56.25$ in^2	$= 2052$ in^4

$$I_{ff} = \Sigma (I_{xx} + Ay^2) = 2052 + 432 + 2052 = 4536 \text{ in}^4$$

DISCUSSION

The total moment of inertia about the neutral (reference) axis of the composite section is 4536 in^4. Although Shapes a, b, and c are the same size, we see that the greatest contribution by far to the total moment of inertia comes from Shapes a and c due to their distance from the reference axis x_{ff}.

Moment of Inertia for Various Steel Sections

The AISC and other trade organizations or manufacturers provide values of I for their products. Examples of I for various cross-sectional steel shapes are shown in Figure A5.14.

A5.3 Section Modulus

Section Modulus and Elastic & Plastic Stage Design

Before we discuss section modulus, we should note that engineering practice uses two independent theoretical approaches to the design of structural members. One approach is based on a material's behavior in the elastic range (elastic stage design), and the other approach is based on a material's behavior in the plastic range (plastic stage design) (see Chapter 13). The engineering theory between the two approaches is beyond the scope of this text, but the reader should simply be aware of the distinction.

Section modulus is another expression of a cross section's ability to resist bending that is convenient for use in formulae for the design of flexural members, such as beams. Section modulus, like moment of inertia, is a measure of the stiffness of a section. There are two ways to express section modulus, S and Z, depending upon the design methodology (elastic or plastic) being used.

The Elastic Section Modulus, S

The elastic section modulus, S, relates to the elastic behavior of flexural members where allowable stresses are kept within the elastic limit. For any given cross section, S is directly proportional to, and derived from, moment of inertia and is given by the formula:

$$S_{xx} = I_{xx}/c$$

where:

S_{xx} = the elastic section modulus about the xx neutral axis

I_{xx} = the moment of inertia about the same xx neutral axis

c = the distance from the xx neutral axis to the extreme fiber of the section

As the formula shows, if I is expressed in inches to the fourth power (in^4) and c is expressed in inches, S is expressed in inches to the third third power (in^3). Examples of c for various cross-sectional shapes about their xx axes are shown in Figure A5.13.

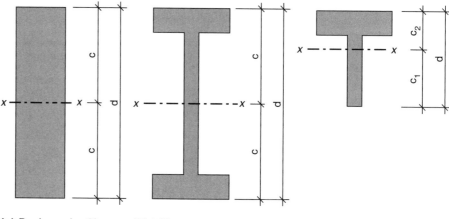

Figure A5.13 c for Various Sections

(a) Rectangular Shape   **(b) I Shape**   **(c) T Shape**

Note that for sections symmetrical about the xx neutral axis, such as those in Figure A5.13a and A5.13b, c = d/2. Also note that for sections unsymmetrical about the xx axis, such as that in Figure A5.13c, there are two values for c.

The Plastic Section Modulus, Z

The plastic section modulus Z relates to the plastic behavior of flexural members, where allowable stresses exceed the elastic limit. Note that "c" does not enter into the calculation of Z, and that Z (like S) is measured in inches to the third power (in^3).

The AISC recently adopted plastic design as the standard methodology for design in steel. The elastic section modulus, S, is no longer applicable in steel design and has been dropped from the AISC manual. Some examples of Z for several common steel shapes are shown in Figure A5.14.

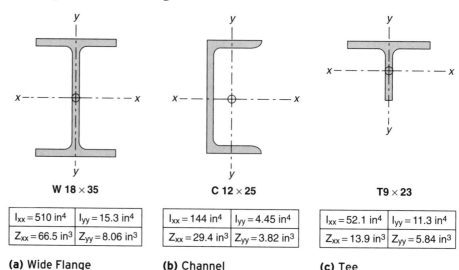

Figure A5.14 Plastic Section Modulus Z for Various Steel Shapes

W 18 × 35

$I_{xx} = 510$ in⁴	$I_{yy} = 15.3$ in⁴
$Z_{xx} = 66.5$ in³	$Z_{yy} = 8.06$ in³

(a) Wide Flange

C 12 × 25

$I_{xx} = 144$ in⁴	$I_{yy} = 4.45$ in⁴
$Z_{xx} = 29.4$ in³	$Z_{yy} = 3.82$ in³

(b) Channel

T9 × 23

$I_{xx} = 52.1$ in⁴	$I_{yy} = 11.3$ in⁴
$Z_{xx} = 13.9$ in³	$Z_{yy} = 5.84$ in³

(c) Tee

Section Modulus, S and Z, for Rectangular Sections

For rectangular cross sections (Figure A5.15) where:

b = width of the cross section

d = depth of the cross section

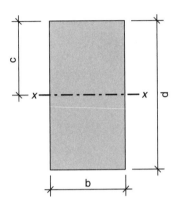

Figure A5.15 A Rectangular Cross Section

S_{xx}, the elastic section modulus about the xx neutral axis, can be expressed by the relationship of I_{xx}/c, or given by:

$$S_{xx} = bd^2/6$$

Z_{xx}, the plastic section modulus about the xx axis, is given by:

$$Z_{xx} = bd^2/4$$

■ EXAMPLE A5.2: The Section Modulus, S and Z, of a Rectangular Cross Section

Determine the elastic and plastic section modulus, S and Z, about the xx neutral axis, for the vertically-oriented 6 in × 12 in rectangular section in Example A5.1 having an I_{xx} of 864 in⁴ (Figure A5.16).

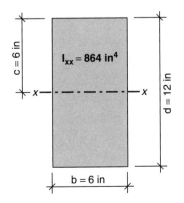

Figure A5.16 S_{xx} and Z_{xx} for a Rectangular Cross Section

To determine the elastic section modulus S_{xx}:

$$\mathbf{S_{xx}} = \mathbf{I/c} = 864 \text{ in}^4/6 \text{ in} = \mathbf{144 \text{ in}^3}$$

or

$$\mathbf{S_{xx}} = \mathbf{bd^2/6} = (6 \times 12^2)/6 = \mathbf{144 \text{ in}^3}$$

To determine the plastic section modulus Z_{xx}:

$$\mathbf{Z_{xx}} = \mathbf{bd^2/4} = (6 \times 12^2)/4 = \mathbf{216 \text{ in}^3}$$

The ratio of Z/S is called the *shape factor* and, for rectangular sections, is always 1.5. The shape factor is of significance in more advanced theoretical analyses of elastic and plastic design.

A5.4 Radius of Gyration

Radius of gyration, denoted by r, is a property of a cross section used to simplify formulae in the design of columns to resist buckling (bending). Radius of gyration is a theoretical concept derived from, and proportional to, moment of inertia, so both must therefore relate to the same specific reference axis.

Understanding Radius of Gyration

Perhaps the best way to visualize the theoretical idea of radius of gyration is to use an example of a rectangular cross section and its xx neutral axis (Figure A5.17).

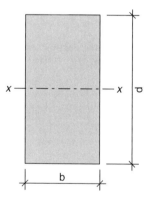

Figure A5.17 A Rectangular Cross Section

Imagine that the area of the section is dissolved and then reconstituted into two parallel lines, one on either side of the neutral axis and each equidistant from it. These two lines represent the concentration of the original area having exactly the same moment of inertia about the neutral axis as the original section. The distance (r_{xx}) from these two theoretical lines to the neutral axis is the radius of gyration (Figure A5.18).

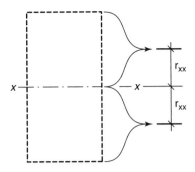

Figure A5.18 Radius of Gyration about xx Neutral Axis

Just as moment of inertia is a measure of the stiffness of a section, so is radius of gyration. For most cross-sectional shapes, we generally refer to two radii of gyration, one for the xx neutral axis and one for the yy neutral axis.

The larger the radius of gyration, the greater the section's resistance to bending, so that if buckling occurs, it will do so about the neutral axis having the least radius of gyration.

For our rectangular example, we can readily see that radius of gyration r_{yy} is less than radius of gyration r_{xx}. Therefore, if buckling occurs, it will do so about axis yy, the neutral axis having the least (i.e., weakest) radius of gyration (Figure 5.19).

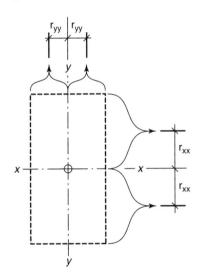

Figure A5.19 Radius of Gyration about xx and yy Neutral Axes

The radius of gyration about a neutral axis is given by the formula:

$$r = \sqrt{(I/A)}$$

where:

r = radius of gyration about a specific reference axis

I = moment of inertia about a specific reference axis

A = cross-sectional area

As the formula shows, if I is expressed in inches to the fourth power (in⁴) and A is expressed in square inches (in²), r is expressed in inches. Although the radius of gyration for basic geometric sections can also be expressed directly in terms of section dimensions (see Table A5.1), let's calculate r for both a rectangle and a circle using the formula $r = \sqrt{(I/A)}$.

■ EXAMPLE A5.3: Radius of Gyration of a Rectangular Section

Let's use the vertically oriented 6 in × 12 in rectangular section, in Examples A5.1 and A5.2, having an I_{xx} of 864 in⁴ and an I_{yy} of 216 in⁴ to calculate the section's radii of gyration about the xx and yy axes (Figure 5.20).

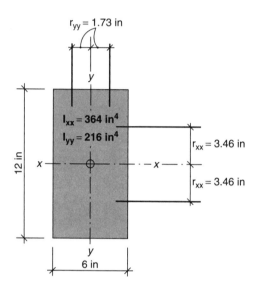

Figure A5.20 xx & yy Radii of Gyration of a Rectangular Section

$$r_{xx} = \sqrt{(I_{xx}/A)} = \sqrt{(864 \ in^4/72 \ in^2)} = \textbf{3.46 in}$$

$$r_{yy} = \sqrt{(I_{yy}/A)} = \sqrt{(216 \ in^4/72 \ in^2)} = \textbf{1.73 in}$$

Since the least radius of gyration in this example is r_{yy}, the section will tend to buckle about the weaker yy axis (Figure A5.21).

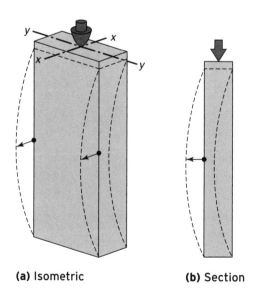

Figure A5.21 Buckling about the Weaker yy Axis

(a) Isometric   **(b)** Section

■ EXAMPLE A5.4: Radius of Gyration of a Circular Section

A circular cross section has a radius of 6 in. What is its radius of gyration about its neutral axes (Figure A5.22)?

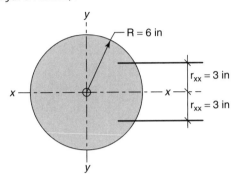

Figure A5.22 Radius of Gyration of a Circular Section

Calculating the moment of inertia:

$$I = \pi R^4/4 = 3.14(6^4)/4 = \textbf{1017.8 in}^4$$

Calculating the area:

$$A = \pi R^2 = 3.14(6^2) = \textbf{113.1 in}^2$$

Calculating the radius of gyration:

$$r = \sqrt{(I/A)} = \sqrt{(1017.8\ in^4/113.1\ in^2)} = \sqrt{(9\ in^2)} = \textbf{3 in}$$

Discussion

Since a circular section is perfectly symmetrical, moments of inertia and radii of gyration about all neutral axes are the same. Therefore, a circle has no least, and no weakest, radius of gyration about its neutral axes (i.e., $I_{xx} = I_{yy}$; $r_{xx} = r_{yy}$).

■ EXAMPLE A5.5:

A Sheet of Paper

To gain a better intuitive sense of radius of gyration, let's experiment with an 8 in × 11 in horizontally-oriented sheet of paper under three different conditions, 1) flat, 2) folded, and 3) rolled. While the paper's behavior will be easy enough to visualize, technically speaking it's all related to the radius of gyration (and, of course, the moment of inertia) of the sheet under the various conditions. To understand how it's related, think of the cross section of the sheet's condition as having an xx neutral axes.

CONDITION 1 (FLAT)

Hold the sheet vertically from the bottom. The sheet flops over simply from its own weight. The sheet cannot even begin to be thought of in structural terms (Figure A5.23a).

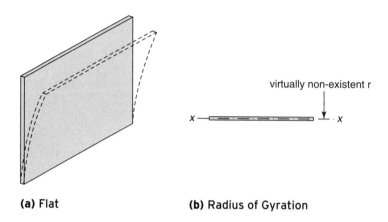

(a) Flat   **(b)** Radius of Gyration

DISCUSSION

Since the sheet has virtually no thickness, all of its cross-sectional material (i.e., area) is virtually coincident with the xx neutral axis. Therefore, its radius of gyration about the xx axis is virtually nonexistent, and the sheet bends about this axis since it has the least radius of gyration (Figure A5.23b).

CONDITION 2 (FOLDED)

Fold the sheet into a series of 1 inch ridges and place it on a level surface. The sheet stands up in support of its weight and can even support a small load carefully placed on top. As the load increases, the sheet eventually flops over as well (Figure A5.24a).

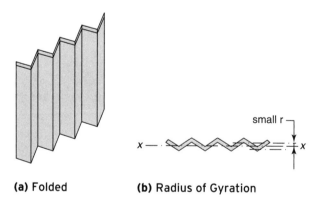

Figure A5.24

(a) Folded   **(b)** Radius of Gyration

DISCUSSION

With the sheet folded into a series of ridges, its cross-sectional material now moves farther from the xx neutral axis. A relatively small radius of gyration is developed about the xx neutral axis, enabling the sheet to provide some resistance to bending about this axis, which is still the axis with the least radius of gyration (Figure A5.24b).

CONDITION 3 (ROLLED)

Take a new sheet and wrap it into a cylindrical tube. Not only does the sheet stand up and support its own weight, but it can now support a relatively substantial load as well (Figure A5.25a).

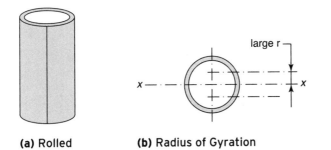

(a) Rolled   **(b)** Radius of Gyration   **Figure A5.25**

DISCUSSION

With the sheet wrapped into a cylindrical tube, its cross-sectional material now moves even farther from the xx neutral axis. A relatively large radius of gyration is developed about the xx neutral axis, enabling the sheet to provide substantial resistance to bending about this, and all, neutral axes, all of which have the same least radius of gyration (Figure A5.25b).

Basic Trigonometry

A6.1 Basic Trigonometric Functions of a Right Triangle

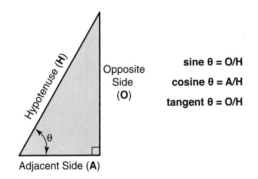

sine θ = O/H

cosine θ = A/H

tangent θ = O/H

Figure A6.1 Basic Trigonometric Functions of a Right Triangle

A6.2 Basic Trigonometric Values of Frequently Used Angles

TABLE A6.1 BASIC TRIGONOMETRIC VALUES OF FREQUENTLY USED ANGLES

Angle	sine	cosine	tangent
0°	0	1.000	0
30°	0.500	0.866	0.577
45°	0.707	0.707	1.000
60°	0.866	0.500	1.732
90°	1.000	0	∞

A6.3 Proportions of Special Right Triangles

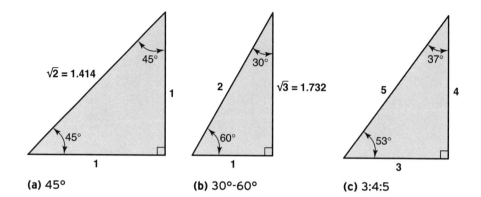

Figure A6.2 Proportions of
Special Right Triangles

(a) 45°   **(b)** 30°-60°   **(c)** 3:4:5

A6.4 The Pythagorean Theorem

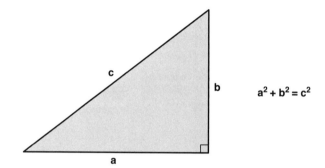

$$a^2 + b^2 = c^2$$

Figure A6.3 The Pythagorean
Theorem

Index